Communications
in Computer and Information Science 1549

More information about this series at https://link.springer.com/bookseries/7899

Ram Krishnan · H. Raghav Rao ·
Sanjay K. Sahay · Sagar Samtani ·
Ziming Zhao (Eds.)

Secure Knowledge Management In The Artificial Intelligence Era

9th International Conference, SKM 2021
San Antonio, TX, USA, October 8–9, 2021
Proceedings

 Springer

Editors
Ram Krishnan
The University of Texas at San Antonio
San Antonio, TX, USA

H. Raghav Rao
The University of Texas at San Antonio
San Antonio, TX, USA

Sanjay K. Sahay
Birla Institute of Technology and Science
Pilani, Rajasthan, India

Sagar Samtani
Indiana University
Bloomington, IN, USA

Ziming Zhao
SUNY Buffalo
Buffalo, NY, USA

ISSN 1865-0929   ISSN 1865-0937 (electronic)
Communications in Computer and Information Science
ISBN 978-3-030-97531-9   ISBN 978-3-030-97532-6 (eBook)
https://doi.org/10.1007/978-3-030-97532-6

This Springer imprint is published by the registered company Springer Nature Switzerland AG
The registered company address is: Gewerbestrasse 11, 6330 Cham, Switzerland

Preface

With the advent of revolutionary technologies such as artificial intelligence (AI), machine learning, cloud computing, big data, and IoT, secure knowledge management (SKM) continues to be an important research area that deals with methodologies for systematically gathering, organizing, and disseminating information in a secure manner. The recent development of AI in the security arena shows a promising future, and there is no doubt that AI can provide new ideas and tools for SKM. This conference on SKM brings together researchers and practitioners from academia, industry, and government on a global scale. The aim of the SKM conference is to present and discuss the most recent innovations, trends, and concerns including practical challenges encountered and solutions adopted with a special emphasis on AI. SKM 2019 was held at the BITS Pilani Goa Campus, India, and past iterations of SKM were held at SUNY at Buffalo, SUNY Albany, NYU, SUNY Stony Brook, UT Dallas, Rutgers University, BITS Dubai, and the University of South Florida. Following the biennial tradition of the Secure Knowledge Management Workshop that began in 2004, SKM 2021 was hosted by the University of Texas at San Antonio, USA, during October 8–9, 2021. The conference took place virtually due to the COVID-19 pandemic.

SKM 2021 received many high-quality submissions, with authors coming from countries such as the USA, India, Austria, Norway, and Ireland. A total of 30 research papers were received by the Technical Program Committee (TPC). The TPC of SKM 2021 comprised researchers and industry practitioners from all corners of the world. Most of the submitted papers received three reviews, and each paper received at least two reviews. The review process was double-blind, and after the careful review process, the top 11 papers were selected for publication in this proceedings volume, with an acceptance rate of 36.6%.

The conference was organized over two days with a very compact schedule. Beyond the technical program of the research papers, the conference was enriched by many other items. The conference program featured three keynotes: James Joshi (University of Pittsburgh) spoke on the privacy challenges we face in the emerging world in his talk titled "Privacy – Challenges and Directions", Stephanie Hazlewood (IBM) spoke on the challenges in using AI for securing organizations in light of attackers armed with AI technology as well ("Cybersecurity: AI vs AI"), and Hsinchun Chen (University of Arizona) spoke on the decade-long effort and journey in building the University of Arizona Eller/MIS AZSecure Cybersecurity Program ("Building the UA/Eller/MIS AZSecure Cybersecurity Analytics Program: My Journey").

The conference also featured a panel on "Women in Cybersecurity", which was chaired by Bhavani Thuraisingham (University of Texas at Dallas) with the support of PhD student volunteer, Alexis Votto. The panel members were Sharmistha Bagchi-Sen (Arizona State University), Nicole Lang Beebe (University of Texas at San Antonio), Elisa Bertino (Purdue University), Heng Xu (American University), and Danfeng (Daphne) Yao (Virginia Tech).

We are very much thankful to the speakers, panelists, and authors for their active participation in SKM 2021. We are also thankful to Springer for providing continuous guidance and support. We extend our heartfelt gratitude to the TPC members and external reviewers for their efforts in the review process. We are indeed thankful to everyone who was directly or indirectly associated with the organizing team of the conference leading to a successful event. We also gratefully acknowledge US National Science Foundation grant 2133980 for partially funding the conference. We hope the proceedings will inspire more research in secure knowledge management, digital payments, and the application of artificial intelligence.

January 2022

Ram Krishnan
H. Raghav Rao
Sanjay K. Sahay
Sagar Samtani
Ziming Zhao

Organization

Steering Committee

Kwiat, Kevin   Air Force Research Laboratory, USA
Memon, Nasir   New York University, USA
Rao, H. Raghav   University of Texas at San Antonio, USA
Thuraisingham, Bhavani   University of Texas at Dallas, USA
Upadhyaya, Shambhu   University at Buffalo, USA

General Chairs

Krishnan, Ram   University of Texas at San Antonio, USA
Rao, H. Raghav   University of Texas at San Antonio, USA

Technical Program Committee Chairs

Samtani, Sagar   Indiana University, USA
Zhao, Ziming   University at Buffalo, USA

Publicity Chairs

Bou-Harb, Elias   University of Texas at San Antonio, USA
Shah, Ankit   University of South Florida, USA

Scientific Chair

Sahay, Sanjay K.   BITS Pilani, Goa Campus, India

Technical Program Committee

Abdelsalam, Mahmoud   Manhattan College, USA
Al-Alaj, Abdullah   Virginia Wesleyan University, USA
Benjamin, Victor   Arizona State University, USA
Bertino, Elisa   Purdue University, USA
Bhatt, Smirti   Texas A&M University, USA
Bose, Indranil   NEOMA Business School, France
Chen, Rui   Iowa State University, USA
Cheng, Yuan   California State University, USA
Chowdhury, Dipanwita Roy IIT Kharagpur, India

Goel, Sanjay	University of Albany, USA
Gupta, Maanak	Tennessee Technological University, USA
Halder, Raju	IIT Patna, India
Hu, Hongxin	University at Buffalo, USA
Hu, Peizhao	Rochester Institute of Technology, USA
Jain, Shweta	City University of New York, USA
Jaiswal, Raj K.	BITS Pilani, Goa Campus, India
Li, Weifeng	University of Georgia, USA
Liang, Yunji	Northwestern Polytechnic University, USA
Liu, Peng	Pennsylvania State University, USA
Masoumzadeh, Amirreza	University at Albany, USA
Medrano, Carlos Rubio	Texas A&M University-Corpus Christi, USA
Mehnaz, Shagufta	Dartmouth College, USA
Mi, Xianghang	University at Buffalo, USA
Mishra, Sumita	Rochester Institute of Technology, USA
Mohaisen, Aziz	University of Central Florida, USA
Nam, Kichan	American University of Sharjah, UAE
Narang, Pratik	BITS Pilani, India
Ninglekhu, Jiwan	InterDigital Communications, USA
Pal, Abhipsa	IIM Kozhikode, India
Park, Jaehong	University of Alabama in Huntsville, USA
Ratazzi, Paul	Air Force Research Laboratory, USA
Rathore, Hemant	BITS Pilani, Goa Campus, India
Ray, Indrakshi	Colorado State University, USA
Santanam, Raghu	Arizona State University, USA
Shah, Ankit	University of South Florida, USA
Shan, Jay	Miami University, USA
Sharma, Ashu	Mindtree, Hyderabad, India
Thakur, Rahul	IIT Roorkee, India
Vaish, Abhishek	IIIT Allahabad, India
Valecha, Rohit	University of Texas at San Antonio, USA
Verma, Rakesh	University of Houston, USA
Wang, Huibo	Baidu Security, USA
Wang, Jingguo	University of Texas at Arlington, USA
Wang, Weihang	University at Buffalo, USA
Xiao, Nan	University of Texas Rio Grande Valley, USA
Yang, Jay	Rochester Institute of Technology, USA
Zhang, Penghui	Arizona State University, USA
Hongyi, Zhu	University of Texas at San Antonio, USA

Abstracts of Invited Talks

Privacy - Challenges and Directions

James Joshi

School of Computing and Information, University of Pittsburgh, PA, USA
jjoshi@pitts.edu

Rapid advances in computing and information technologies are enabling a hyper-connected world. Enabled by such connectivity and the growing computational power/infrastructures at our disposal, innovative Artificial Intelligence (AI) and Machine Learning (ML) techniques are increasingly being deployed in various applications. Innovations in AI/ML is further being fueled by huge amounts of data that is continuously collected in myriad of ways, including data that has or can reveal highly privacy-sensitive information about us. While AI/ML technologies and the huge amounts of data available can be used for immense benefits for our society, privacy issues pose as a huge potential roadblock. Globally, there is also increasing number of privacy regulations being introduced to address privacy challenges related to access to and use of data by analytic engines and AI/ML-enabled applications. In this talk, he discuss the current privacy challenges that we face in emerging world that is increasingly reliant on technologies and some directions for research. He also briefly overview the National Science Foundation's Secure and Trustworthy Cyberspace program, and other programs that are aligned with the themes of this conference.

Building the UA/Eller/MIS AZSecure Cybersecurity Analytics Program: My Journey

Hsinchun Chen

University of Arizona, Eller College of Management, Management Information
Systems Department, Tucson, AZ 85721, USA
hchen@eller.arizona.edu

In this talk, a decade-old effort and journey in building the University of Arizona
Eller/MIS AZSecure Cybersecurity Program has been discussed. Based on $15M+
funding from the National Science Foundation (NSF) SaTC (Secure and Trustworthy
Cyberspace), ACI (Advanced Cyber Infrastructure), and SFS (CyberCorps Scholarship-
for-Service) programs since 2012, our research team at the Eller/MIS Artificial Intelligence (AI) Lab has developed significant Cybersecurity Analytic research in: (1) Dark
Web Analytic for studying international hacker community, forums, and markets; (2)
Privacy and PII (Personal Identifiable Information) Analytic for identifying and alleviating privacy risks for vulnerable populations; (3) Adversarial Malware Generation and
Evasion for adversarial AI in cybersecurity; and (4) Smart Vulnerability Assessment for
scientific workflows and OSS (Open Source Software) vulnerability analytics and mitigation. Our research advances the development of large-scale longitudinal cybersecurity
data (e.g., hacker forms, darknet markets, stolen email accounts, malware source code
and binary, GitHub OSS, scientific VMs) and advanced AI and DL/ML (deep learning
and machine learning) based algorithmic and representational innovations (e.g., transfer learning, attention mechanism, multi-view learning, transformer) inspired by unique
cybersecurity domain-specific characteristics, practices and opportunities. As a leader in
advanced cybersecurity education, University of Arizona has received the CAE-CD/R/
CO cybersecurity designations from NSA/DHS and significant SFS fellowship funding
from NSF.

Cybersecurity: AI vs AI

Stephanie Hazlewood

Security Automation, IBM Security, Canada
stephanie@ca.ibm.com

In the rapidly transforming business domain of today applications have become modular and containerized. Large amounts of data generated from business processes serve as shared resources for conducting advanced analytic and building robust Artificial Intelligence (AI) models. In the current state-of-the-art AI cybersecurity, there exist many complexities such as the presence of too many vendors and alerts. AI is a double-edged sword as it is used by both attackers as well as cybersecurity professionals, to mount attacks and defend against them. In essence, AI addresses three key business issues – prediction, automation and optimization.

Security threats that organizations face continue to increase exponentially. However, AI-infused security solutions bring speed and accuracy to help businesses proactively protect their assets, more accurately detect threats, and respond faster when security incidents arise. The future of cybersecurity converges with AI strengths and thus this talk focuses on how Trusted AI systems can be implemented that provide fair, explainable, and robust business insights. She also discuss how security solutions must defend against attackers that use AI to enhance the speed and accuracy of their own attacks.

Women in Cyber Security at the International Conference on Secure Knowledge Management in the Artificial Intelligence Era

Bhavani Thuraisingham[1], Alexis Votto[2], Sharmistha Bagchi-Sen[3], Nicole Beebe[4], Elisa Bertino[5], Heng Xu[6], and Daphne Yao[7]

[1] The University of Texas at Dallas, USA
bhavani.thuraisingham@utdallas.edu
[2] The University of Texas at San Antonio, USA
Alexis.Votto@utsa.edu
[3] Arizona State University, USA
Sharmistha.Bagchi-Sen@asu.edu
[4] The University of Texas at San Antonio, USA
Nicole.Beebe@utsa.edu
[5] Purdue University, USA
bertino@purdue.edu
[6] American University, USA
xu@american.edu
[7] Virginia Tech, USA
danfeng@vt.edu

Secure Knowledge Management (SKM) Workshop/Conference was the first venue to host an event on Women in Cyber Security. With a grant from the National Science Foundation, Profs. Sharmistha Bagchi-Sen, Shambhu Upadhyaya, and H. Raghav Rao, all from the University of Buffalo, hosted the first Women in Cyber Security panel at SKM 2004. Since then the panel was organized at various SKM events. The most recent panel was chaired by Prof. Bhavani Thuraisingham at SKM 2021 on October 09, 2021 and coordinated by Ms. Alexis Votto. The panelists were Profs. Sharmistha Bagchi- Sen, Nicole Beebe, Elisa Bertino, Heng Xu, and Daphne Yao. Each of the panelists discussed their work in cyber security and as well as opportunities and challenges for women in cyber security. Sharmistha discussed her work on geography and security as well as the need to focus on Diversity, Equity add Inclusion (DEI). Nicole discussed her initial work for the Air Force in cyber security and her more recent research in academia in areas such as digital forensics. She also discussed opportunities for research grants in cyber security. Elisa discussed her initial work in database management and then her work in cyber security. In particular she discussed her early research in secure database systems and then how she migrated into secure wireless networks and 5G technologies. Heng discussed her research in data privacy, fairness in artificial intelligence and her most recent work in cyber security governance. She also discussed aspects of social responsibility as well as the need for change to lead the future. Finally, Daphne discussed

A panel discussion chaired by Bhavani Thuraisingham and coordinated by Alexis Votto.

her research on crypto systems, certifying data breaches as well anomaly detection. She also discussed the workshop she co-founded on Women in Cyber Security Research (Cyber-W) and about overcoming racism and sexism in one's career. She emphasized that persistence is important and never to give up. She also discussed about how some women face the impostor syndrome and the need to get help from others. After the panel positions, the audience asked several questions. For example, one of the questions asked was to discuss the challenges for women in cyber security. One panelist answered that early in her career one of the bosses essentially mentioned that women need to have a thick skin in engineering. Also, when she was a tenure track assistant professor, one colleague asked her why do you want to go for tenure? I thought you would want to be in the Mommy track. She also added that there are roadblocks for women and they have to work extremely hard to get ahead. She said that it is very important to prioritize. Another panelist mentioned that we have come a long way compared to, say, the 1980s. She ignores such comments as it is not easy to convince others to change their behavior. Another panelist mentioned that some women have left their careers not because of one or two comments, but due to the community not supporting them. For example, female faculty that take maternity leave may not have published as much during their leave. When such faculty are being criticized for this it's very important that other faculty explain the reasons and support the female faculty. One panelist mentioned that the challenges are even more for BIPOC (Black, Indigenous, and People of Color) women and there is a concrete ceiling for them. Another panelist mentioned that we need policies to support women as well as men and also focus on the inequity in research areas. For example, it's harder to publish in some areas and this has to be recognized. The panel chair mentioned that none of us would be where we are now if not for the women who came before us. She also added that she would never have been in the position she is in now fifty years ago.

Another question from the audience was how to select an area for research and get funding for the research projects. There was an interesting discussion on this topic. It depends on whether you are in, say, Computer Science (where funding and top tier conference publications are important) and Business (where journal publications are important). It was felt that one has to also pursue one's passion. Another panelist discussed the importance of interdisciplinary research and the challenges involved such as bringing in behavioral scientists into cyber security research. The panel chair also mentioned that when she did not mention her title in an email, she was referred to as a student from the University of Texas at Dallas. She felt that this is subconscious bias because her name was a foreign sounding one. For example, had her name been a very English sounding name such a mistake may not have been made. Finally, the chair asked each panelist for their ending statements with respect to her research as well as on supporting women. One panelist mentioned that we need more data for research. She added that advancing women including BIPOC women is critical. Another panelist mentioned to follow your passion. She also cautioned not to swing the pendulum too far and we must not promote a person just because she is a woman or from an underrepresented minority community. A third panelist mentioned that we need to motivate our students and carry out systematic research. A fourth panelist mentioned that we need a pipeline of women so that the representation of women continues to increase. Another panelist mentioned that research depends on the stage you are in. For example, before tenure focus on the publications and grants, But after tenure you need it make an impact with your research. Finally, a panelist mentioned that we need an end-to-end plan for research. She also added that the concrete ceiling comment made earlier is very true. Finally, she offered that we should not be unhappy as it could destroy us. We must be positive and do the best we can. The panel chair agreed with the panelists that we cannot change others and not to be unhappy when others are mean to us. We must support each other. The panel chair has mentioned that a high income career is a must for every woman and a person from the underrepresented minority community. She emphasized that this is especially true for women. She ended the panel by saying "what better way to have an intellectually stimulating and yet a high income career than pursuing one in cyber security".

Contents

Intrusion and Malware Detection

Adversarial Robustness of Image Based Android Malware Detection Models

Hemant Rathore[1]($\boxtimes$), Taeeb Bandwala[1], Sanjay K. Sahay[1], and Mohit Sewak[2]

[1] Department of CS and IS, Goa Campus, BITS Pilani, Sancoale, India
{hemantr,f20170940,ssahay}@goa.bits-pilani.ac.in
[2] Security and Compliance Research, Microsoft R&D, Hyderabad, India
mohit.sewak@microsoft.com

Abstract. The last five years have shown a tremendous increase in the number of Android smartphone users. So has been the case with malicious Android applications that aim to jeopardize user data, security, and privacy. Most existing Android malware detection engines find it challenging to keep up with the pace of incoming malware and their sophistication of evasion techniques against the detection engines. This has prompted researchers to delve into using machine learning and deep learning algorithms to construct state-of-the-art malware detection models. However, research indicates that these detection models might be vulnerable to adversarial attacks prompting a thorough investigation. Therefore, we first propose a image based malware detection pipeline that uses an embedding layer-based hybrid CNN named E-CNN that uses Android permissions and intents as features for malware detection. The permission and intent based E-CNN detection models achieved baseline accuracy of 93.48% and 76.7% respectively. We then act as an adversary and propose the ECO-FGSM adversarial evasion attack against the above detection models. The ECO-FGSM attack converts malware samples into adversarial malware samples so that they are forcefully misclassified as benign by the detection models. The proposed attack achieved a high fooling rate of 55.72% and 99.97% against permission and intent based E-CNN detection models, respectively. We also identified a list of most vulnerable permissions and intents to generate adversarial samples. We then use adversarial retraining as a defense strategy to counter the ECO-FGSM attack against the detection models. The adversarial defense helped improve the baseline accuracies of permission and intent based E-CNN detection models by 3.41% and 11.4%, respectively. We reattack the adversarially retrained models using the ECO-FGSM attack to validate their adversarial robustness. We found a reduction in the fooling rate by 23.28% and 97.55% against permission and intent-based E-CNN detection models, respectively. Finally, we conclude that investigating the adversarial robustness of the malware detection models is an essential step that helps improve their performance and robustness before real-world deployment.

Keywords: Android · Adversarial robustness · Convolutional Neural Network · Evasion attack · Malware detection

© Springer Nature Switzerland AG 2022
R. Krishnan et al. (Eds.): SKM 2021, CCIS 1549, pp. 3–22, 2022.
https://doi.org/10.1007/978-3-030-97532-6_1

1   Introduction

Smartphones have become an indispensable part of our lives owing to their wide range of usage, ease of use, and portability. As a result, smartphone users have grown drastically in the last decade [18]. Notably, the number of active Android users rose from 1.4 billion in 2015 to over 2.8 billion in 2020. The android operating system has a significant global market share of over 71% in the smartphone segment in the first financial quarter of 2021 [1]. Furthermore, the number of Android applications (apps) and their developers in the ecosystem has also grown exponentially in the last few years. Many of these applications have access to sensitive information stored on the smartphone. This has attracted many malware developers to craft malicious Android applications that can exploit the system or application vulnerabilities for malicious purposes. As a result, the total number of malicious applications increased dramatically from over 2.2 million in January 2015 to over 30 million in May 2021 [2], threatening the Android ecosystem. Existing malware detection techniques include signature, heuristic, and behavior-based detection algorithms [29]. However, these techniques are highly human-driven and cannot handle the high growth rate of malware in the ecosystem. Therefore researchers have started to explore new techniques like machine learning and deep learning for malware detection [18,29].

Existing literature suggests that the development of malware detection models using machine learning and deep learning require feature extraction followed by the use of classification/clustering algorithm [29]. For instance, Giang et al. (2015) proposed a method that scores an application's security based on its permission usage pattern and then used a decision tree cluster which achieved an accuracy of 85% for malware detection [5]. Feizollah et al. (2017) used android intents and explored BayesianNetwork algorithm configurations to achieve high detection rates for android malware samples [6]. Some studies also explored Convolutional Neural Network (CNN) for the malware detection task. Huang et al. (2018) transformed the bytecode of classes.dex extracted from android archive file into an image and passed it to a CNN for malware detection [12]. Ganesh et al. (2017) proposed a CNN-based malware detection method that investigates permission patterns [7]. However, recent studies have shown that these machine learning and deep learning based classifiers are prone to adversarial attacks [19,22,24,25].

Researchers have developed a taxonomy for threat modeling by categorizing adversarial attacks based on the adversary's goals, knowledge, and capabilities [4,31]. The adversary can perform falsification attacks that include *false-positive attack* wherein a negative sample is forcefully misclassified as positive, and vice versa in the case of *false-negative attack*. Adversary's knowledge about the system includes information about dataset (train and test data), feature set, classification algorithm and model architecture & its parameters. The white-box scenario assumes that the adversary has complete information about the system, whereas the black-box scenario assumes the adversary has zero information. Adversarial attack specificity considers whether the adversary performs a

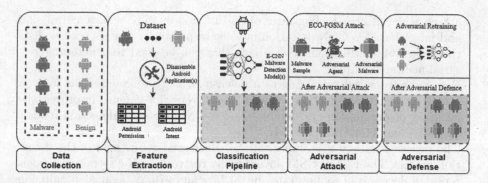

Fig. 1. Proposed workflow to improve the adversarial robustness of image-based android malware detection models

forceful misclassification to a specific class of samples (targeted-attack) or just any misclassification from the actual output classes (non-targeted attack).

In the light of existing work, we propose a novel malware detection pipeline that uses a hybrid CNN classifier named E-CNN (Embedding Convolutional Neural Network) which is based on an embedding layer. We perform static analysis of Android applications (malware and benign) and extract two feature sets: permissions and intents. Then the hybrid CNN architecture is used to develop a permission-based E-CNN malware detection model and an intent-based E-CNN malware detection model. However, these detection models might be vulnerable to evasion-based adversarial attacks. Therefore, we developed a custom evasion attack strategy, namely ECO-FGSM (Embedding COsine similarity based Fast Gradient Sign Method) that aims to convert malware samples into adversarial malware samples that are forcefully misclassified as benign by the malware detection models. The ECO-FGSM attack is designed to add only those perturbations which do not break the syntactic, structural, functional, and behavioral integrity of the android application. Also, the attack is intended to convert maximum malware samples into adversarial malware samples with minimum perturbation(s) in each malware sample. Furthermore, the ECO-FGSM attack aims to find permission and intent based adversarial vulnerabilities in the models. These vulnerabilities are thoroughly investigated post-attack, and we then propose adversarial retraining as a defense mechanism to counter the attack. We re-attacked the detection models using ECO-FGSM to validate the effectiveness of the proposed defense mechanism. Finally, we made the following contributions through this work:

- We designed a novel malware detection pipeline namely E-CNN that involves a hybrid embedding-based CNN classifier. The permission and intent based E-CNN malware detection models achieved accuracies of 93.48% and 76.7%, respectively.
- We proposed an adversarial evasion attack named ECO-FGSM to find and exploit the vulnerabilities in malware detection models. The ECO-FGSM

attack achieved high fooling rates of 55.72% and 99.97% against permission and intent based E-CNN detection models, respectively. The attack also lists the vulnerable permissions and intents that can be used to generate adversarial malware samples.

- We used adversarial retraining as a defense strategy to counter the evasion attack against the detection models. The adversarial defense improved the accuracy of permission and intent based E-CNN malware detection models by 3.41% and 11.4%, respectively.
- The defense strategy also improved the adversarial robustness of the detection models. The ECO-FGSM adversarially reattack on the retrained models reported decrease in fooling rates by 23.28% and 97.55% against permission and intent based E-CNN detection models.

The rest of the paper is organized as follows. Section 2 explains the proposed framework, adversarial attack, and defense strategy. Section 3 discusses the experimental setup, followed by experimental results in Sect. 4. Section 5 lists related work in the domain, and Sect. 6 concludes the paper.

2   Proposed Framework for Adversarial Robustness

In this section, we will start with a brief discussion on the proposed workflow and classification pipeline. Later we will discuss the design of ECO-FGSM evasion attack and adversarial retraining defense strategy against malware detection models.

2.1   Proposed Framework Workflow

We have divided the proposed workflow into five basic modules which are as follows:

1. *Data Collection:* The first step involves collecting android applications from verified authentic sources to create a dataset with a fairly equal distribution of benign and malware samples.
2. *Feature Extraction:* The second step involves static malware analysis of the collected android applications in the dataset to extract different features for each sample. We have extracted two static features, namely android permission and android intent.
3. *Classification Pipeline:* The third step involves preprocessing of the features followed by designing, training, and testing the android malware detection models using classification algorithms. Their performance can be analyzed using accuracy, area under the ROC curve etc.
4. *Adversarial Attack:* The fourth step is to design and execute the proposed ECO-FGSM adversarial evasion attack strategy against the malware detection model. The evasion attack is designed to exploit vulnerabilities and generate adversarial samples for forceful misclassifications in detection models. The attack design also ensures that the perturbations do not break the android applications' syntactic, structural, functional, and behavioral integrity.

5. *Adversarial Defense:* The fifth step is to design a defense strategy to counter the evasion attack for improving the robustness of the malware detection models. The performance evaluation of the final malware detection model can be conducted using accuracy, area under the ROC curve, fooling rate, etc.

2.2 Structure of the Classification Pipeline

The classification pipeline is divided into the following two parts:

Preprocessing Function (Tokenizer). This function performs a custom tokenizing operation on the feature vectors of each android sample. As explained in Sect. 3.3, this operation gives a distinct identification to each feature value (permission/intent) in the feature vector which is recognizable by the embedding layer [8] used in the malware detection models. Hence, at the end of this operation, each feature value in the feature vector would be associated with a distinct token value depending on its position in the vector.

Classification Model (E-CNN). E-CNN is an image-based CNN that uses an embedding layer to implicitly transform processed-feature vectors into a 2D image. The image resembles a *footprint* of the sample and is processed by *Conv2D* layers followed by subsequent DNN layers to generate the class probability. We set the class probability threshold as 0.5 for classification. It means that a *probability* $>= 0.5$ would imply a malware sample (*classlabel* $= 1$) and a *probability* <0.5 would imply a benign sample (*classlabel* $= 0$). We developed two E-CNN malware detection models, each of which is trained separately on two distinct feature vectors namely, permission and intent.

2.3 Adversarial Evasion Attack Using ECO-FGSM

We propose a novel Embedding COsine similarity based Fast Gradient Sign Method (ECO-FGSM) which is a targeted, white box evasion attack. It uses the gradients of a network to generate perturbations which are added to the original malware sample to convert them into an adversarial malware sample. The FGSM attack proposed by Goodfellow et al. cannot be applied directly to the malware detection models since they use an embedding layer [9]. We can visualize the E-CNN malware detection model in two parts:

– The *embedding layer* whose input is a processed feature vector and output is a 2D image.
– The *CNN network* following the embedding layer whose input is the 2D image and output is a class probability.

The FGSM section of the adversarial attack is concerned with the second part of the above visualization. It creates signed perturbations with respect to each pixel position in the 2D image that enters the CNN layers. It does so by computing the gradients of the loss function with respect to each pixel in the image with an objective to maximize the loss function.

$$P = sign(\frac{\partial Loss(\theta, X, Y)}{\partial X}) \tag{1}$$

where *Loss* represents the Loss function which in our case is binary_cross_entropy, θ represents the model parameters, X represents the input image which is the one created by the embedding layer, Y represents the output label which in our case would be 1 for malware and 0 for benign, *sign* represents the signum function, and P represents the resulting perturbation array.

The gradients are internally back computed using the chain rule of derivatives. Each signed value in the perturbation array P represents the direction of perturbation which maximizes the loss function.

The second part of the ECO-FGSM attack involves the problem of translating the gradients computed by FGSM to valid perturbations within the binary feature vector. To accomplish this, we interpret that the first part of the $E - CNN$ model gives a $2D$ output image which is basically an array of adjacently placed embedding vectors. Similarly, we consider P to be an array of adjacently placed gradient vectors, each of which corresponds to the gradient of their respective positional embedding vectors. For each position in the binary feature vector, we have two possible embedding vectors that correspond to either 0 or $1 - bit$ value. The addition of $1 - bit$ perturbation simply implies that the embedding vector in the image changes from $0 - bit$ to its $1 - bit$ counterpart.

$$a = embedding[bit\_index]_{1-bit} - embedding[bit\_index]_{0-bit} \tag{2}$$
$$b = P[bit\_index] \tag{3}$$
$$cosim(a, b) = \frac{(a \cdot b)}{|a||b|} \tag{4}$$

Hence, for each of the gradient vectors present in P, we compute a *similarity score* which is the cosine similarity between the gradient vector and the difference between $1 - bit$ and $0 - bit$ embedding vectors at that position. We then sort the positions in the decreasing order of their similarity scores. The idea is higher the similarity score is, the earlier the perturbation should be added. This is then used by the attack which selects $0 - bit$ positions in the base feature vector and adds $1 - bit$ perturbations in order. The maximum possible number of perturbations in subsequent attack steps is increased gradually in the experimental setup.

In summary, the ECO-FGSM attack aims to find the most vulnerable permission or intent in the feature vector of a malware sample which is then added to convert it into an adversarial malware sample that is forcefully misclassified as benign by the malware detection models. The addition of permission or intent does not change the properties of the original malware sample. Moreover, we are only allowing addition of perturbations and not the reverse because removing permission or intent can adversely affect the compilation dependency of the malware sample.

2.4   Defence Strategy Using Adversarial Retraining

We propose adversarial retraining as the defense strategy that involves retraining the malware detection models on an augmented dataset containing all the original samples from the dataset and the adversarial malware samples. It is a simple yet effective strategy to improve the performance of the detection model. Goodfellow et al. (2014) and Huang et al. (2016) showed that adversarial training improves the robustness of deep learning based models [9, 14]. Goodfellow et al. (2014) also showed that training on the adversarial samples could provide regularization for DNNs. They injected adversarial examples into the dataset while continually generating new adversarial examples at every step of the attack. This helped in improving the generalization capability of the model [9]. Kurakin et al. (2017) also showed how adversarial training could significantly increase model robustness against adversarial examples [15]. Thakur et al. (2020) showed how retraining neural networks with adversarial images could effectively defend against white-box attacks. They first trained DNNs on CIFAR10 and Tiny-ImageNet datasets and attacked them using FGSM strategy [26]. Then they retrained the models with adversarial samples and the fooling rate was decreased to more than half, which suggested a significant improvement in robustness. Referring to the above works and given that we are also performing an evasion attack on the image based CNN models. We expect that adversarial retraining would update the model weight parameters and hence would make them more robust to subsequent rounds of attack and improve their generalization ability.

3   Experimental Setup

In the section, we first describe the procedure used for collecting malware and benign android applications to form a dataset, followed by the process of feature extraction from applications. Later in the section, we discuss details regarding the classification pipeline, followed by a discussion on various performance metrics used during the work.

3.1   Dataset Collection

The first module in the proposed workflow is data collection (Fig. 1). The dataset consists of both malware and benign android applications downloaded from authentic sources. The malware set consists of all the samples from the well-known Drebin dataset proposed by Arp et al. [3]. The dataset contains 5545 android malicious application from various malware families like *FakeInstaller*, *Plankton*, *GingerMaster*, *Iconosys* etc. The Drebin dataset is well studied and has more than 1500 citations as of June 2021. The benign set consists of android applications downloaded from Google Play Store. We developed a crawler to parse and download android applications belonging to various categories from Play Store. All the applications are validated using VirusTotal (an ensemble antivirus service developed and maintained by Google). VirusTotal uses more than 60 most popular antiviruses including *AVG*, *BitDefender*, *F-Secure*, *Kaspersky*, *Norton*, *McAfee*, *Trend Micro*. The downloaded applications are then validated for their complete *benignness*. An application is discarded if it is flagged as malware by even a single antivirus engine. The final dataset contains 5545 android malicious applications and 5545 benign applications.

3.2 Feature Extraction

The malware detection models are built using features that can help in classifying malware and benign samples. Static features are extracted by parsing the application code without executing it, whereas dynamic features are extracted by executing the applications in a controlled environment. Android permission, intent, API call, opcode frequency etc., are examples of static features, while network traffic, system call etc., are examples of dynamic features [20,21,23,29]. We have first constructed comprehensive list of two static features, namely Android permission and intents using official android documentation. The number of permissions and intents were 195 and 273, respectively. We then extracted permission and intent, from all the android applications available in the dataset. We used *APKTOOL* (an open-source reverse engineering tool) to disassemble android applications. Then a parser scans through the android application to extract permissions and intents used in that application. Finally, two separate feature vectors, namely *Android permission* and *Android Intent* were developed where a row represents the android application, and a column represents the presence of a particular permission/intent in that application. We developed two separate feature vectors to validate the performance of the E-CNN malware detection models, ECO-FGSM attack, and adversarial retraining defense strategy.

3.3 Classification Pipeline

Tokenization is a crucial step for any model that uses an embedding layer. The token-encoder function is designed specifically for the proposed E-CNN models that use permission or intent feature vectors. The encoding procedure is as follows:

$$\text{Let } arr \text{ represent a feature vector and } N = len(arr) \tag{5}$$
$$\text{For } i^{th} \text{ bit in } arr: \tag{6}$$
$$arr[i] = i + (arr[i] * N) \tag{7}$$

Hence, if i^{th} bit is 0, a token value i is assigned to that position and if i^{th} bit is 1, token value $(i + N)$ is assigned inplace. The benefit of this is that we get

Table 1. Structure of permission/intent based E-CNN malware detection model(s)

Layer	E-CNN (Permission) Output shape	E-CNN (Intent) Output shape
Embedding 1	(None, 195, 50)	(None, 273, 50)
Reshape 1	(None, 195, 50, 1)	(None, 273, 50, 1)
Conv2d 1	(None, 195, 50, 30)	(None, 273, 50, 20)
Activation 1	(None, 195, 50, 30)	(None, 273, 50, 20)
Max pooling2d 1	(None, 97, 25, 30)	(None, 136, 25, 20)
Conv2d 2	(None, 97, 25, 60)	(None, 136, 25, 50)
Activation 2	(None, 97, 25, 60)	(None, 136, 25, 50)
Max pooling2d 2	(None, 48, 12, 60)	(None, 68, 12, 50)
Flatten 1	(None, 34560)	(None, 40800)
Dense 1	(None, 512)	(None, 512)
Dense 2	(None, 256)	(None, 256)
Dense 3	(None, 64)	(None, 64)
Dense 4	(None, 1)	(None, 1)
Activation 3	(None, 1)	(None, 1)
Trainable parameters	17,879,633	21,074,703

$(2 * N)$ different possible encoding values for our feature vector which can then be fed into the embedding layer.

The E-CNN model takes in a tokenized input feature vector (permission or intent) of an android application and feeds it into an embedding layer that transforms the vector into a 2D-array equivalent image. It is then followed by a reshape layer to meet the input requirement of a stacked-2D array of $depth = 3$ for the next convolutional layers. The CNN layers process this array, and the resulting output features are subsequently used by lower DNN layers for classification.

We designed two separate models, namely the permission-based E-CNN model and the intent-based E-CNN model. However, some implementation-specific characteristics are common for the both models. We are using $2D$ convolution layers with *kernel_size* of $(3, 3)$ and *padding* hyperparameter set to *same*. The hyperparameters *strides* and *dilation_rate* are set to $(1, 1)$. These Conv2D layers are followed by *MaxPooling2D layers* that reduce the output feature map's size. The hyperparameters including *pool_size* are set to $(2, 2)$, *strides* and *padding* are set to their default values of *none* and *valid* respectively. The output feature map obtained from CNN is flattened and fed into a DNN for classification. The *kernel initializer* and *bias initializer* for all layers have been set to their *default values*, *glorot_uniform* and *zeros* respectively. We have also added intermediate *dropout layers* to control overfitting. The loss function used for both the models is *binary_cross_entropy*, and the optimizer's choice is varied based on the performance reported in training and testing. Table 1 shows the structure of the permission and intent based E-CNN malware detection models.

3.4   Performance Metrics

We have used the following performance metrics to evaluate the malware detection models, ECO-FGSM adversarial evasion attack, and defense strategy:

- *True Positive (TP)* corresponds to the number of malware applications that are correctly classified as malware by the detection model.
- *False Positive (FP)* corresponds to the number of benign applications that are falsely flagged as malware by the detection model.
- *True Negative (TN)* corresponds to the number of benign applications that are correctly classified as benign by the detection model.
- *False Negative (FN)* corresponds to the number of malware applications that are falsely flagged as benign by the detection model.
- *Accuracy* (Acc) corresponds to the ratio of the number of samples that are correctly classified (malware or benign) and the total number of predictions by the detection model.
- *AUC* aka Area Under the receiver operating characteristic Curve is created by plotting true positive rates and false positive rates at various threshold values for the detection model.
- *Precision* corresponds to the ratio of the number of correctly predicted malware samples with respect to the total number of malware predictions made by the detection model.
- *Recall* corresponds to the ratio of correct malware predictions by the detection model with respect to the total number of malware samples in the dataset.
- *F1* score corresponds to the harmonic mean of precision and recall.
- *Fooling Rate (FR)* corresponds to the percentage of malware samples successfully converted into adversarial malware samples (from the set of malware samples) using evasion attack strategy against the detection model.

4   Experimental Results

This section first discusses the experimental results achieved by permission and intent based E-CNN malware detection models. Later in the section, we explain the results achieved by ECO-FGSM attack against detection models and adversarial retraining as the defense strategy.

4.1   Permission/Intent Based E-CNN Malware Detection

The third step in the proposed workflow (Fig. 1) is to design, train, test, and benchmark the baseline malware detection models. As discussed in Sect. 3.3, we have created two separate E-CNN malware detection models, first uses permission as feature input, and the second uses intent as feature input. Table 2 shows the baseline performances of the above two malware detection models.

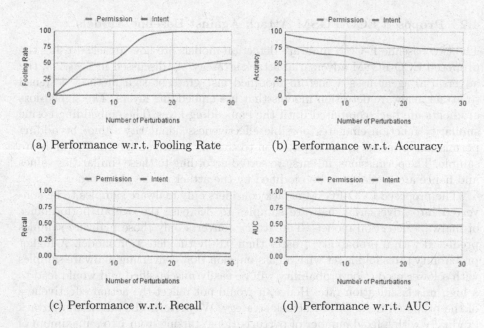

(a) Performance w.r.t. Fooling Rate   (b) Performance w.r.t. Accuracy

(c) Performance w.r.t. Recall   (d) Performance w.r.t. AUC

Fig. 2. Performance of permission/intent based E-CNN malware detection model(s) during ECO-FGSM adversarial attack

Table 2. Performance of baseline permission/intent based E-CNN malware detection model(s)

Feature	Model	Acc	AUC	F1 score	Precision	Recall
Permission	E-CNN	93.48	0.9343	0.9318	0.9454	0.9186
Intent	E-CNN	76.70	0.7638	0.7318	0.8297	0.6545

The permission-based E-CNN malware detection model achieved a high classification accuracy of 93.48%. It also reported a high AUC score of 0.9343, which shows that the model can adequately classify both malware and benign samples. Furthermore, we observe a similar pattern in F1, Precision, and Recall with the scores 0.9318, 0.9454, and 0.9186 respectively for the permission-based detection model. It signifies that the permission-based model distinguishes malware and benign samples with balanced performance in terms of precision and recall. The intent-based E-CNN malware detection model accomplishes a classification accuracy of 76.7% and an AUC of 0.7638. The intent-based detection model achieved a high precision score of 0.8297 compared to the recall score, which was 0.6545. Hence, the above results show that the permission-based E-CNN malware detection model is more accurate than the intent-based detection model. On the other hand, the AUC score signifies that both the models are not overfitting any particular class (malware/benign), and detection models are well balanced.

4.2   Proposed ECO-FGSM Attack Against Baseline Models

The two baseline E-CNN malware detection models are now attacked using the proposed ECO-FGSM adversarial attack strategy. As discussed in Sect. 2.3, the adversarial agent uses a custom modified fast gradient sign method designed to attack malware detection models that use embedding layers. The signed-loss gradients are back-computed until the embedding layer. The embedding cosine similarity function emulates possible effectiveness (similarity value) by adding permission or intent in the application to convert it into an adversarial malware sample. The permissions/intents are sorted according to these similarities values and hence are available to be modified by the attack in the given order.

The proposed ECO-FGSM attack considers only malware samples to be converted into adversarial malware samples to decrease the overall performance of malware detection models. The attack converts only those malware samples predicted with a probability greater than 0.8 by the detection model. A higher probability threshold is set with an assumption that converting malware samples with a lower prediction probability will be easily misclassified and would lead to a high misclassification rate. Hence, it would not reflect the actual effectiveness of the proposed ECO-FGSM attack strategy. We perform the adversarial attack gradually with a fixed number of perturbations starting from 1 to a maximum of 30 modifications in each malware sample. The attack is terminated early only if the malware sample is forcefully misclassified as benign by the E-CNN detection model. The ECO-FGSM attack is designed to add permission/intent in malware samples and thus does not break the syntactic, structural, functional, and behavioral integrity of the modified android application. The effectiveness of the ECO-FGSM attack is quantified using fooling rate, which is the percentage of malicious samples successfully converted into adversarial malware samples that are forcefully misclassified as benign by the E-CNN malware detection model.

Figure 2a shows the variation in fooling rate achieved by the proposed ECO-FGSM attack against the permission/intent based malware detection model. The adversarial attack gradually increased the number of perturbations from 1 to 30, after which the performance saturates. The blue line shows the fooling rate achieved by the ECO-FGSM attack against the permission-based E-CNN detection model. The attack achieves a maximum fooling rate of 55.72% with a maximum of 30 perturbations. The increase in the fooling rate is quite gradual against the permission-based detection model. On the other hand, the ECO-FGSM attack achieves a 99.97% fooling rate against the intent-based E-CNN detection model, which is highlighted using the red line. There is a significant increase in the fooling rate as we move from 1 to 5 perturbations and 10 to 15 perturbations against intent-based detection models. The near 100% fooling rate against the intent-based model suggests that the permission-based model is comparatively more robust in malware classification than its intent-based counterpart. We can also infer that the proposed ECO-FGSM attack is quite effective as it achieves a fooling rate greater than 50% against both the E-CNN detection models.

Table 3. Most vulnerable permissions/intents and their modification percentage

	Android permission	Percentage
1	android.permission.DISABLE_KEYGUARD	5.39
2	android.permission.FORCE_BACK	4.11
3	android.permission.ACTIVITY_RECOGNITION	3.76
4	android.permission.CHANGE_NETWORK_STATE	3.54
5	android.permission.BIND_INCALL_SERVICE	3.45
6	android.permission.BIND_INPUT_METHOD	3.45
7	android.permission.BIND_MIDI_DEVICE_SERVICE	3.45
8	android.permission.BIND_NFC_SERVICE	3.45
9	android.permission.ACCESS_NETWORK_STATE	3.41
10	android.permission.READ_PROFILE	3.27
	Total	**37.28**
	Android intent	Percentage
1	android.intent.action.AIRPLANE_MODE	9.91
2	android.intent.action.ALL_APPS	9.91
3	android.intent.category.APP_FILES	8.30
4	android.intent.action.SEND	5.79
5	android.intent.action.TIMEZONE_CHANGED	4.47
6	android.intent.extra.shortcut.INTENT	4.32
7	android.intent.action.INSTALL_FAILURE	4.05
8	android.intent.extra.EXCLUDE_COMPONENTS	4.01
9	android.intent.extra.LOCUS_ID	3.94
10	FILL_IN_SELECTOR	3.89
	Total	**58.58**

Accuracy refers to the fraction of samples correctly classified as malware or benign by the E-CNN malware detection model. Figure 2b shows the variation in classification accuracy of two detection models as the number of perturbations are increased in malware samples using ECO-FGSM attack. We observe that increasing the maximum number of perturbations will gradually decrease the accuracy of permission/intent based E-CNN malware detection models. The graph suggests that both detection models found it difficult to correctly classify the adversarial samples and thus verify the success of ECO-FGSM attack against detection models. The classification accuracy decreased by 26.6% from 95.29 (before attack) to 69.94 (after attack) for the permission-based E-CNN detection model. Similarly, the intent-based E-CNN detection model showed an accuracy drop of 39.09% from 78.78 (before attack) to 47.98 (after attack), indicating an even greater loss in the model's classification ability as compared to its permission counterpart.

Recall denotes the fraction of correct malware predictions with respect to the total number of malware samples (including adversarial samples, if any) in the dataset. It is an important measure as it is concerned with only malicious samples and hence would reflect the effectiveness of ECO-FGSM attack and performance of malware detection model. Figure 2c depicts the decrease in recall for permission/intent based E-CNN malware detection models. The recall dropped by 55.03% from 0.9356 (before attack) to 0.4207 (after attack) for the permission-based model. However, the recall drop in the case of the intent-based model was more drastic, as evident from the graph. It dropped by 93% from 0.6727 (before attack) to 0.0471 (after attack). This observation goes in hand with the near 100% fooling rate achieved by the ECO-FGSM attack in the case of intent based detection model.

Figure 2d shows the variation in AUC during the ECO-FGSM attack on permission/intent based E-CNN malware detection model(s). Similar to the accuracy trend, the AUC score of the permission-based E-CNN detection model decreased by 27.02% from 0.9526 (before attack) to 0.6952 (after attack). Whereas in the intent-based E-CNN model, AUC dropped by 39.8% from 0.786 (before attack) to 0.4732 (after attack). The higher percentage drop of AUC in the intent-based detection model suggests that it is less adversarial robustness against ECO-FGSM than its permission-based counterpart.

We tabulated the results of post-adversarial attack investigation in Table 3. It shows the top ten android permissions that were added the maximum number of times to malware samples for converting them into adversarial malware samples during the ECO-FGSM attack. We observe that these permissions added benign nature in malware samples, making it difficult for the permission-based E-CNN detection model to classify them as malware. The list of top three android permissions use to generate adversarial malware samples are *android.permission.DISABLE_KEYGUARD*, *android.permission.FORCE_BACK* and *android.permission.ACTIVITY_RECOGNITION*. We can also conclude that adding these top 10 *Vulnerable Permissions* into malicious samples can be helpful in easily generating adversarial malware samples. Similarly, Table 3 shows the top ten intents that were added maximum times to malicious samples for converting them into adversarial malware samples by ECO-FGSM attack against intent-based E-CNN malware detection model. The top 3 intents, namely *android.intent.action.AIRPLANE_MODE*, *android.intent.action.ALL_APPS* and *android.intent.category.APP_FILES* are added 9.91%, 9.91% and 8.30% respectively to generate adversarial samples. These top 10 *vulnerable intents* can also be used in the future to easily generate adversarial malware samples.

4.3   Adversarial Retraining and Robustness of Models

The result of the ECO-FGSM evasion attack showed that the permission/intent based E-CNN malware detection model(s) are vulnerable to adversarial attacks. We then explored adversarial retraining as the defense strategy to counter the

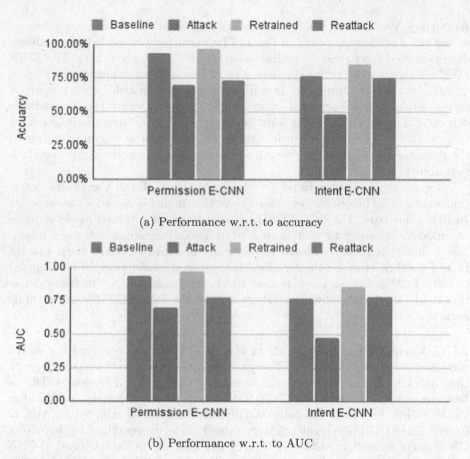

(a) Performance w.r.t. to accuracy

(b) Performance w.r.t. to AUC

Fig. 3. Performance (Accuracy and AUC) of permission/intent based E-CNN malware detection model(s) during baseline, ECO-FGSM evasion attack, adversarial defense, and ECO-FGSM reattack on retrained model(s) (Color figure online)

attack and improve the robustness of the E-CNN detection models. The augmented dataset included the original dataset (malware and benign samples) and adversarial malware samples with correct labels generated during the ECO-FGSM attack. Random oversampling was used to handle class imbalance in the augmented dataset. Then, permission and intent based E-CNN malware detection models were retrained on the augmented dataset. The same 80–20 train-test split ratio was used to retrain-test both the malware detection models. Additionally, we again performed the ECO-FGSM attack on newly trained malware detection models to examine the effect of adversarial retraining on the adversarial robustness of the detection models.

Accuracy Variations. Figure 3a depicts the variations in accuracy observed across the workflow proposed in Fig. 1. The permission-based E-CNN malware detection model achieved a baseline accuracy of 93.48% (blue bar). The ECO-FGSM attack on the permission-based model reduced the model's accuracy to 69.94% (red bar), a drop of 25.18% from the baseline model. Later, the adversarial retrained model achieved an accuracy of 96.67% (yellow bar) for malware detection. Finally, ECO-FGSM reattack on retrained model dropped its accuracy to only 72.95% (green bar), which suggests that adversarial retraining improved the robustness of the malware detection model, thereby improving its classification ability.

We observe a similar trend for the intent-based E-CNN malware detection model. The baseline intent-based detection model achieved an accuracy of 76.70% (blue bar). The ECO-FGSM attack on the intent-based model reduced the model's accuracy to 47.97% (red bar). The adversarially retrained intent-based detection model achieved an accuracy of 85.44% (yellow bar). Finally, ECO-FGSM reattack on the retrained intent-based model dropped its accuracy to only 74.83%. It also suggests that the intent-based E-CNN malware detection model is adversarially more robust against the ECO-FGSM attack than its permission counterpart.

AUC Variations. Figure 3b shows the AUC variations observed across the proposed workflow in Fig. 1. It follows a very similar trend to the accuracy graph (Fig. 3a). Concerning the permission-based E-CNN malware detection model, the baseline model achieved an AUC of 0.9343, which is then reduced to 0.6952 after the ECO-FGSM attack. The adversarially retrained model achieved an AUC of 0.9668. The ECO-FGSM reattack on retrained model dropped its AUC to 0.7696. We observe a similar AUC variation in the case of the intent-based E-CNN malware detection model. The baseline model accomplishes an AUC of 0.7638, which is reduced to an AUC value of 0.4731 after the ECO-FGSM attack. The adversarial retrained model accomplished an AUC of 0.854. The ECO-FGSM reattack on retrained model dropped the AUC to only 0.7776. Therefore, we can conclude that the intent-based E-CNN malware detection model is adversarially superior to the permission-based model against the ECO-FGSM evasion attack.

5   Related Work

Researchers have investigated machine learning and deep neural network approaches to construct various android malware detection systems, which have shown promising results. Aung et al. (2013) proposed a permission-based android malware detection system that used a random forest classifier and achieved 91.78% accuracy [32]. Yerima et al. (2014) used permission and code based features in a Bayesian classifier and attained 93% accuracy [30]. Verma et al. (2016) used permission and intent based features with the J48 decision tree classifier and achieved 94% classification accuracy [27]. Naway et al. (2019) fed a combination of features including permissions and intents into a DNN to achieve 95.31% accuracy [17].

Some studies also explored Convolutional Neural Network (CNN) for the malware detection task. However, we explore an alternate approach using a CNN model that has an embedding layer. The advantage is that the image conversion occurs implicitly within the detection model and thus may not be accessible to a black-box attacker for adversarial perturbations. Also, the embedding layer gives a more concrete feature representation of android samples owing to a larger number of feature parameters. It is also retrainable which enhances the robustness of detection models. We also achieve a higher baseline accuracy for malware detection using permissions on a comparatively larger dataset.

There has been limited investigation on the robustness of malware detection models based on machine learning and deep learning algorithms in terms of adversarial attacks and defenses. Grosse et al. (2017) used FGSM to craft adversarial samples against a malware detection model and explored adversarial retraining as the defense mechanism [11]. Their attack gave misclassification rates of up to 63% against a dense neural network that directly processed binary feature vectors of samples extracted from the DREBIN dataset. Liu et al. (2019) used a genetic algorithm to create adversarial malware samples against machine learning based malware classifiers that were trained on the DREBIN dataset [16]. In another related study, Grosse et al. (2016) used the Jacobian-based Saliency Map attack to create adversarial samples [10]. They used adversarial retraining and defensive distillation for defense against a DNN malware classifier trained on the DREBIN dataset. They achieved misclassification rates ranging from 60% to 80%. There have been some other studies concerning black-box attacks on malware detection as well. Hu et al. (2017) used a generative adversarial network to create adversarial samples in a black box setting [13]. There has been minimal work on attacking malware detection models based on a neural network that uses embedding layer(s). Xu et al. (2020) used cosine similarity in a gradient-based attack to create adversarial perturbations for text classification models [28]. Kurakin et al. (2017) attacked a CNN model using FGSM. However, we propose a modified FGSM attack on an embedding-based CNN model in the malware domain [15]. The attack achieved almost 100% fooling in the case of the android intents feature. The advantage of the proposed attack over other white-box attacks lies in its simplicity and efficiency due to its low processing overheads.

6   Conclusion

This paper explored the adversarial robustness of an image-based malware detection model. The paper first proposed a novel malware detection pipeline to construct the E-CNN models which is a hybrid CNN design with an embedding layer. The designed permission and intent based E-CNN malware detection models achieved classification accuracies of 93.48% and 76.7% respectively. Literature suggests that much work has already been done on malware detection using CNNs and DNNs. However, our paper moves one step further and investigates the adversarial robustness of these malware detection models. Therefore, we proposed an evasion-based adversarial attack strategy named ECO-FGSM to convert malware samples into adversarial malware samples that are forcefully misclassified as benign by the malware detection models. The attack achieved high fooling rates of 55.72% and 99.97% against the permission and intent based E-CNN malware detection models, respectively. We also list the most vulnerable permissions and intents that can be added to malicious samples to convert them into adversarial malware samples that can fool the detection models. Finally, we developed adversarial retraining as a defense strategy to counter the adversarial attack and improve the robustness of the detection models. The adversarial defense improved the accuracy of permission and intent based E-CNN detection models by 3.41% and 11.4% over their baseline performances, respectively. The ECO-FGSM reattack after adversarial retraining showed that the fooling rates decreased by 23.28% and 97.55% against permission and intent E-CNN models, respectively. Hence, we conclude that investigating the robustness of a malware detection model with adversarial attack and defense is an essential step that helps improve its overall performance before any real-world deployment.

References

1. Android Statistics (2021). https://www.businessofapps.com/data/android-statistics/. Accessed June 2021
2. AVTEST. https://portal.av-atlas.org/malware/statistics. Accessed June 2021
3. Arp, D., Spreitzenbarth, M., Hubner, M., Gascon, H., Rieck, K.: DREBIN: effective and explainable detection of android malware in your pocket. In: Network and Distributed System Security (NDSS) Symposium, vol. 14, pp. 23–26 (2014)
4. Barreno, M., Nelson, B., Joseph, A.D., Tygar, J.D.: The security of machine learning. Mach. Learn. **81**(2), 121–148 (2010). https://doi.org/10.1007/s10994-010-5188-5
5. Duc, N.V., Giang, P.T., Vi, P.M.: Permission analysis for android malware detection. In: 7th VAST-AIST Workshop "Research Collaboration: Review and perspective" (2015)
6. Feizollah, A., Anuar, N.B., Salleh, R., Suarez-Tangil, G., Furnell, S.: Androdialysis: analysis of android intent effectiveness in malware detection. Comput. Secur. **65**, 121–134 (2017)
7. Ganesh, M., Pednekar, P., Prabhuswamy, P., Nair, D.S., Park, Y., Jeon, H.: CNN-based android malware detection. In: International Conference on Software Security and Assurance (ICSSA), pp. 60–65. IEEE (2017)
8. Gibert, D.: Convolutional Neural Networks for Malware Classification. University Rovira i Virgili, Tarragona, Spain (2016)
9. Goodfellow, I.J., Shlens, J., Szegedy, C.: Explaining and harnessing adversarial examples. In: International Conference on Learning Representations (ICLR) (2015)
10. Grosse, K., Papernot, N., Manoharan, P., Backes, M., McDaniel, P.: Adversarial perturbations against deep neural networks for malware classification. arXiv preprint arXiv:1606.04435 (2016)

11. Grosse, K., Papernot, N., Manoharan, P., Backes, M., McDaniel, P.: Adversarial examples for malware detection. In: Foley, S.N., Gollmann, D., Snekkenes, E. (eds.) ESORICS 2017. LNCS, vol. 10493, pp. 62–79. Springer, Cham (2017). https://doi.org/10.1007/978-3-319-66399-9_4
12. Hsien-De Huang, T., Kao, H.Y.: R2–D2: color-inspired convolutional neural network (CNN)-based android malware detections. In: IEEE International Conference on Big Data (Big Data), pp. 2633–2642. IEEE (2018)
13. Hu, W., Tan, Y.: Generating adversarial malware examples for black-box attacks based on GAN. arXiv preprint arXiv:1702.05983 (2017)
14. Huang, R., Xu, B., Schuurmans, D., Szepesvári, C.: Learning with a strong adversary. In: International Conference on Learning Representations (ICLR) (2016)
15. Kurakin, A., Goodfellow, I., Bengio, S.: Adversarial machine learning at scale. In: International Conference on Learning Representations (ICLR) (2017)
16. Liu, X., Du, X., Zhang, X., Zhu, Q., Wang, H., Guizani, M.: Adversarial samples on android malware detection systems for IoT systems. Sensors 19(4), 974 (2019)
17. Naway, A., Li, Y.: Using deep neural network for android malware detection. Int. J. Adv. Stud. Comput. Sci. Eng. 7(12), 9–18 (2018)
18. Qiu, J., Zhang, J., Luo, W., Pan, L., Nepal, S., Xiang, Y.: A survey of android malware detection with deep neural models. ACM Comput. Surv. (CSUR) 53(6), 1–36 (2020)
19. Rathore, H., Sahay, S.K., Nikam, P., Sewak, M.: Robust android malware detection system against adversarial attacks using q-learning. Inf. Syst. Front. 23, 1–16 (2020)
20. Rathore, H., Sahay, S.K., Rajvanshi, R., Sewak, M.: Identification of significant permissions for efficient android malware detection. In: Gao, H., J. Durán Barroso, R., Shanchen, P., Li, R. (eds.) BROADNETS 2020. LNICST, vol. 355, pp. 33–52. Springer, Cham (2021). https://doi.org/10.1007/978-3-030-68737-3_3
21. Rathore, H., Sahay, S.K., Thukral, S., Sewak, M.: Detection of malicious android applications: classical machine learning vs. deep neural network integrated with clustering. In: Gao, H., J. Durán Barroso, R., Shanchen, P., Li, R. (eds.) BROADNETS 2020. LNICST, vol. 355, pp. 109–128. Springer, Cham (2021). https://doi.org/10.1007/978-3-030-68737-3_7
22. Rathore, H., Samavedhi, A., Sahay, S.K., Sewak, M.: Robust malware detection models: learning from adversarial attacks and defenses. Forensic Sci. Int. Digit. Investig. 37, 301183 (2021)
23. Sewak, M., Sahay, S.K., Rathore, H.: DeepIntent: implicitintent based android IDS with E2E deep learning architecture. In: IEEE 31st Annual International Symposium on Personal, Indoor and Mobile Radio Communications, pp. 1–6. IEEE (2020)
24. Sewak, M., Sahay, S.K., Rathore, H.: DOOM: a novel adversarial-DRL-based Op-code level metamorphic malware obfuscator for the enhancement of IDS. In: Adjunct Proceedings of the 2020 ACM International Joint Conference on Pervasive and Ubiquitous Computing and Proceedings of the 2020 ACM International Symposium on Wearable Computers, pp. 131–134 (2020)
25. Sewak, M., Sahay, S.K., Rathore, H.: DRLDO: a novel DRL based de-obfuscation system for defence against metamorphic malware. Def. Sci. J. 71(1), 55–65 (2021)
26. Thakur, N., Ding, Y., Li, B.: Evaluating a simple retraining strategy as a defense against adversarial attacks. arXiv preprint arXiv:2007.09916 (2020)
27. Verma, S., Muttoo, S.: An android malware detection framework-based on permissions and intents. Def. Sci. J. 66(6), 618 (2016)
28. Xu, J., Du, Q.: TextTricker: loss-based and gradient-based adversarial attacks on text classification models. Eng. Appl. Artif. Intell. 92, 103641 (2020)

29. Ye, Y., Li, T., Adjeroh, D., Iyengar, S.S.: A survey on malware detection using data mining techniques. ACM Comput. Surv. (CSUR) **50**(3), 1–40 (2017)
30. Yerima, S.Y., Sezer, S., McWilliams, G.: Analysis of Bayesian classification-based approaches for android malware detection. IET Inf. Secur. **8**(1), 25–36 (2013)
31. Yuan, X., He, P., Zhu, Q., Li, X.: Adversarial examples: attacks and defenses for deep learning. IEEE Trans. Neural Netw. Learn. Syst. **30**(9), 2805–2824 (2019)
32. Zarni Aung, W.Z.: Permission-based android malware detection. Int. J. Sci. Technol. Res. **2**(3), 228–234 (2013)

DyPolDroid: Protecting Users and Organizations from Permission-Abuse Attacks in Android

Carlos E. Rubio-Medrano[1]([✉]), Matthew Hill[2], Luis M. Claramunt[3],
Jaejong Baek[3], and Gail-Joon Ahn[4]

[1] Texas A&M University-Corpus Christi, Corpus Christi, TX, USA
carlos.rubiomedrano@tamucc.edu
[2] Tempe, AZ, USA
[3] Arizona State University, Tempe, AZ, USA
{lclaramu,jbaek7}@asu.edu
[4] Samsung Inc., Seoul, Republic of Korea
gahn@asu.edu

Abstract. Android applications are extremely popular, as they are widely used for banking, social media, e-commerce, etc. Such applications typically leverage a series of *Permissions*, which serve as a convenient abstraction for mediating access to security-sensitive functionality, e.g., sending data over the Internet, within the Android Ecosystem. However, several *malicious* applications have recently deployed attacks such as data leaks and spurious credit card charges by *abusing* the Permissions granted initially to them by unaware users in good faith. To alleviate this pressing concern, we present DyPolDroid, a dynamic and semi-automated security framework that builds upon Android Enterprise, a device-management framework for organizations, to allow for users and administrators to design and enforce so-called *Counter-Policies*, a convenient user-friendly abstraction to restrict the sets of Permissions granted to potential malicious applications, thus effectively protecting against serious attacks without requiring advanced security and technical expertise. Additionally, as a part of our experimental procedures, we introduce Laverna, a fully operational application that uses permissions to provide benign functionality at the same time it also abuses them for malicious purposes. To fully support the reproducibility of our results, and to encourage future work, the source code of both DyPolDroid and Laverna is publicly available as open-source.

Keywords: Permission-abuse attacks · Access control · Android Enterprise

1 Introduction

In recent years, there has been an increase in the number of malicious applications in the Android Ecosystem [1], targeting users with a large variety of attacks, e.g.,

---

M. Hill—Independent Researcher.

R. Krishnan et al. (Eds.): SKM 2021, CCIS 1549, pp. 23–36, 2022.
https://doi.org/10.1007/978-3-030-97532-6_2

harvesting private data [2], making unwanted credit card charges [3], retrieving the location of users [4], etc. Whereas the root causes for such attacks have been largely explored in the literature [5], an increasing number of applications look to use and abuse the permissions granted legitimately by users to carry out attacks. These so-called *Permission-Abusing Applications* (PA-Apps) initially pose as *benign* and request users to grant a seemingly normal set of permissions to deliver some *harmless* functionality, e.g., sorting out contact information. However, they later *abuse* the granted permissions to facilitate attacks, e.g., leaking the user's contacts to a remote server via the Internet [6, 7].

Also recently, *Android Enterprise* (AE) [8] has emerged as a convenient framework for monitoring and configuring Android devices in a remote fashion, e.g., automatically installing and uninstalling apps and services. These features allow for AE administrators, *AE-Admins* for short, to manage and enforce security policies protecting users and organizations from costly attacks, e.g., by automatically removing *previously-known* malicious apps from devices at once. In such a context, AE-Admins may also want to prevent the deployment of attacks carried out by PA-Apps that are *unknown* beforehand, and may be downloaded and installed on devices by users at any moment of time. However, solving such a problem involves the following challenges:

1. *Detection.* How to detect *previously-unknown* PA-Apps running on devices?
2. *Prevention.* How to efficiently prevent PA-Apps from carrying out attacks?.
3. *Administration.* How to help AE-Admins to deploy protections against PA-Apps to several different devices in an straightforward and efficient way?
4. *Flexibility.* How to keep protections against PA-Apps up-to-date with respect to changes in the configuration of devices, i.e., the installation of new apps?.
5. *Adoption.* How to protect users from PA-Apps without requiring security expertise and/or modifications to either devices, the OS, or PA-Apps?.

To address these challenges, this paper presents `DyPolDroid` (Dynamic Policies in Android), a dynamic, semi-automated security framework for effectively detecting and neutralizing PA-Apps by means of the following:

1. *Detection.* `DyPolDroid` starts by identifying a series of *Behavioral Patterns*: pairs of Permissions that, if used in combination inside the code of a potential PA-App, may facilitate a successful attack, e.g., combining the `Internet` and `Read-Contacts` permissions to perform a data leak [9].
2. *Prevention.* Then, `DyPolDroid` allows for users and AE-Admins to easily write *Counter-Policies* restricting the occurrence of Behavioral Patterns within Android apps. Later, such Counter-Policies are evaluated and translated into *Device Policies*: lists of permissions that are allowed or denied for each potential PA-App, and are sent for enforcement on devices via the AE.
3. *Administration.* Also, `DyPolDroid` allows for AE-Admins to easily configure and deploy default security Counter and Device Policies restricting the permissions patterns that may be abused by potential PA-Apps, thus effectively preventing them from carrying out attacks on AE-managed devices.
4. *Flexibility.* In addition, up-to-date information on the specific configuration of each device can be also retrieved by means of the AE, and later leveraged

to create custom Counter-Policies that can not only account for previously-unknown, newly-installed PA-Apps, but may also enforce other relevant organizational policies, e.g., restricting gaming apps during office hours.

5. *Adoption.* Finally, DyPolDroid requires no manual, user-made configurations of devices, nor it requires modifications to the device OS, the supporting hardware, nor modifications to the code of potential PA-Apps, as required by other approaches in the literature [10,11], which greatly increases its suitability and convenience for being successfully deployed in practice.

Overall, this paper makes the following contributions:

1. We present a description of PA-Apps, including their relationship with other types of malicious apps for Android that have been studied in the literature.
2. We introduce DyPolDroid, which provides an effective solution for counter-acting PA-Apps at the same time it offers an convenient degree of automation that requires no advanced security expertise from either users or AE-Admins.
3. As a part of our experimental procedure, we also introduce Laverna, a fully operational PA-App, which uses permissions to provide benign functionality, e.g., send automated text messages to phone contacts, at the same time it also abuses them for malicious purposes, e.g., leaking the name and phone of all contacts to a remote server over the Internet.
4. Finally, to support the reproducibility of our experimental results, and to encourage future work based on our reported findings, the source code of both DyPolDroid and Laverna is publicly available as open-source [12].

This paper is organized as follows: Sect. 2 presents some background on the technologies later explored in the paper, and provides a concise definition of the problem that is then later addressed in Sect. 3. We provide a description of a preliminary procedure we have conducted to evaluate the effectiveness of DyPolDroid in Sect. 4, and then discuss some future work and conclude the paper in Sect. 6. A preliminary version of this paper appeared as a poster abstract in the Proceedings of the 6th IEEE European Symposium on Security and Privacy 2021 (Euro S&P 2021) conference [13].

2   Background and Problem Statement

2.1   Android Permissions

In the Android Ecosystem, apps must request and obtain so-called *Permissions*, which serve as convenient abstractions for mediating accesses to the resources of the host device, e.g., sending data over the Internet, turning the camera on and off, sending SMS texts and calls, etc. Android Permissions have been extensively studied in the literature, and have seen a number of changes over the years [14–16]. Historically, there are two major recognizable eras: the *all-or-nothing* era, and the *run-time* era. Prior to Android 6.0, all permissions requested by an app needed to be granted by users at installation time; users were presented with a list of permissions to accept or deny once the app have been downloaded but before installation could begin. If users would choose to deny the requested permissions, the installation of the app would fail. With the release of Android 6.0, the permission model was modified such that apps needed to request access to a permission the first time that they wanted to use it, which allowed for a more fine-grained approach in which users would accept or reject each permission individually [17]. Finally, once a permission is granted to an app, it can be used repeatedly by the instructions of the app's code to access the functionality *guarded* by it, e.g., using the `Internet` permission to access the Internet.

2.2   Android Enterprise

Android Enterprise (AE) is a device management framework that allows for organizations to remotely monitor and configure Android-run devices, e.g., automatically installing and uninstalling apps without extensive user intervention [8]. In addition, for security purposes, AE leverages the permission model described before to dynamically update, e.g., grant or deny, the permissions requested by individual apps, thus allowing for AE administrators to remotely allow or restrict the functionality of the apps installed on a managed device at will. Devices can be remotely managed in two different modes: in the *Fully-Managed* mode, devices may have their configurations set remotely by an AE administrator, leaving little room for users to change the settings of the device. Alternatively, in the *Bring-Your-Own-Sevice* (BYOD) mode, devices may allow for two different profiles to be configured and co-exist inside a device: a *work* profile fully controlled by an AE as described before, and a *user* profile that can be left for users to configure at will, e.g., downloading and installing apps at will.

In addition, leveraging the features provided by AE, administrators can also obtain real-time device configuration data, which may allow them to dynamically send and install, a.k.a., *push*, customized, app-specific permissions on the device depending on the current configuration and any other related context information. This introduced a convenient approach for remote security management that removes the need of instrumenting the device itself, the device OS, the code of apps (APK files), or any other supporting API, as required by previous approaches in the literature [18]. However, this approach for remotely updating permissions may be in fact limited by the network bandwidth available to the device at a given moment of time, which may affect the deployment of immediately needed changes, e.g., denying permissions to a potentially malicious app that has been just detected by AE as installed in the managed device. Also, AE is currently available to devices running versions of Android greater than 5.0.*, and the BYOD mode discussed before is only available to versions of Android running an API level 23 to 29. For the purposes of this paper, we will assume the devices implementing our approach are managed by an existing AE, follow the Android version features just mentioned, and implement either the fully-managed mode or the BYOD mode with a work profile as discussed before.

2.3   The Behavior of Android Applications

For the purposes of this paper, we define *Application Behavior*, or simply *Behavior* for short, as any functionality depicted by an app when executed. Examples

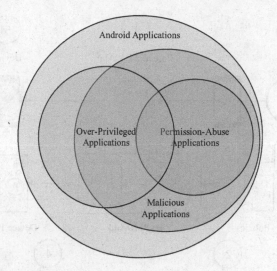

Fig. 1. Classifying Apps in Android based on Behavior. In this paper, we are interested in detecting and neutralizing PA-Apps, which are always regarded as malicious.

include, but are not limited to: gaming, social networking, picture-taking, etc., Conversely, an *Attack* is a well-recognized and highly-undesirable behavior, which may have a negative effect on the user and/or the device. Illustrative examples may include the violation of user privacy via leaking of user contacts, or a financial affectation via unwanted texts or calls.

Having said this, an app is said to be *Benign* if it strictly provides the behavior expected by the user, as stated either by means of a formal or informal documentations and/or descriptions, without causing any affectation to the user or the device. In contrast, a *Malicious* app attempts to subvert the normal, intended use of the expected behavior in an attempt to cause an unwanted affectation either to the user or the device itself [10,11]. In addition, an *Over-Privileged* app requests more permissions than the ones needed to provide its expected benign behavior, and can either neglect such *extra* permissions, thus staying as a benign app, or can actively use them in a malicious way [19–22].

Finally, a *Permission-Abusing* app (PA-App) is a seemingly benign app that is also secretly malicious: its formal or informal usage documentation states that it uses permissions in an expected, harm-free way, e.g., for sending messages to contacts via the Internet, but it may also use them in a malicious, unwanted, and potentially user-harming way as well, e.g., for leaking contacts data to a remote server [3], installing tracking software [4] or collecting user data [2].

2.4 Problem Statement

For the purposes of this paper, we assert that apps that request access to permissions and knowingly misuse them are malicious, i.e., they are PA-Apps, as such permissions may allow for them to successfully carry out attack(s). Therefore, *we*

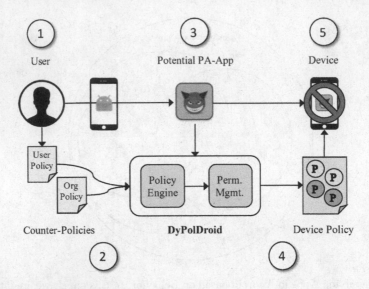

Fig. 2. How DyPolDroid Works: a User signs up for an Android Enterprise (1) and moves on to write Counter-Policies (2), which are later evaluated against the Attack Patterns obtained from any installed PA-Apps (3), producing a Device Policy that is then sent to the Device (4). As a result, PA-Apps have their permissions blocked (5).

aim to detect all potential apps installed on devices that may be PA-Apps, and we also aim to prevent them from successfully exploiting any granted permissions at run-time. Following Fig. 1, detecting all potential over-privileged apps that may or may not be malicious is out of scope of this paper. Also, the detection and prevention of all other malicious Android apps that carry out attacks by means of other techniques other than the abuse of permissions, e.g., dynamic library updates [23], is also out of scope.

3 Our Approach: Dynamic Permission Updates for Potential PA-Apps via the Android Enterprise

To address the problem just described, we now introduce DyPolDroid (Dynamic Policies in Android): a dynamic security framework graphically shown in Fig. 2, in which both users and AE-Admins can actively restrict the behavior of PA-Apps, thus preventing the occurrence of costly attacks in Android devices.

We start in Sect. 3.1 by introducing the concept of *Behavioral Patterns*: pairs of permissions which, if used together within an app's code, may facilitate permission-abusing attacks. Then, we move on to describe in Sect. 3.2 how users and AE-Admins can write so-called *Counter-Policies* for restricting Behavioral Patterns in Android apps. As it is further described in Sect. 3.3, such patterns are in turn discovered by analyzing the data flow of potential PA-Apps installed on a device, and are key component for ultimately producing so-called *Device Policies*, which, as it will be shown in Sect. 3.4 are subsequently enforced by leveraging the dynamic permission updates provided by the AE.

```
1   <Rule RuleId="Laverna_Attacks" Effect="Deny">
2    <Target>
3     <AnyOf> <AllOf> <Match Id="boolean-equal">
4      <AttributeValue>true</AttributeValue>
5       <AttributeDesignator AttributeId="Laverna"/>
6     </Match> </AllOf> </AnyOf>
7      <AnyOf> <AllOf> <Match Id="boolean-equal">
8       <AttributeValue>true</AttributeValue>
9       <AttributeDesignator AttributeId="Steal_Contacts"/>
10    </Match> </AllOf>
11     <AllOf><Match Id="boolean-equal">
12      <AttributeValue>true</AttributeValue>
13      <AttributeDesignator AttributeId="Steal_Messages"/>
14    </Match></AllOf> </AnyOf>
15   </Target>
16  </Rule>
```

Listing 1.1. A Counter-Policy for the Laverna PA-App.

3.1   Behavioral Patterns

Following the description started in Sect. 2.1, we define a *Behavioral Pattern* as a sequence of permissions required by apps to execute either a benign behavior or an attack [9,24]. As an example, the gaming behavior may include the pattern: (CAMERA, INTERNET), whereas a contact-leaking attack may require an pattern such as (READ_CONTACTS, INTERNET). Android apps, including PA-Apps, may in turn depict different behavioral patterns, and there may be an overlap between the permissions exhibited in benign and attack patterns, e.g., the Internet permission being simultaneously used for sending messages (benign) and leaking private data (attack) as just discussed.

3.2   Writing Counter-Policies

Initially, Counter-Policies are written using a series of *templates* depicting a subset of XACML, the *de facto* language for authorization and access control [25]. Users and AE-Admins are then able to protect their device by specifying a variety of rules including features like: which applications can be installed, the default permission policy of any newly installed application, and what potential attacks the user would like to defend against. More interestingly, rules may also include what Behavioral Patterns may be allowed for Android apps that are installed on the device in the future. As an example, Listing 1.1 shows an excerpt of a Counter-Policy for Laverna, a self-developed PA-App that will be featured in Sect. 4. Two Behavioral Patterns, namely, *Steal_Contacts* and *Steal_Messages*, which correspond to the namesake attacks, are specified in lines 7–10 and 11–14. Figure 3 presents a graphical depiction of the process just discussed: Behavioral Patterns can be leveraged to construct custom Counter-Policies, which are then

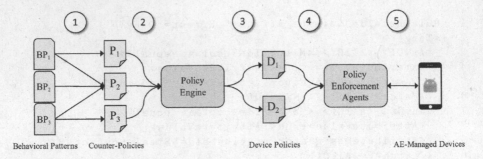

Fig. 3. From Behavioral Patterns to Device Policies: Templates describing Behavioral Patterns are leveraged by users and AE-Admins to write Counter-Policies (1), which are then fed as an input to `DyPolDroid`'s Policy Engine (2), so they can be turned into Device Policies (3). Later, Device Policies are handled by a Policy Enforcement Agent (4), which also retrieves up-to-date device configuration data from the Device (5).

subsequently processed by `DyPolDroid` to create Device Policies. In addition, Counter-Policies leverage the conflict resolution features provided by XACML for the case when multiple policies are applied to the same device, allowing for `DyPolDroid` to resolve conflicts before any resulting policies are sent to the user's device, as show in Fig. 3 (2).

3.3 Discovering Behavioral Patterns

Our Behavioral Patterns are inspired by a set of predetermined attack vectors that were found to be common place across a number of known malicious apps [9]. Those vectors can be represented as a sequence of instructions mapping data from a *source* instruction to a *sink* instruction within the app's code. Normally, both source and sink instructions will include a function call to an Android Class Function (ACF) performing a *sensitive* functionality operation, which will be in turn *guarded* by a given Android Permission. For example, the Behavioral Pattern: (`READ_CONTACTS, INTERNET`), may be depicted within a PA-App code as a sequence of instructions depicting the flow of sensitive data, e.g., user's contact information, in which the first instruction extracts the contacts (source) and the last one sends them to a remote server via the Internet (sink).

To detect the occurrence of Behavioral Patterns within potential PA-Apps, `DyPolDroid` leverages *Taint Tracking* [26], a well-known data flow analysis technique. Initially, data flow sequences are obtained from the APK file of the PA-App by leveraging FlowDroid [27]. Then, for each sequence, its source and sink instructions are cross-referenced against a list containing a series of *mappings* between ACFs and the Permissions such ACFs require for successful execution, as mentioned before. If the permissions mapped to both the sink and source instructions are found to depict a Behavioral Pattern P, then the permissions included in P are returned as a result for further processing, as detailed next.

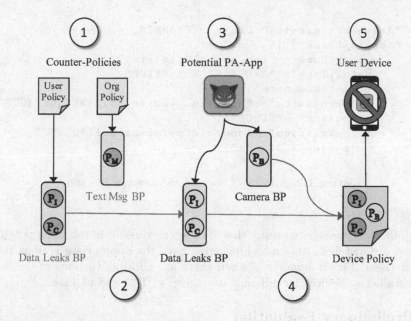

Fig. 4. Creating Device Policies in `DyPolDroid`. The set of *authorized* permissions from each Behavioral Pattern is obtained by evaluating Counter-Policies (1) (2), whereas the set of *observed* permissions is obtained via Taint Tracking analysis on potential PA-Apps (3). Later, the set of *resulting* permissions is calculated by comparing the denied and the requested permissions, and it is later encoded as a Device Policy (4), which is set out to the Device for enforcement via the AE (5).

3.4 Device Policies and Enforcement

Figure 4 gives an overview of how Device Policies are created. First, the set of *authorized* permissions is calculated by evaluating the Counter-Policies that may be relevant under the current context, e.g., the AE, the organization, the user, the device, etc. Second, the set of *observed* permissions, as depicted by the code of a potential PA-App, is obtained by means of the procedure described in the previous Section. Third, the set of *resulting* permissions is obtained by intersecting the sets of authorized and observed permissions. These resulting permissions are then updated within the Device Policy to allow or block their future usage. Listing 1.2 shows a sample Device Policy that blocks the READ_CONTACTS (lines 6–7) and READ_SMS (lines 8–9) permissions for the Laverna PA-App that will be discussed in Sect. 4.

Once a newly-generated Device Policy is received by the AE, it is forwarded to the device following the procedures described in Sect. 2.2. Once received, the policy will immediately begin to apply. If there are any conflicts between the user's device and the new-applied policy, e.g., an installed application is not allowed by the policy, the device manager will freeze the profile until the device is compliant with the policy, e.g., forcing the user to manually uninstall the offending PA-App. Finally, `DyPolDroid` uses a SHA 256 hash in conjunction with

```
 1   { "defaultPermissionPolicy": "PROMPT",
 2     "applications": [{
 3       "packageName": "com.example.laverna",
 4       "installType": "REQUIRED_FOR_SETUP",
 5       "permissionGrants": [
 6         { "permission": "android.permission.READ_CONTACTS",
 7           "policy": "BLOCK"},
 8         { "permission": "android.permission.READ_SMS",
 9           "policy": "BLOCK"}
10     ]}
```

Listing 1.2. A Device Policy for the Laverna PA-App.

the application package to ensure that if different versions of the same potential PA-App are installed, only matching apps have the appropriate actions taken against them. This is important when there are multiple versions of the same app installed on devices for different users, e.g. v1.1.33 and v1.1.34.

4   Preliminary Evaluation

For the purposes of evaluating our approach, we have developed Laverna: a *proof-of-concept* PA-App that requests several permissions for benign functioning, getting full access to the user's contacts, real time location, and SMS so it can serve as a messaging application. However, it also silently exploits the granted permissions to collect and leak data to a remote server when the user is messaging another user. The leaked data includes the contact's full name and phone number and the messages sent, including who the sender and receiver are. The Counter-Policy shown in Listing 1.1 gives the response to the different types of attacks a users wants to defend against. In this case the two attacks are: *Steal_Contacts*, and *Steal_Messages*. Should any of the attacks be found when analyzing the application, the action taken against the used permissions will be to deny them. This change in allowed permissions is reflected in the JSON-based Device Policy shown in Listing 1.2.

In our experiments, Laverna was downloaded on an experimental device, and a user was allowed to select what permissions can be granted before installed such PA-App. Our tests show that DyPolDroid was able to block this application from collecting the user's data and sending it off the device. Since a subset of the permissions requested by Laverna were found to be malicious, the default policy was overridden to block them on the device. While this approach does not preemptively block the leaking of user data, once DyPolDroid has been performed its analysis future cases will mitigate such attacks.

5   Related Work

As described in Sect. 1, several different approaches in the literature have addressed the problem of malicious applications in Android. In such regard,

DyPolDroid is not the first attempt at increasing the security of mobile devices, nor the first to propose fine-grained device policies. In this section, we compare DyPolDroid with previous work, describe similarities and sources of inspiration, and also clarify key differences that add up to the novelty of our approach.

VetDroid [24] was intended to discover and vet undesirable behaviors in Android applications, by analyzing how permissions are used to access (sensitive) system resources, and how these resources are further utilized by the application, allowing for security analysts to easily examine the internal sensitive behaviors of an app. Our description of PA-Apps, presented in Sect. 2, is inspired on this idea. DyPolDroid goes as step further by introducing the concept of attack patterns in Sect. 3.3 to identify malicious behavior in potential PA-Apps.

Kratos [5] is a vendor independent tool for detecting errors in Android security enforcement. It allows for potential permission misuse to be more easily located by creating a call graph of the Android system image, and marking each entry-point to the graph. The nodes in the graph are annotated with security relevant information. The taint analysis depicted by DyPolDroid, which is described in Sect. 3.3, follows a similar approach. However, we aim to detect well-defined attack patterns on the sequences of method calls exhibited by potential PA-Apps. If a pattern is detected, it may be then subsequently restricted by means of a Counter and a related Device Policy.

Slavin et al. [28] proposed a technique to automatically detect policy violations due to errors or omissions within Android applications. They were able to classify these violations into two categories: strong and weak violations. The former is when an application fails to state the data collection purpose, while the latter is when the application vaguely describes its data collection process. DyPolDroid depicts a similar approach in which potentially malicious PA-Apps are identified by the attack patterns they depict within their code. However, the restriction of such PA-Apps may not only depend on their successful identification, but also on the Counter and Device policies as illustrated in Sect. 3.4.

DroidCap [29] introduced OS-level support for so-called *capability-based* permissions in Android, which provided further separation of privileges within an application by modifying the Android Zygote and IPC. Whereas this technique may able to provide a fine-grained, more specific approach for defeating malicious apps, it still requires modifications to the Android OS itself, which can be a considerable barrier for its adoption in practice. In contrast, since DyPolDroid relies on the remote configuration features of the AE, it requires no modification to the OS of the managed devices.

BorderPatrol [30] leverages the *Bring Your Own Device* (BYOD) paradigm, similar to the *work* profile discussed in Sect. 2.2. It protects devices by creating a customized Mobile Device Manager that leverages fine-grained contextual information, thus providing a more fine-grained approach than the AE. However, since BorderPatrol uses the Xposed Module Repository [31], it requires root access to managed devices, which may introduce additional trouble [32].

Finally, Reaper [33] provides real-time analysis of Android apps, in an effort to augment and complement the Android Permission System, thus potentially counteracting ongoing attacks. As with `DyPolDroid`, Reaper leverages dynamic analysis of Android APK files to detect permission abuse, and also uses stack trace info of the running process for further processing. However, it also leverages the Xposed framework, thus, it also requires root access to devices.

6   Conclusions and Future Work

PA-Apps are still an ongoing problem for Android Ecosystems. In such regard, `DyPolDroid` offers an effective and convenient solution that requires no root access to user's devices nor any modifications to the code of PA-Apps: two constraints that have limited the deployment in practice of previous approaches.

As a matter of ongoing and future work, we are currently analyzing several PA-Apps to identify Attack Patterns and potential templates for Counter-Policies that can effectively defeat them. We plan to use this insight to conduct a study in which users sign up for an experimental Android Enterprise. Then, we aim to collect data on how the devices are used, and verify whether `DyPolDroid` was able to accurately detect when permissions were improperly abused. Also, we will collect data regarding the level of user satisfaction with respect to the restrictions observed in the functionality of potential PA-Apps as a result of using `DyPolDroid`. Finally, we must notice that the Android Open Source Project does not maintain a complete mapping of the public permission functions, which is required by our analysis described in Sect. 3.3. In the past, there have been noticeable attempts to determine these, namely Axplorer [34], and PScout [35]. However, at the moment of publication of this paper, the aforementioned approaches were no longer up-to-date with newer versions of Android. Therefore, we plan to further work on this issue, as should more up-to-date mappings become available in the future, the accuracy of `DyPolDroid` will likely increase.

Acknowledgments. This work is partially supported by a grant from the National Science Foundation (NSF-SFS-1129561), a grant from the Center for Cybersecurity and Digital Forensics at Arizona State University, and by a startup funds grant from Texas A&M University – Corpus Christi.

References

1. ZDNet: Play store identified as main distribution vector for most android malware (2020). https://www.zdnet.com/article/play-store-identified-as-main-distribution-vector-for-most-android-malware/
2. The New York Times: The Lesson We're Learning From TikTok? It's All About Our Data (2020). https://www.nytimes.com/2020/08/26/technology/personaltech/tiktok-data-apps.html

3. Wired: A barcode scanner app with millions of downloads goes rogue (2020). https://www.wired.com/story/barcode-scanner-app-millions-downloads-goes-ro gue/

4. Android Authority: Report: Hundreds of apps have hidden tracking software used by the government (2020). https://www.androidauthority.com/government-tracking-apps-1145989/

5. Shao, Y., Ott, J., Chen, Q.A., Qian, Z., Mao, Z.: Kratos: discovering inconsistent security policy enforcement in the android framework. In: Proceedings of the Network and Distributed System Security Symposium (NDSS), January 2016

6. Sunday Express: Android's biggest issue is far worse than we ever imagined, new research proves (2020). https://www.express.co.uk/life-style/science-technology/1362551/Android-Google-Play-Store-malware-problem-researc

7. PC Magazine: Android Users Need to Manually Remove These 16 Infected Apps (2020). https://www.pcmag.com/news/android-users-need-to-manually-remove-these-17-infected-apps

8. Google: Android Enterprise (2021). https://www.android.com/enterprise/

9. Arora, A., Peddoju, S.K., Conti, M.: PermPair: android malware detection using permission pairs. IEEE Trans. Inf. Forensics Secur. **15**, 1968–1982 (2020)

10. Vidas, T., Votipka, D., Christin, N.: All your droid are belong to us: a survey of current android attacks. In: Proceedings of the 5th USENIX Conference on Offensive Technologies, Series WOOT 2011. USENIX Association, USA, p. 10 (2011)

11. Zachariah, R., Akash, K., Yousef, M.S., Chacko, A.M.: Android malware detection a survey. In: 2017 IEEE International Conference on Circuits and Systems (ICCS), pp. 238–244 (2017)

12. Hill, M., Rubio-Medrano, C.E.: DyPolDroid Github Repository (2021). https://github.com/sefcom/DyPolDroid

13. IEEE: The 6th IEEE European symposium on security and privacy (2021). http://www.ieee-security.org/TC/EuroSP2021/

14. Felt, A.P., Chin, E., Hanna, S., Song, D., Wagner, D.: Android permissions demystified. In: Proceedings of the 18th ACM Conference on Computer and Communications Security, Series CCS 2011, pp. 627–638. ACM, New York (2011)

15. Felt, A.P., Ha, E., Egelman, S., Haney, A., Chin, E., Wagner, D.: Android permissions: user attention, comprehension, and behavior. In: Proceedings of the Eighth Symposium on Usable Privacy and Security. ACM, New York (2012)

16. Ramachandran, S., et al.: Understanding and granting android permissions: a user survey. In: 2017 International Carnahan Conference on Security Technology (ICCST), pp. 1–6 (2017)

17. Google: Permissions on android (2021). https://developer.android.com/guide/topics/permissions/overview

18. Enck, W.: Analysis of access control enforcement in android. In: Proceedings of the 25th ACM Symposium on Access Control Models and Technologies, Series SACMAT 2020, pp. 117–118. ACM, New York (2020)

19. Wei, X., Gomez, L., Neamtiu, I., Faloutsos, M.: Permission evolution in the android ecosystem. In: Proceedings of the 28th Annual Computer Security Applications Conference, Series ACSAC 2012, pp. 31–40. ACM, New York (2012)

20. Wang, H., Guo, Y., Tang, Z., Bai, G., Chen, X.: Reevaluating android permission gaps with static and dynamic analysis. In: 2015 IEEE Global Communications Conference (GLOBECOM), pp. 1–6 (2015)

21. Calciati, P., Gorla, A.: How do apps evolve in their permission requests? a preliminary study. In: 2017 IEEE/ACM 14th International Conference on Mining Software Repositories (MSR), pp. 37–41 (2017)

22. Wu, S., Liu, J.: Overprivileged permission detection for android applications. In: ICC 2019-2019 IEEE International Conference on Communications (ICC), pp. 1–6 (2019)
23. Zhauniarovich, Y., Ahmad, M., Gadyatskaya, O., Crispo, B., Massacci, F.: Stadyna: addressing the problem of dynamic code updates in the security analysis of android applications. In: Proceedings of the 5th ACM Conference on Data and Application Security and Privacy, pp. 37–48. ACM, New York (2015)
24. Zhang, Y., et al.: Vetting undesirable behaviors in android apps with permission use analysis. In: Proceedings of the 2013 ACM SIGSAC Conference on Computer and Communications Security, Series CCS 2013, pp. 611–622. ACM, New York (2013)
25. OASIS Standard: eXtensible Access Control Markup Language (XACML) Version 3.0, 22 January 2013. http://docs.oasis-open.org/xacml/3.0/xacml-3.0-core-spec-os-en.html
26. Zhu, D.Y., Jung, J., Song, D., Kohno, T., Wetherall, D.: TaintEraser: protecting sensitive data leaks using application-level taint tracking. SIGOPS Oper. Syst. Rev. **45**(1), 142–154 (2011)
27. Arzt, S., et al.: FlowDroid: precise context, flow, field, object-sensitive and lifecycle-aware taint analysis for android apps, Series PLDI 2014, pp. 259–269. ACM, New York (2014)
28. Slavin, R., et al.: Toward a framework for detecting privacy policy violations in android application code. In: Proceedings of the 38th International Conference on Software Engineering, Series ICSE 2016, pp. 25–36, New York (2016)
29. Dawoud, A., Bugiel, S.: DroidCap: OS support for capability-based permissions in android. In: Proceedings of the Network and Distributed System Security Symposium (NDSS) (2019)
30. Zungur, O., Suárez-Tangil, G., Stringhini, G., Egele, M.: BorderPatrol: securing BYOD using fine-grained contextual information. In: 2019 49th Annual IEEE/IFIP International Conference on Dependable Systems and Networks (DSN) (2019)
31. Drupal: Xposed Module Repository (2021). https://repo.xposed.info/
32. Gasparis, I., Qian, Z., Song, C., Krishnamurthy, S.V.: Detecting android root exploits by learning from root providers. In: 26th USENIX Security Symposium. Vancouver, BC: USENIX Association, pp. 1129–1144, August 2017. https://www.usenix.org/Conf./usenixsecurity17/technical-sessions/presentation/gasparis
33. Diamantaris, M., Papadopoulos, E.P., Markatos, E.P., Ioannidis, S., Polakis, J.: REAPER: real-time app analysis for augmenting the android permission system, Series CODASPY 2019, pp. 37–48. ACM, New York (2019)
34. Backes, M., Bugiel, S., Derr, E., McDaniel, P., Octeau, D., Weisgerber, S.: On demystifying the android application framework: Re-visiting android permission specification analysis. In: Proceedings of the 25th USENIX Conference on Security Symposium, Series SEC 2016, pp. 1101–1118 (2016)
35. Au, K.W.Y., Zhou, Y.F., Huang, Z., Lie, D.: PScout: analyzing the android permission specification. In: Proceedings of the 2012 ACM Conference on Computer and Communications Security, Series CCS 2012, pp. 217–228, New York (2012)

Metacognitive Skills in Phishing Email Detection: A Study of Calibration and Resolution

Yuan Li[1]([✉]), Jingguo Wang[2], and H. Raghav Rao[3]

[1] University of Tennessee at Knoxville, Knoxville, TN 37996, USA
yli213@utk.edu
[2] University of Texas at Arlington, Arlington, TX 76019, USA
jwang@uta.edu
[3] University of Texas at San Antonio, San Antonio, TX 78249, USA
hr.rao@utsa.edu

Abstract. Metacognition plays important roles in human judgments. In this study, we study two types of metacognitive skills, namely calibration and resolution, in individuals' judgments of phishing emails. Drawing upon the Probabilistic Mental Model (PMM) and past research on phishing detection, we examine individual- and task-related factors and their impacts on both skills. Results from an online survey experiment show that task-related factors (i.e., email familiarity, judgment time, variability of judgment time, and task easiness) influence calibration while both task- and individual-related factors (i.e., online transaction experience, victimization experience, email entity familiarity, and variability of judgment time) influence resolution. Interventions to improve individuals' metacognition in phishing email detection are discussed.

Keywords: Detection of phishing email · Metacognition · Calibration · Resolution · Probabilistic Mental Model

1 Introduction

Humans are an integral part of defense against phishing emails, as technological solutions are insufficient to stop phishing attacks [1, 27, 35, 50]. The ability of a person to distinguish phishing emails from legitimate emails is a key element in cybersecurity. Thus, phishing email detection has been a popular topic of research in recent years [4, 21, 45, 46].

Literature shows that people suffer from judgmental bias such as overconfidence when detecting phishing emails [20, 46], which explains why they fall victim to phishing attacks even after training [21]. Such kind of bias reflects their deficiency in metacognitive skills. Recently, scholars have started to examine metacognition in phishing detection [9, 46], with the goals to recognize roots in the metacognitive bias and design interventions to improve individuals' metacognitive skills for phishing detection. Other than

R. Krishnan et al. (Eds.): SKM 2021, CCIS 1549, pp. 37–47, 2022.
https://doi.org/10.1007/978-3-030-97532-6_3

overconfidence, calibration and resolution represent two important skills in metacognition [52]. Calibration refers to the skill to correctly assign judgmental confidence based on accuracy, and resolution refers to the skill of a person to distinguish correct judgments from incorrect judgments. Both skills influence how a person processes information in a judgmental task and how the judgment may influence subsequent behavior (e.g., seeking more information, or committing the decision). While calibration and resolution have been widely studied in judgmental literature [25, 52], their applications in phishing detection research have been scarce [9].

This study answers these questions: 1) What are the metacognitive skills of a person in the context of phishing email detection? And, 2) what factors influence a person's metacognitive skills in phishing detection? We first present the conceptualizations of the skills, and then draw upon the Probabilistic Mental Model [17, 22] and the phishing detection literature [11, 21, 43–45, 48] to study the impact of a few antecedent factors on both skills. Lastly, we report an online experiment conducted to survey respondents and empirically test the effects of the antecedents.

2   Calibration and Resolution: Conceptualizations

Two important metacognitive skills are calibration and resolution [52]. Both are based on probabilistic judgments, i.e., how likely an email is a phishing email. By assigning a confidence level to a judgment, the person's metacognitive skills can be measured. Accordingly, calibration represents the reliability of a person in correctly assigning confidence levels to individual judgments. It is examined by employing a series of judgments and aggregating the discrepancies between confidence and accuracy across the judgments [34, 41]. Higher calibration means the person is more reliable and credible in the judgments [42].

Resolution, in contrast, represents a person's capability to distinguish correct judgments from incorrect judgments, thus reflecting their diagnosticity or discriminability [23]. It resolves an inherent issue in calibration when a person assigns the same confidence level to all the judgments: for example, a person randomly predicts the sex of a new-born baby with a 50% confidence [29], yielding perfect calibration but zero value for prediction. Resolution resolves this issue by grouping the judgments based on their similarities (i.e., same confidence levels) and examining the correctness of judgments in those groups. This is based on the premise that for judgments at the same confidence level, they should exhibit similar attributes and thus have the same results (i.e., right or wrong). If a person feels confident about some judgments and those judgments are all correct (i.e., true positive or true negative), or the person feels uncertain about some judgments and those judgments are all incorrect, the person is said to have strong resolution skills to discern the correct and incorrect judgments. Thus, resolution has practical value for prediction [36].

3   Theoretical Basis and Hypotheses

We draw upon the Probabilistic Mental Model (PMM) [17, 22] to study the mechanisms of a person's calibration and resolution skills. The model suggests that when making a probabilistic judgment, a person develops a PMM for the task through inductive inference, placing the task (i.e., judging an email) in a larger context called reference class (that includes similar emails received earlier) and determines the conditional probability of the event based on the context. The PMM links the specific constitution of the problem with that of the reference class stored in long-term memory, and the reference class provides information cues to judge if the email is a phish [17].

The amount of information cues inferred from the reference class and the ecological probability (i.e., chance of occurrence) of the event determine judgmental confidence and accuracy, which then influence calibration and resolution [6, 7]. For example, both grammatical errors and suspicious addresses are cues for phishing emails [12, 13], but their ecological probabilities may differ: compared to grammatical errors, the existence of suspicious email addresses is a stronger signal of phishing emails. Thus, if a person makes the judgment solely based on grammatical errors, judgmental confidence will be low or misjudgment may occur; but if the person uses the suspicious email addresses as the basis of judgment, the person may be more confident and accurate.

Two general sources of bias exist in probabilistic judgment: one deals with limited knowledge or experience of the individual regarding the ecological probabilities of the events (called external errors), and the other deals with the difficulty of recalling reference class from long-term memory (called internal errors) [22]. For external errors, the literature suggests that different individuals may have different knowledge or experience with phishing attacks, and their attention to signals may differ due to individual and task related factors [43]. Regarding this, we focus on a few previously verified factors that are closely related to judgments: online transaction experience, victimization experience, email familiarity, and source/business entity familiarity. The first two factors deal with individual characteristics while the latter two deal with situational or task attributes. Research on cognitive competence [19] suggests that these factors influence the abilities of a person to recognize information cues from emails and to detect phishing emails.

For internal errors, we study factors that influence one's ability in fetching reference class or signals from long-term memory, including time spent in judging emails and variability of judgment time, as time is key to effective processing of information in judgmental tasks [3, 31, 47]. In addition, we include task easiness in the study, which may also influence the observed calibration and resolution skills of a person due to the well-known hard-easy effect [17, 22]. The impacts of the external and internal error factors on calibration and resolution are discussed as follows.

First, we argue that personal experience deals with subjective knowledge about prior objects or events [18]. Online transaction experience refers to the extent to which a person uses Internet to conduct transactions. Such experience is positively related to the individual's ability in accomplishing online tasks [34]. Online experience helps to accumulate information cues about potential online threats, therefore increasing the reference class for judging new threats and enhancing the resolution skill of the person. In general, Internet savvy individuals have greater knowledge and are more capable of distinguishing phishing emails than amateurs [49]. This suggests a positive impact of online transaction experience on resolution. Since experience may improve both accuracy and confidence at the same time, resulting in no change in calibration [34], we therefore do not expect its impact on calibration. This leads to the following hypotheses regarding phishing email detection:

H1: A person's online transaction experience (a) does not influence the person's calibration skill but (b) increases the resolution skill.

Second, being a prior victim of phishing attacks provides more specific experience with phishing attack. It may help reduce overconfidence in phishing email detection [46], as the person is more aware of the true ecological probability (i.e., correctness or actual occurrence) of phishing emails, which enables the person to adjust confidence judgment accordingly. Thus, the person, after being victimized, would become more aware of the existence and prevalence of phishing emails, and would therefore pay more attention to information cues of potential phishing emails. This suggests an increase in calibration skill. Additionally, prior victimization experience may help the person to develop appropriate mental models (i.e., PMM) to process new emails, yielding a more confident judgment. Prior victimization may also make a person more cautious about phishing attacks, drawing more attention to information cues in emails and decreasing the threshold to recognize a phishing email. This leads to improved resolution skill in discerning potential phishing emails. Therefore, we hypothesize:

H2: A person's victimization experience with phishing attack increases (a) the calibration skill and (b) the resolution skill of the person.

Third, literature on cognitive competence [19] suggests that individuals feel more confident in a context where they believe they are knowledgeable or familiar than in a context where they believe they are uninformed and unfamiliar. General knowledge about, and familiarity with, a context influences their abilities in interpreting information cues in the context and the subsequent judgments. Perceived familiarity with the source/business entity refers to the extent to which one feels acquainted with the source or business entity in an email: for instance, the name and logo of the company in the email are known to the person. Unfortunately, the same look-and-feel may be used to deceive individuals, as people may react more favorably to a known business entity than an unknown one [28]. Thus, emails sent from a known source significantly increase user susceptibility to phishing [30]. If an email is sent from an unfamiliar business, the person may become vigilant and examine the entirety of the email. Therefore, we expect that perceived source/business entity familiarity causes people to feel trusted and less concerns, leading to poor judgment and reduced calibration and resolution. We hypothesize:

H3: A person's perceived familiarity with the business entity in the email decreases (a) the calibration skill and (b) the resolution skill of the person.

Fourth, we argue that, similarly, perceived email familiarity may increase one's confidence in judgment, leading to overconfidence and miscalibration. This can be interpreted as familiarity with business entity: the same look-and-feel in an email may deceive the user and cause the drawing of early conclusion without further inspecting the entirety of the email. On the other hand, perceived email familiarity may help boost the resolution skill: if a person has seen the email before, he or she may have had a mental model about the email, and can retrieve the model for direct judgment (with a high confidence) instead of relying on external information cues or signals that may lead to biased judgment. We hypothesize:

H4: A person's email familiarity (a) decreases the calibration skill while (b) increases the resolution skill.

Fifth, the efforts a person puts on processing emails may influence judgmental skills. Judgment time is defined as the time elapsed from the moment the person receives an email to the moment the judgment is made. Literature in behavioral decision making shows that cognitive effort (such as time) and accuracy are closely related [32]. In a study on perceptual judgment, Baranski and Petrusic [5] found that increasing demand for judgmental speed decreased the resolution skill of the subjects. For human detection of errors, Klein et al. [24] found that effort affected detection performance through changes in discriminability: by paying closer attention to information, an individual might be better able to distinguish errors from correct data values. In terms of phishing detection, less judgment time means, in general, that a person is unable or unwilling to recall all relevant emails in the reference class from long-term memory, or does not adequately detect signals in the emails but rushes to decision to save efforts. As a result, calibration and resolution skills will both weaken. If more time is spent examining the emails, a more solid reference class may be recalled and more information cues may be processed, leading to improved judgment. Thus, we hypothesize:

H5: The time a person spends in judgment (i.e., judgment time) increases (a) the calibration skill and (b) the resolution skill of the person.

Sixth, how individuals allocate cognitive resources in judgments is also an important factor. When resources such as time are limited and attention is diverted, proper recognition of information cues may not occur and the outcome may result in false beliefs [3]. Variability in attention influences subsequent judgments [23], as when a person deals with many emails daily, which is the case in the era of digital communication. Greater variability in judgment time is associated with the tendency to use heuristic rules that rely on less or selective information [33], leading to bias [16]. Therefore, we hypothesize:

H6: A person's variability of judgment time decreases (a) the calibration skill and (b) the resolution skill of the person.

Last, calibration and resolution can be influenced by the difficulty of the tasks. This is known as the hard-easy effect [22, 23]: in the calibration literature, it is widely recognized that people are overconfident in judging difficult tasks and underconfident for easy tasks, suggesting a positive effect of ease of tasks on calibration [5, 23]. Similarly, easy tasks are found to be associated with increased resolution skills [5, 37]: from the signal detection perspective [51], easy tasks imply that the signals of phishing emails are strong, resulting in improved discriminability of the person. Thus, we hypothesize:

H7: The easiness of detection tasks increases (a) the calibration skill and (b) the resolution skill of a person.

4 Research Method and Results

An online experiment was conducted to study individuals' phishing email detection abilities. The subjects each judged a group of 16 emails randomly picked from a pool of phishing and legitimate emails, and the images of the emails were presented sequentially to each subject in the web browser. The subjects then judged whether each email was legitimate or not, and how confident they were (with a score of 50 to 100). They also answered questions regarding other research constructs. Following the suggestion by Schneider [37], we employed equal proportions of phishing and legitimate emails in the study to avoid truth-bias or lie-bias in judgments.

Table 1 shows the measurements of the independent variables. As our unit of analysis is individual, we obtained the mean value of business entity familiarity, and mean value of email familiarity, across the group of emails for each subject. This captured the subject's overall familiarity with the source/business entities and emails. Online transaction experience and victimization experience were each measured by summing the values of corresponding items. For each email, the time spent to make judgment was recorded online; the total time spent on the 16 emails was then calculated to measure judgment time. Following prior literature [8, 33, 39], the coefficient of variation (CV) of the time spent on each email was calculated to measure variability of judgment time. Task easiness was derived from the results of all the email judgments.

Table 1. Measurement of independent variables.

Independent variables	Measurement methods
Online transaction experience	1) Buying products or services online with a credit card, a debit card, or a payment service such as PayPal 2) Accessing bank accounts (such as checking, saving, mortgage) online 3) Paying bills (such as electronic, utility, credit cards, loans) online 4) Buying and selling stocks or mutual funds online
Victimization experience	1) Someone used or attempted to use your credit cards without permission 2) Someone used or attempted to use your accounts such as your wireless phone account, bank account or debit/check cards without your permission 3) Someone used or attempted to use your personal information without permission to obtain new credit cards or loans, run up debts, open other accounts, or commit other frauds
Business entity familiarity	How familiar do you think you are with the business entity indicated in the email?
Email familiarity	Have you personally received or seen this particular email before this survey?
Judgment time	Recorded online
Variability of judgment time	The coefficient of variation (CV) of the time spent on the emails was calculated
Task easiness	The mean value of the easiness of judging the emails that a subject received, where the easiness of each email was derived from the proportion of subjects who judged the same email correctly

The dependent variables (i.e., calibration and resolution) are derived based on the formulas provided by Björkman [7]. Control variables were each measured with a single item. A total of 592 valid observations were obtained in the experiment.

We ran multiple liner regressions to test the hypotheses. The results are reported in Table 2. First, online transaction experience has no significant effect on calibration, but has a positive effect on resolution, supporting H1. Victimization experience has no significant effect on calibration, rejecting H2a, but it has a positive effect on resolution, supporting H2b. Source/business entity familiarity has no significant effect on calibration, rejecting H3a, but it has a negative effect on resolution, providing support for H3b. Email familiarity has a negative effect on calibration as it increases CI, but its effect on resolution is insignificant, providing support for H4a but not H4b. Judgment time has a positive effect on calibration as it reduces CI, but its effect on resolution is insignificant for RI, providing mixed support for H5. H6 is fully supported, as variability of judgment time increases CI and reduces RI, suggesting that variability in decision time reduces both calibration and resolution. Finally, task easiness increases calibration as it reduces CI, but its effect on resolution is insignificant, providing support for H7a but not H7b.

Table 2. Results of multiple liner regressions.

Independent variables	(a) CI[a]			(b) RI		
	β	t-value	p-value	β	t-value	p-value
Online transaction experience (H1)	.075	1.727	.085	.155	3.543	.000
Victimization experience (H2)	−.048	−1.183	.237	.091	2.196	.029
Business entity familiarity (H3)	.057	1.280	.201	−.101	−2.212	.027
Email familiarity (H4)	.099	2.323	.021	.054	1.245	.213
Judgment time (H5)	−.135	−3.197	.001	.071	1.669	.096
Variability of judgment time (H6)	.150	3.513	.000	−.137	−3.157	.002
Task easiness (H7)	−.128	−3.223	.001	−.050	−1.238	.216
Number of emails per day	.002	0.055	.956	.040	0.993	.321
Gender	−.054	−1.344	.179	.044	1.078	.281
Age	.000	0.007	.994	−.077	−1.833	.067
Education	.017	0.428	.668	−.010	−0.255	.798
R^2	.086			.057		

[a] As CI is a penalty score, it is opposite to the calibration skills; thus, a positive regression coefficient means reduced calibration skills, and vice versa.

5 Discussion and Conclusions

5.1 Contributions of the Study

The research makes two contributions. First, the introduction of calibration and resolution skills provides a new perspective in studying individuals' phishing detection abilities that goes beyond prior literature on detection accuracy and overconfidence [20, 38, 46]. Accuracy is critical to judgmental performance, but it alone cannot fully characterize a person's phishing detection abilities. As the relationship between confidence and accuracy reflects how a person processes information for judgment [3], this study therefore provides new insight into a person's phishing detection abilities and adds to the portfolio of cybersecurity skills recognized in prior literature [10].

Second, factors recognized in prior literature, such as individual characteristics, have been studied for their impact on general knowledge questions [26], restricting their applicability in phishing email detection. Our study is among the first to provide empirical evidence of the factors in this field. Importantly, the finding of the different impacts of individual characteristics and task attributes not only provides support to prior literature [34, 40], but also has implications for research and practice (discussed below).

5.2   Implications of the Study

For theory, our study suggests that in studying individuals' phishing detection abilities, the focus should move beyond judgmental accuracy and examine metacognitive skills in terms of calibration and resolution. This will extend knowledge of individuals' reliability and diagnosticity in phishing email detection. If a person exhibits high accuracy but low calibration and/or resolution, it could be that the person is underconfident in the judgments or the judgmental task is not challenging enough to elicit the person's actual abilities.

Another important implication is the use of both calibration and resolution to assess the effectiveness of fraud detection algorithms or models in Artificial Intelligence (AI). People are not very good at detecting deception [15]; thus, intelligent agents are provided for additional help, such as AI-based phishing email filters [2]. The challenge is that an accurate model, developed from one dataset with a certain threshold, may perform poorly in another dataset [14] since the threshold can be manipulated to achieve the best performance in the first dataset. Thus, to select an effective intelligent agent, the underlying models should be tested using calibration and resolution measures in addition to traditional accuracy measure.

5.3   Limitations of the Study

The study has a few limitations that may be addressed in future research. First, the online experiment was not conducted in a controlled environment, which may cause bias. Thus, future research may employ other methods, such as field experiments, to verify the findings. Second, we did not control for the subjects' own abilities to detect phishing emails, which may also influence their calibration and resolution skills. Future research may expand the current study to incorporate personal ability factors.

References

1. Abbasi, A., Zahedi, F.M., Zeng, D., Chen, Y., Chen, H., Nunamaker, J.F.: Enhancing predictive analytics for anti-phishing by exploiting website genre information. J. Manag. Inf. Syst. **31**(4), 109–157 (2015)

2. Abbasi, A., Zhang, Z., Zimbra, D., Chen, H., Nunamaker, J.J.F.: Detecting fake websites: the contribution of statistical learning theory. MIS Q. **34**(3), 435–461 (2010)
3. Alba, J.W., Hutchinson, J.W.: Knowledge calibration: what consumers know and what they think they know. J. Consum. Res. **27**(2), 123–156 (2000)
4. Anderson, B.B., Vance, A., Kirwan, C.B., Jenkins, J.L., Eargle, D.: From warning to wallpaper: why the brain habituates to security warnings and what can be done about it. J. Manag. Inf. Syst. **33**(3), 713–743 (2016)
5. Baranski, J.V., Petrusic, W.M.: The calibration and resolution of confidence in perceptual judgments. Percept. Psychophys. **55**, 412–428 (1994)
6. Björkman, M.: Knowledge, calibration, and resolution: a linear model. Organ. Behav. Hum. Decis. Process. **51**(1), 1–21 (1992)
7. Björkman, M.: Internal cue theory: calibration and resolution of confidence in general knowledge. Organ. Behav. Hum. Decis. Process. **58**(3), 386–405 (1994)
8. Brucks, M.: The effects of product class knowledge on information search behavior. J. Consum. Res. **12**(1), 1–16 (1985)
9. Canfield, C.I., Fischhoff, B., Davis, A.: Better beware: comparing metacognition for phishing and legitimate emails. Metacogn. Learn. **14**(3), 343–362 (2019). https://doi.org/10.1007/s11 409-019-09197-5
10. Carlton, M., Levy, Y., Ramim, M., Terrell, S.: Development of the MyCyberSkills™ iPad app: a scenarios-based, hands-on measure of non-it professionals' cybersecurity skills. Pre-ICIS Workshop on Information Security and Privacy (SIGSEC). Fort Worth, Texas (2015)
11. Chen, R., Wang, J., Herath, T., Rao, H.R.: An investigation of email processing from a risky decision making perspective. Decis. Support Syst. **52**(1), 73–81 (2011)
12. Dhamija, R., Tygar, J.D., Hearst, M.: Why phishing works. Inf. Syst. Educ. J. **13**(5), 581–590 (2006)
13. Downs, J.S., Holbrook, M.B., Cranor, L.F.: Decision Strategies and Susceptibility to Phishing, vol. 79 (2006). https://doi.org/10.1145/1143120.1143131
14. Ferri, C., Hernández-Orallo, J., Modroiu, R.: An experimental comparison of performance measures for classification. Pattern Recogn. Lett. **30**(1), 27–38 (2009)
15. George, J.F., et al.: The role of e-training in protecting information assets against deception attacks. MIS Q. Exec. **7**(2), 85–97 (2008)
16. Gigerenzer, G.: How to make cognitive illusions disappear: beyond "heuristics and biases." Eur. Rev. Soc. Psychol. **2**, 83–115 (1991)
17. Gigerenzer, G., Hoffrage, U., Kleinbolting, H.: Probabilistic mental models: a Brunswikian theory of confidence. Psychol. Rev. **98**, 506–528 (1991)
18. Hadar, L., Sood, S., Fox, C.R.: Subjective knowledge in consumer financial decisions. J. Mark. Res. **50**(3), 303–316 (2013)
19. Heath, C., Tversky, A.: Preference and belief: ambiguity and competence in choice under uncertainty. J. Risk Uncertain. **4**(1), 5–28 (1991)
20. Hong, K.W., Kelley, C.M., Tembe, R., Murphy-Hill, E., Mayhorn, C.B.: Keeping up with the Joneses: assessing phishing susceptibility in an email task. Proc. Hum. Fact. Ergon. Soc. Ann. Meet. **57**(1), 1012–1016 (2013). https://doi.org/10.1177/1541931213571226
21. Jensen, M.L., Dinger, M., Wright, R.T., Thatcher, J.B.: Training to mitigate phishing attacks using mindfulness techniques. J. Manag. Inf. Syst. **34**(2), 597–626 (2017)
22. Juslin, P., Olsson, H., Mats, B.: Brunswikian and Thurstonian origins of bias in probability assessment: on the interpretation of stochastic components of judgment. J. Behav. Decis. Mak. **10**(3), 189–209 (1997)
23. Keren, G.: On the calibration of probability judgments: some critical comments and alternative perspectives. J. Behav. Decis. Mak. **10**(3), 269–278 (1997)
24. Klein, B.D., Goodhue, D.L., Davis, G.B.: Can humans detect errors in data? Impact of base rates, incentives, and goals. MIS Q. **21**(2), 169–194 (1997)

25. Koriat, A.: Metacognition: Decision Making Processes in Self-Monitoring and Self-Regulation. Wiley, New Jersey (2015)
26. Krug, K.: The relationship between confidence and accuracy: current thoughts of the literature and a new area of research. Appl. Psychol. Crim. Just. 3(1), 7–41 (2007)
27. Kumaraguru, P., Sheng, S., Acquisti, A., Cranor, L.F., Hong, J.: Teaching Johnny not to fall for phish. ACM Trans. Internet Technol. 10(2), 1–31 (2010)
28. Li, Y.: The impact of disposition to privacy, website reputation and website familiarity on information privacy concerns. Decis. Support Syst. 57(6), 343–354 (2014)
29. Liberman, V., Tversky, A.: On the evaluation of probability judgments: calibration, resolution, and monotonicity. Psychol. Bull. 114(1), 162 (1993)
30. Moody, G., Galletta, D., Dunn, B.: Which phish get caught? An exploratory study of individuals' susceptibility to phishing. Eur. J. Inf. Syst. 26(6), 564–584 (2017)
31. Palmer, M.A., Brewer, N., Weber, N., Nagesh, A.: the confidence-accuracy relationship for eyewitness identification decisions: effects of exposure duration, retention interval, and divided attention. J. Exp. Psychol. 19(1), 55–71 (2013)
32. Payne, J.W.: Task complexity and contingent processing in decision making: an information search and protocol analysis. Organ. Behav. Hum. Perform. 16(2), 366–387 (1976)
33. Payne, J.W.: Contingent decision behavior. Psychol. Bull. 92(2), 382–402 (1982)
34. Pillai, K.G., Hofacker, C.: Calibration of consumer knowledge of the web. Int. J. Res. Mark. 24(3), 254–267 (2007)
35. Rao, J.M., Reiley, D.H.: The economics of spam. J. Econ. Perspect. 26(3), 87–110 (2012)
36. Schmid, C.H., Griffith, J.L.: Multivariate Classification Rules: Calibration and Discrimination. Wiley, New Jersey (2005)
37. Schneider, S.L.: Item difficulty, discrimination, and the confidence-frequency effect in a categorical judgment task. Organ. Behav. Hum. Decis. Process. 61(2), 148–167 (1995)
38. Sheng, S., Magnien, B., Kumaraguru, P., Acquisti, A., Cranor, L.F.: Anti-Phishing Phil: the Design and Evaluation of a Game That Teaches People Not to Fall for Phish. Carnegie Mellon University, Pittsburgh (2007)
39. Stone, D.N.: Overconfidence in initial self-efficacy judgments: effects on decision processes and performance. Organ. Behav. Hum. Decis. Process. 59(3), 452–472 (1994)
40. Stone, E.R., Opel, R.B.: Training to improve calibration and discrimination: the effects of performance and environmental feedback. Organ. Behav. Hum. Decis. Process. 83(2), 282–309 (2000)
41. Tang, F., Hess, T.J., Valacich, J.S., Sweeney, J.T.: The Effects of visualization and interactivity on calibration in financial decision-making. Behav. Res. Account. 26(1), 25–58 (2014)
42. Tenney, E.R., Spellman, B.A., Maccoun, R.J.: The benefits of knowing what you know (and what you don't): how calibration affects credibility. J. Exp. Soc. Psychol. 44(5), 1368–1375 (2008)
43. Vishwanath, A., Herath, T., Chen, R., Wang, J., Rao, H.R.: Why do people get phished? Testing individual differences in phishing vulnerability within an integrated, information processing model. Decis. Support Syst. 51(3), 576–586 (2011)
44. Wang, J., Herath, T., Chen, R., Vishwanath, A., Rao, H.R.: Phishing susceptibility: an investigation into the processing of a targeted spear phishing email. IEEE Trans. Prof. Commun. 55(4), 345–362 (2012)
45. Wang, J., Li, Y., Rao, H.R.: Overconfidence in phishing email detection. J. Assoc. Inf. Syst. 17(11), 759–783 (2016)
46. Wang, J., Li, Y., Rao, H.R.: Coping responses in phishing detection: an investigation of antecedents and consequences. Inf. Syst. Res. 28(2), 378–396 (2017)
47. Weber, N., Brewer, N.: Confidence-accuracy calibration in absolute and relative face recognition judgments. J. Exp. Psychol. 10(3), 156–172 (2004)

48. Wright, R.T., Jensen, M.L., Thatcher, J.B., Dinger, M., Marett, K.: Influence techniques in phishing attacks: an examination of vulnerability and resistance. Inf. Syst. Res. **25**(2), 385–400 (2014)
49. Wright, R.T., Marett, K.: The influence of experiential and dispositional factors in phishing: an empirical investigation of the deceived. J. Manag. Inf. Syst. **27**(1), 273–303 (2010)
50. Wu, M., Miller, R.C., Garfinkel, S.L.: Do security toolbars actually prevent phishing attacks? In: Proceedings of the SIGCHI Conference on Human Factors in Computing Systems ACM, pp. 601–610. Quebec, Canada (2006)
51. Xiao, B., Benbasat, I.: Designing warning messages for detecting biased online product recommendations: an empirical investigation. Inf. Syst. Res. **26**(4), 793–811 (2015)
52. Yeung, N., Summerfield, C.: Metacognition in human decision-making: confidence and error monitoring. Philos. Trans. Royal Soc. Biol. Sci. **367**(1594), 1310–1321 (2012)

Secure Knowledge Management

Deep Reinforcement Learning for Cybersecurity Threat Detection and Protection: A Review

Mohit Sewak[1]([✉]), Sanjay K. Sahay[2], and Hemant Rathore[2]

[1] Security and Compliance Research, Microsoft R&D, Pune, India
mohit.sewak@microsoft.com
[2] Department of CS and IS, BITS Pilani, Sancoale, Goa, India
{ssahay,hemantr}@goa.bits-pilani.ac.in

Abstract. The cybersecurity threat landscape has lately become overly complex. Threat actors leverage weaknesses in the network and endpoint security in a very coordinated manner to perpetuate sophisticated attacks that could bring down the entire network and many critical hosts in the network. Increasingly advanced deep and machine learning-based solutions have been used in threat detection and protection. The application of these techniques has been reviewed well in the scientific literature. Deep Reinforcement Learning has shown great promise in developing AI-based solutions for areas that had earlier required advanced human cognizance. Different techniques and algorithms under deep reinforcement learning have shown great promise in applications ranging from games to industrial processes where it is claimed to augment systems with general AI capabilities. These algorithms have recently also been used in cybersecurity, especially in threat detection and endpoint protection, where these are showing state-of-the-art results. Unlike supervised machine and deep learning, deep reinforcement learning is used in more diverse ways and are empowering many innovative applications in the threat defense landscape. However, there does not exist any comprehensive review of these unique applications and accomplishments. Therefore, in this paper, we intend to fill this gap and provide a comprehensive review of the different applications of deep reinforcement learning in cybersecurity threat detection and protection.

Keywords: Deep Reinforcement Learning · Network IDS · Endpoint detection · Adversarial attacks · Advanced Threat Protection

1 Introduction

With the exponential rise in data, the need for its protection from theft and damage has become particularly important. The modern-day attacks are much more sophisticated, and when paired with the rise in cloud services, smartphones, and the Internet of Things (IoT) devices, we now have a complex defense scenario amidst a myriad of new cybersecurity threats that did not exist a few

© Springer Nature Switzerland AG 2022
R. Krishnan et al. (Eds.): SKM 2021, CCIS 1549, pp. 51–72, 2022.
https://doi.org/10.1007/978-3-030-97532-6_4

decades ago. Coordinated attacks that initially intrude via the network layer, and then infect multiple hosts in quick successions are not uncommon even for non-state/military networks and hosts now. Therefore, a robust Managed (Threat) Detection and Response (MDR) system is necessary to provide integrated security for the network and endpoint from threats and malicious activities.

Deep Reinforcement Learning (DRL) is gaining popularity in various fields ranging from games to industrial processes and cyber-physical systems. It has recently started gaining traction in various aspects of cybersecurity as well. Though there exist surveys on use of DRL in security [29], but their focus is not MDR. Therefore, in this paper, we have presented a review of the various applications of DRL-based techniques and how they have improved various aspects of MDR. As shown in Fig. 4, the MDR integrates two important threat detection and prevention systems as follows:

- Intrusion (Detection &) Prevention System (IDPS/IPS): an IDPS/IPS is an intrusion detection and prevention system. The IDPS/IPS works in conjunction with one or more Intrusion Detection Systems (IDS).
- Endpoint Detection & Response system (EDR): The role of an EDR system is to secure the endpoints. Modern EDR also integrates the Host IDS (HIDS), besides the Endpoint Protection Platform (EPP), and Advanced Threat Protection (ATP).

The market for EDR solutions is growing at a rapid pace, from \$238 Mn. in 2015 to \$1.54 Bn. in 2020 while that of the global Intrusion Detection And Prevention Systems (IDPS) is projected to grow by 5.4% (from USD 4.8 Bn. in 2020 to USD 6.2 Bn. by 2025) [24]. The major factors responsible for these changes include the increasing number of attacks, the rising privacy and security awareness, etc. Hence the need to use the best technologies and frameworks to keep up with the rapidly growing market is necessary. DRL offers advanced solutions for many of the needs of both IDS and EPP, and with the increasing funding trends in advanced Artificial Intelligence (AI) based solutions in this area, we believe that a review of the different applications of DRL in various aspects of threat detection and protection is very much needed at this stage.

The rest of the paper is organised as follows. In Sect. 2 we provide a brief introduction on the diverse types of DRL techniques. Next, we provide a similar introduction of the MDR, IDS and EDR systems, along with their respective taxonomies in Sect. 3. Next, we describe and analyse the different arts that use DRL in the IDS space in Sect. 4, and in the endpoint space in Sect. 5. Finally we conclude the paper in Sect. 6.

2   About Deep Reinforcement Learning

Reinforcement learning (RL) [40] is the field of machine learning (ML) that deals with sequential decision-making involving an agent which learns the desired action policy (behavior) incrementally while interacting with the environment. RL explores the different states of an environment using an explore-exploit

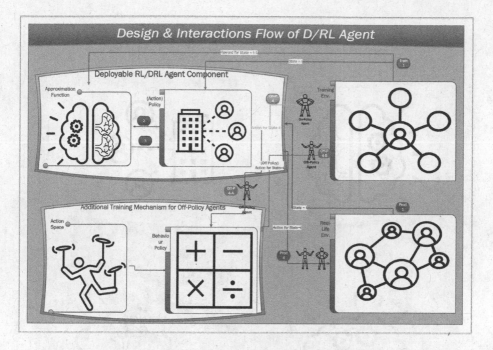

Fig. 1. Interaction of different types of D/RL agents

mechanism/policy and hence the RL agent does not require complete knowledge or control of the environment. The exploration policy of an off-policy agent could be different from its action policy. Whereas, for an on policy-agent, a stochastic action policy also aids the exploration of the environment. This is as shown in Fig. 1.

RL is different from any supervised ML or Deep Learning (DL) algorithm. Where supervised ML/DL aims to either maximize a likelihood function or minimize a loss function to estimate/predict an optimal value against a specific record, RL tries to maximize total (absolute or discounted) reward over a trajectory of observations. The observations in an LR context comprises of a set of states, each of these states individually may closely resemble the input of a supervised RL/DL problem. Therefore, an RL/DRL problem may house within itself a supervised learning ML/DL algorithm to provide an estimate against an individual state, which will be helpful for the agent to determine the policy to maximize the overall reward. This is where the distinction between RL (also known as Classical RL) and Deep Reinforcement Learning (DRL) [4,21] comes in. In RL, the approximation function is either a simple classical ML algorithm or even a non-ML model, like a tabular-memory structure as in the case of Q-Learning [33]; whereas in DRL [40], such approximation functions are invariably a DL algorithm. This distinction is illustrated in Fig. 2.

DL-based approximators as used in DRL are well suited for handling and extracting insights from high-dimensional sensory inputs. These algorithms can

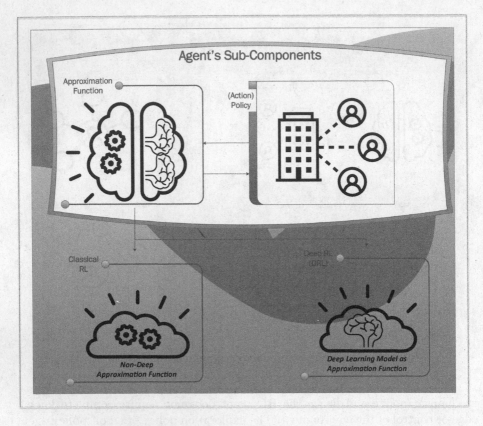

Fig. 2. Classical RL vs. Deep RL (DRL)

process states consisting of inputs ranging from raw image frames to complex raw sensor data. Where classical RL needs human expertise to extract domain-relevant insightful features from the input states, the DL model in the DRL algorithm can automatically extract complex non-linear features from raw-input features, thus making them ideal for learning complex and dynamic real-world processes.

A DRL-based algorithm could be further sub-divided into value approximation-based algorithm [41] or policy-based [46] approaches and algorithm. This distinction is based upon the underlying utility that the approximation function is targeted to estimate. This is illustrated in Fig. 3. If the approximation algorithm aims to estimate the value of being in a future state, which further influences the policy of the agent, then such approach and hence the algorithm falls under the value (approximation based) D/RL approaches. The common value based DRL algorithms are as follows [40]:

– Deep Q-networks [27]
– Double DQN [49]
– Dueling DQN (or Dueling network architecture for Q-Learning) [52]

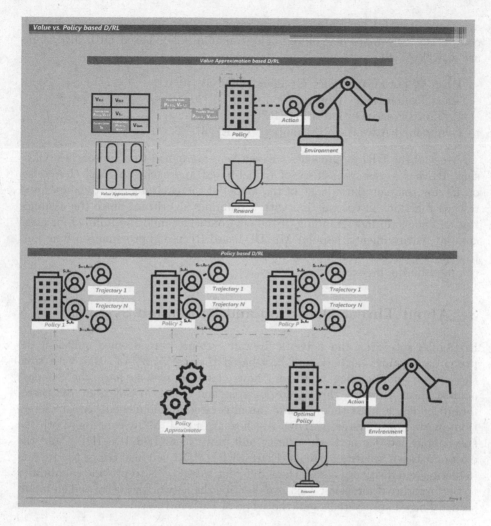

Fig. 3. Difference between value-based and policy-based D/RL approaches

Further there are some not so popular approaches also, like the Distributional DQN, and the AE-DQN [55].

The policy approximation-based methods on the other hand optimize a performance utility function as the objective (typically the expected cumulative reward) by finding a good policy. As compared to estimating the value function that in turn is used to greedily reach an optimal policy as in value-based approaches, the policy-based approach offers a direct solution to optimizing the policy that leads to taking action trajectories that maximize the reward. But since the policy-based approach deals with distributions of complex trajectories instead of simple scalar values, finding a gradient of such distribution and thereby optimizing it becomes challenging. Therefore, although policy-based approaches are more powerful for real-life applications, they are also mathematically and computationally more demanding. The common policy-based DRL algorithms are as follows [40]:

- Deep Deterministic Policy Gradient (DDPG) [40]
- Trust Region Policy Optimization (TRPO) [36]
- Proximal Policy Optimization (PPO) [38]
- Generalized Advantage Estimation (GAE) [37]

Most of the DRL approaches covered here are model-free approaches. Classical RL has a vast repository of model-based approaches as well that relies on having complete knowledge of the model of the environment (dynamics and reward function) in conjunction with a planning algorithm. Since the assumption of complete understanding of the environment cannot be fulfilled for large complex environments, popular ML/DL-based RL use approximation functions to estimate the utility of a proxy function under the assumed model of the environment during its exploration.

3   About Threat Detection and Protection Systems

Erstwhile, anti-virus and network firewall systems were deemed sufficient for protection against network and host-based threats [34,35,43]. But with time the nature and potency of threats have changed, and so have the defences against them. Now the threats do not arise and attack in isolation, and therefore defending against them requires an integrated and managed (threat) detection and response system (MDR). As shown in Fig. 4, MDR combines both the sub-components for network security and prevention (IDS/IPS/IDPs) and the endpoint-based security systems (EDR/EPP). MDR can also triage the threats detection and discovery across these different subsystems to provide capabilities to perform threat forensics. Next, we describe the network security and endpoint security-based sub-systems and the scope of DRL in these.

3.1   Taxonomy of Intrusion Detection and Prevention Systems

On the network protection end, the need for dedicated network log and anomaly detection components were felt. Vendors offered both software-based and hardware solutions to suit unique needs and budget requirements. Such integrated network threat detection system is generically now called a Network-based Intrusion detection System (NIDS) [15,31,32]. By definition, such NIDS protected an entire local network or sub-network. But similar network threat detection needs were also felt broadly at the level of the network perimeter, individual applications (contained in a VM or container), and at the individual host level. Therefore, taking clues from the NIDS and adding to it platform-specific detection resources and techniques, IDS for the perimeter (PIDS), VM (VIDS), and

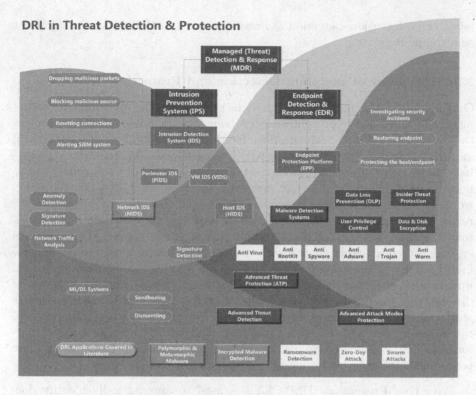

Fig. 4. Taxonomy of threat detection & protection systems in cybersecurity and scope for DRL

hosts (HIDS) were also developed [22]. Of these, the more popular research coverage is the NIDS followed by the HIDS [9]. The PIDS and the VIDS mostly use scaled/modified versions of NIDS and hence are not extensively covered in the research literature. HIDS resides on the host machine and interacts with the OS to determine malicious activities or processes by analysing various host activities like system calls, apps, and file access logs, etc. The NIDS has 2 components; one based on signature matching which provided definite signals; and another based on analysis of log files and configurations, which provided statistical trends and anomalies which need to be interpreted into signals of distinct types. Where a threat detected from a definitive analysis like signature matching could be immediately blocked by the system, others discovered based on statistical methods were relayed as events to a Security Information and Event Management (SIEM) system, monitored by domain experts who can do additional analysis to confirm an attack or malicious network traffic and trigger appropriate actions. Popular signature matching algorithms used in a NIDS is based on the Aho-Corasick algorithm [30]. The Intrusion Prevention System, as shown in Fig. 4 includes sub-systems to automate and actively block some such threats. Such systems are called the Intrusion Prevention Systems (IPS) when they exist as a separate layer, or an Intrusion Detection & Prevention System (IDPS) when these exist as a composite system.

3.2   Taxonomy of Endpoint Detection and Protection Systems

On the host protection end, the anti-virus system was the predominant mechanism. But this failed to prevent many evolving threats. Some initial host protection systems combined both the Host Intrusion Detection System (HIDS) [15] and the anti-virus system. Like the NIDS, the HIDS [9] also uses a monitoring-based approach to generate threat detection. But instead of monitoring the live network traffic and the resultant generated log files like the NIDS, the HIDS would monitor the running processes, changes in the operating system (OS) registry, and other configurations. Instead of sending the events to a SIEM system, the changes are blocked until admin privileges are granted. The anti-virus system as used in earlier generation host protection modules used to be predominantly based on signature matching techniques and hence required a periodical update to its signature repository to detect any new threats. Since malware are of diverse types ranging beyond just viruses, therefore soon such anti-virus systems started including signatures for other threats like the Trojans [48], Worms [18], Spyware, Adware, etc. As shown in Fig. 4, modern Endpoint Protection Platforms (EPP) [13] as used by many enterprises today, also includes one or more components listed below beside the malware detection system.

- Data Loss Prevention (DLP): This is used to automatically identify documents and records containing personal and confidential information and prevent their accidental leakage and enforce policies around its usage and archival.
- Insider Threat (IT) Protection: This component detects any malicious intent by an internal employee to steal or leak confidential data/credentials of critical systems of an enterprise.
- Data & Disk Encryption: This module encrypts the data and the disk to mitigate impacts arising from asset thefts.
- User Privilege Control: This module assists in enforcing different policies based upon the access privilege of different users.

In wake of the advanced threats arising from advanced second-generation malware modern EPP platforms also comprise an Advanced Threat Protection (ATP) sub-system [19], which may consist of advanced ML/DL-based malware detection and protection components.

4   DRL for Network Intrusion Detection Systems (NIDS)

NIDS monitors maliciousness in the network traffic in a host agnostic manner. These are included in the larger umbrella of managed (thread) detection and response systems to provide comprehensive protection coupled with endpoint protection systems. Since these systems are host-agnostic they cannot leverage many popular host-specific file detection techniques and rely on analysis of the network statistics and binary packet data and header information. Before managed NIDS systems, network audit data were manually screened and analyzed to detect any malicious activity or a possible attack. But such methods were not scalable with the increasing network sizes, which led to the popularity of managed NIDS. NIDS analyses multiple sources ranging from application traces, user command data, and network packets to detection signals of attack or malicious payloads.

Of late, the two predominant methods that the NIDS used to detect threats were *signature* based identification [30], called the *SNIDS* and (*s*tatistical) anomaly detection [7], called the *ANIDS*. SNIDS methods rely on a database of pre-extracted signatures from different network payloads and a corresponding label for each extracted signature. Such methods are very efficient but often could not detect similar threats in the absence of an exactly matching signature. Also, such methods are useful mainly for malicious payload detection. The ANIDS on the other hand extracts patterns of different statistical measures to detect any shift from normal network activity and flags such an event. Such events are relayed to a Security Information and Event Management (SIEM) system, monitored by domain experts who can do additional analysis to confirm an attack or malicious network traffic and trigger appropriate actions.

The size of the network that a managed NIDS monitors is large and depending upon the strictness of threshold to any security event such ANIDS could generate high frequency and volume of detection/identification events. When ANIDS is a part of an overarching IPS/IDPS, additional rule-based blocking/analysis/throttling actions could be triggered. But an automatic blockage/throttling of network traffic based on statistical anomalies is sub-optimal and may impact the network speed and latency for critical services. Therefore, such ANIDS are often coupled with ML/RL/DRL-based or hybrid systems. Such ML/RL-based systems could also be part of the active management done by IPS instead of the IDS. Recently DRL has also become popular for detecting an anomaly in the ANIDS systems. We review some recent art in this regard as shown in Fig. 5 and in the following sub-sections, grouped by the objective of using DRL in ANIDS.

4.1   DRL for Anomalous Network Traffic (Binary) Classification

As shown in Fig. 2, the DRL consists of a DL approximator. In value-based DRL (Fig. 3), this estimator comprises a DL model architecture to estimate the state (V) or state-action (Q) value. Though DRL, as opposed to DL are conceived for tasks with sequential attribution for rewards, if we ignore this aspect, and map the instantaneous reward directly to a softmax function, then the DRL essentially works as a DL algorithm with an episode of unity size, and no accumulation or discounting of rewards for past attribution.

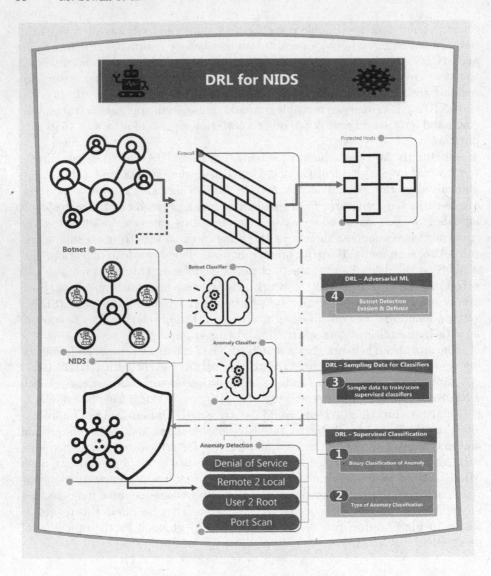

Fig. 5. Application of DRL in NIDS

Some arts that use DRL as a similar supervised DL learner are as follows:

– Gülmez et al. [14] discussed a DRL-based approach for network intrusion detection and evaluated it on NSL-KDD [11] and UNSW-NB15 [10] datasets, which are the two most commonly used standardized datasets of network-anomalies. The results demonstrated that the DRL method achieved an F-scores of ≥ 0.96 in both datasets. The DL approximator used here is a Multi-Layer Perceptron (MLP) based Deep Neural Network (DNN) [45]. As with any DNN, the effectiveness of the DRL model here also was significantly affected by the structure of the DNN.

- Feng-Hsu et al. [16] also used the same datasets (NSL-KDD [11] and UNSW-NB15 [10]) and also proposed a DRL-based classification approach for ANIDS. But they adopted an alternate testing approach, and in addition to using a standardized dataset for evaluation, they evaluated their system on a real campus NIDS as well, which had exponentially a larger network traffic flow. They also compared their DRL-based classification approach with three other ML-based classifiers (based on Random Forest, Support Vector Machine, and Multi-Layer Perceptron).
- Kamalakanta Sethi et al. [39] presented a *context-adaptive* IDS using DRL. Their main intention of replacing a DL-based classifier with a DRL-based classifier was to achieve a balance between detection accuracy and False Positive Rate (FPR). They noted that balancing between the accuracy and the FPR (robustness) using classical ML techniques is challenging, and by using DRL this could be achieved.

Since all the 3 papers have worked with the same datasets, we can compare the results for each dataset. Here is a short comparative summary of results from these work on the two standardized datasets that all of these use.

- Evaluation of NSL-KDD dataset [11]: Though the model proposed by Gülmez gave a 97% accuracy with a precision of 98% and a recall of 96%, and the model used by Feng-Hsu gave an accuracy of 91.4% their results are not directly comparable as they did not mention their FPR and for such classification accuracy alone could not be the basis of comparison. Feng-Hsu also claimed that DRL based approach gave better results when compared with the three classical ML techniques used and presented in their papers (RF, SVM, and MLP-DNN). The DQN based model used by Kamalakanta et al., though had a reduced accuracy rate of 81.80% on the dataset (when compared to the other two models), was able to reduce the FPR to 2.6%.
- Evaluation of UNSW-NB15 dataset [10]: The model proposed by Gülmez, again gave higher (but not directly comparable) accuracy of 96%, at a 95% precision, and a recall of 97%. Like the results on NSL-KDD, the model used by Feng-Hsu gave a balanced result of 92% across all the evaluation metrics on UNSW-NB15. The results presented by Kamalakanta on the other hand again had a reduced accuracy rate of 85.09% and the False Positive Rate of 3.3%.

4.2 DRL for Anomalous Activity Type Classification in Network Traffic

Most DL classifiers could classify both binary and multi-class problems. Therefore, while using DRL predominantly as a DL-based classifier, the detection type is only limited to the availability of classes in the standardized dataset. The popular NSL-KDD dataset [11] for ANIDS, comes in various sizes, and difficulty levels for two types of classification problems; a binary class dataset to predict the presence of anomalous activity and a 5-class dataset, which has four types of anomalous activities, and the fifth class representing normal traffic. The arts in this sub-section cover identification of one or more of these types of anomalies. These are listed below:

- Ekachai Suwannalai et al. [47] presented a DQN based approach for a five-label classification problem and compared the results with two other ML-based approaches, the Recurrent Neural Network (RNN) and the Adversarial Reinforcement Learning with SMOTE (AESMOTE). The model was trained on two standardized datasets, the NSL-KDD and the KDDTest+. They demonstrated that this approach gave superior performance than the other two non-DRL approaches.
- Yandong et al. [25] used a DRL based framework which was based on an actor-critic based approach, called the Deep DPG (DDPG) (a policy-based method mention in Sect. 2). The state space consisted of these 8 features namely the number of bytes and packets transmitted and those received, and the switch port number, etc. They used a conditional reward function as shown in Eq. 1:

$$\text{Reward} = \begin{cases} -1 & \text{Load}_s > U_s \\ \lambda p_b + (1 - \lambda)(1 - p_a) & \text{Load}_s \leq U_s \end{cases} \tag{1}$$

They claimed that the proposed algorithm was capable of learning efficient mitigation policies and could mitigate an adverse Distributed Denial of Service (DDoS) attack in real-time. They also tested their framework on five other scenarios with different attack dynamics to prove the robustness of their system.

4.3   DRL for Sampling Anomalies

There is more that DRL can do as compared to DL, especially for scenarios that involve sequential decision-making beyond simple prediction on a static record. The art in this section covers approaches where RL/DRL are used to assist an ML/DL-based classification system instead of replacing it. This is done by selecting either the candidate input dataset for training or for scoring with these classifiers.

Lopez-Martin et al. [26] used DRL to selectively sample the training data used for training the Ml-based anomaly detection models. They used the four most popular DRL agent algorithms the DQN, the DDQN, the Policy Gradient (PG), and the Actor-Critic (AC). Of these, the DDQN gave the best results with all metrics including the accuracy, F1 score, precision, and recall $\approx$89%. They also benchmarked their DRL model's performance against ML-based techniques like Logistic Regression, SVM, Random Forest. The result indicated that where the DRL-based methods had improved accuracy, F1 score, and recall but algorithms like Adaboost generated better precision of 97%.

4.4 DRL for Botnet Detection Evasion

A botnet [1] is a malware-infected computer network that is under the control of a master attack perpetuating machine known as the bot-herder. With such a sophisticated network of malicious systems, the bot-herder is capable of carrying out a massive, coordinated attack. Common botnet attacks include DDoS, financial breaches, Email spams, etc. Therefore, the identification of such botnets in the network becomes very crucial but is also very challenging. As per work·by Rajab et al. [1] up to 27% of connections and 11% of DNS domains are infected by a botnet. Contemporary botnets use evasion techniques to avoid detection by even potent ML/DL-based ANIDS. Therefore, recently DRL is being used to understand how botnets could evade detection from ANIDS and then bolster defences against such evasions. Next, we present some work that has used DRL in the area of botnet detection-evasion, such that effective defences could be created against a real evading botnet.

Giovanni Apruzzese et al. [3] suggested that a more resilient and robust botnet detection system can be developed through adversarial training. Two datasets were used to train the model, namely the CTU and BOTNET which trained two DRL agents based on DDQN and Deep-SARSA. The agent in their DRL system changes the binary sequence of a malicious network traffic flow with one of the available sequences of binaries until the embedded detector could not detect it as malicious. The results showed that by contaminating the training set by 1%, the evasion rate increased by 25% approximately.

Where Giovanni Apruzzese et al. [3] worked on action-selection based policy, Di Wu et al. [53] proposed an action-elimination based policy for a DQN agent. They used a dataset made by combining benign samples from IOST 2010 dataset and botnet samples are taken from the *Malware Capture Facility Project*. They gave an instantaneous reward of 10 units for a successful evasion. Interestingly, no penalty was given to the agent on failed evasion. Their action also included a simple pre-determined set of modifications to the binary traffic. Their results showed an evasion ranging from 70% to 80% on various botnet samples (namely the Nerris, Rbot, Zeus, and Geodo), which was significantly higher than the available baseline.

5 DRL for Endpoint Detection and Protection Systems

An endpoint is the last line of defense for any host machine/device. Also, this is the only component that sees the file in its entirety as an executable program compatible with the host's operating system (OS), and hence offers opportunities for complex feature extraction and processing. Therefore, this is the most matured component from the perspective of the application of ML/DL/DRL techniques.

With the evolving malware threats from advanced second-generation malware and ransomware, there is little that NIDS could do for their detection. Also, many such malware postpone any malicious activity that could be captured by a dynamic analysis system. Second-generation malware could use techniques like

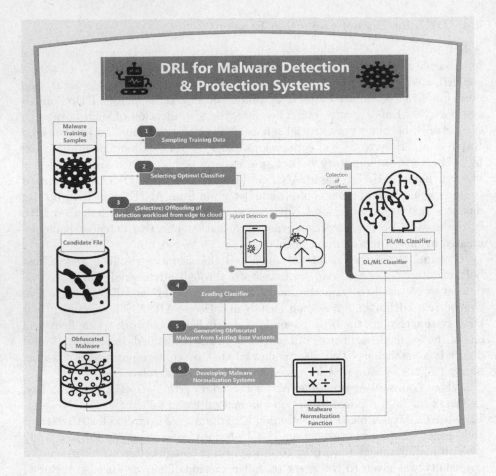

Fig. 6. Applications of DRL in malware detection & protection systems

obfuscation [6] to change its structure and evade classical anti-virus programs. Therefore, the ATP-based systems, invariably use some form of ML for advanced threat detection and protection.

Also, the use of DRL in endpoint security is much more advanced than for NIDS as covered in Sect. 4. There are two broad ways that DRL is used for ATP in an EDR/EPP as shown in Fig. 6, these are enumerated below and detailed in the following subsections.

5.1   DRL for Assisting Existing Classification System

In this subsection, various DRL applications are discussed to enhance the efficiency or effectiveness of classification by an existing ML/DL-based malware classification system. These applications fall under the following three types as discussed next.

Sampling Data for Training a Malware Classifier: The SOTA ML and DL-based classifiers require a large amount of data on which they can train and learn. The supervised models are trained on a standardized network-anomaly dataset and learn to extract the best features from these datasets. The files, however, cannot be scanned indefinitely online by the systems and their execution needs to be halted by the heuristics employed by the engine somewhere.

A DRL-based supervised learner was proposed by Yu Wang et al. [51] to determine when the emulation process should stop optimally based on the state information generated. Many Personal Executable (PE) files produced from Microsoft's anti-malware engine were used as the dataset to train the model. The agent can perform two types of actions continue (C) and halt (H) and was rewarded based on 2 criteria: firstly, based on the sequence lengths of the emulation, the shorter the sequence, the higher the reward (so that the agent tries to halt the process faster) and secondly the prediction accuracy.

The results from their work indicated that the DRL model was able to halt the execution of around 91% of samples on which the model was tested. The true positive rate (61% improvement) and false positive rate (1% improvement) also improved when compared to the best baseline model presented by Ben Athiwaratkun et al. [5].

Selecting Optimal Classifier for a Candidate Detection: The modern-day threat detectors and classifiers use multiple detectors to increase their detection rates. Such models could be scaled horizontally using cloud infrastructure to reduce the computation time even with multiple candidate detection. The idea of using selected classifiers for candidate detection, and subsequently querying additional malware detectors was suggested, instead of using an ensemble of all the classifiers, and then aggregate their predictions. This approach may reduce the overall computation cost of a candidate file's inference. But such targeted detection requires intelligent decision-making dynamically based on the incoming candidate's file's features. This is where DRL can help.

Yoni Birman et al. [8] presented a DRL-based approach to implement a 'cost-aware' malware detection approach to maintain a balance between first the need to have multiple ML classifiers for sophisticated detection and second for total computation cost for a candidate detection. They proposed to have such a cost-aware mechanism as a part of a Malware Detection as service (MDaaS) approach. Their system used an Actor-Critic agent and an action-space denoted by the array as in Eq. 2, where N is the number of detectors, M is the Maximum number of detectors per action, and c the binary class for the file.

$$c + \sum_{i=1}^{M} \binom{N}{i} \tag{2}$$

Further, as a reward, the correct classifications are assigned a fixed reward, and a penalty proportional to the computational cost involved during the classification was imposed. This helped in learning the behavior of not scoring against the classifiers that will have little or no contribution as a misclassification from these will incur a penalty for the DRL.

Their system was successfully able to maintain a similar level of accuracy as obtained by aggregating inferences from all available classifiers and reduced the computational cost by around 87%. They benchmark their system using a large number of the balanced dataset of PE files collected from the security department of a large organization and using three prominent cloud architectures namely the on-premise, AWS EC2, and AWS Lambda.

Selective Offloading of Edge Detection Workloads to Cloud Based Detection: Mobile endpoints offer greater challenges as compared to PC and Servers. This is because of the availability of limited computation power for neural processing with any ML/DL-based system and battery/power constraints. Therefore, these systems invariably need to decide the optimal state of balance between edge detection and server/cloud offloading of candidate detection. This is again an area where DRL can help.

In this regard, Xiaoyue Wan et al. [50] suggested a DQN based approach (and a hotbooting-Q strategy) to determine a strategy of selectively offloading detection from the endpoints on edge devices to a cloud-based detection setup. This is like the Q-Learning-based strategy proposed by Yanda Li et al. [20], however, Yanda et al.'s method resulted in convergence, especially for larger networks. The use of DQN instead of classical Q-Learning resulted in faster convergence along with the higher accuracy, which was 24.5% more than the traditional Q-learning-based approach as proposed by Yanda.

5.2   DRL for Adversarial Attacks on Existing Classifiers and Subsequent Defense

In this subsection, we will discuss the applications of DRL to generate adversarial samples to evade an existing malware classifier. Metamorphic malware could use techniques like obfuscation [6] to similarly evade a classifier, though in a more organic manner than conventional adversarial-ml. We therefore also include arts to generate metamorphic malware and DRL-based techniques to defend against them also in this section. These applications fall under the following three types as discussed next.

Evading Malware Classifier: Advances in adversarial-ML have proved that a DL-based classifier is very sensitive towards samples with adversarial noise. Such DL-based classifiers could be easily evaded by strategically adding noise in the candidate file's feature to lower the overall detection probability sufficiently to reverse the detection. These types of attacks are known as score-based attacks in adversarial-ml and are widely covered in DL literature. Earlier Generative Adversarial Networks (GAN) based techniques were used for this effect, but recently DRL based techniques are becoming popular.

Anderson et al. [2] used a DQN based agent for malware evasion. The action space of their setup consisted of included basic adding, creation, and manipulation-based actions; and they used a binary unity reward for a successful evasion. They demonstrated a median evasion rate of 72% using their method.

In [12] Fang Z et al. also used a DQN agent system to evade anti-malware engines and named it DQEAF. The DQN agent is trained on samples that are screened as malicious using the online VirusTotal service. Four such agents are trained on four different families of malware under the Win32 platform including 'Backdoor', 'Trojan', 'Worm', and 'Email'. The agent would append randomly generated bytes to the file features, libraries, and sections to the sample PE file to change their signatures. They also used a binary unity or 0 reward scheme as Anderson et al., but with a different calculation for reward as shown in Eq. 3

$$r_t = 20^{(-\text{TURN}-1)/\text{MAXTURNS}} \times 100 \tag{3}$$

The RL learning episode would terminate on successful evasion. The results showed a slightly higher evasion success rate of 75%. The similarity in results between the work of Fang et al. and Anderson et al. is expected due to the similar algorithm used on a similar dataset but is not comparable as Fang et al. did not use a standardized dataset.

Generating Obfuscated Malware: Advanced Threat Protection (ATP), is one of the most powerful features for any Endpoint detection/protection system. As shown in Fig. 4, the ATP intends to protect against next/second generation threats like oligomorphic, polymorphic, and metamorphic malware. Of these, metamorphic malware is the most dangerous. Metamorphic malware could change their code body using techniques like obfuscation, and in doing so they could virtually infect every connected host in the entire network evading all types of current generation detection techniques including those based on sophisticated DL-based detection mechanisms. Some of the popular malware obfuscation techniques used include dead/junk code insertion, register reassignment, subroutine reordering, code transposition, etc. [54] So far, the threat from these systems, though was high on impact or 'value at stake' perspective, not so much from a 'probability of occurrence'. This is because such malware is overly complex to develop.

Sewak et al. [44], showed how an adversarial-ML-based DRL system, using PPO agents could be used to generated obfuscated and metamorphic malware. Their system could be used to create such metamorphic malware of most of the existing non-metamorphic malware currently available in abundance. They created multiple PPO-based DRL agents as an adversary to ML-based malware detectors. There is a similar coverage of DRL as an adversarial to ML/DL-based classifiers in NIDS in Sect. 4.4 for Botnet evasions. The techniques covered in this section are based upon popular value-based DRL agents like the DQN. As highlighted by Sewak et al., the problem of obfuscation even at the opcode level; which is the highest abstracted level at which the functionality of a metamorphic malware could be preserved; is too complex to be effectively and efficiently solved by such popular DRL agent algorithms. This is because when the problem is converted into an equivalent single-task MDP, it leads to an extremely high cardinality action space, for which the existing popular DRL agent algorithms as we covered in Sect. 4.4 do not scale well.

Interestingly, Sewak et al. also argued that existing art in adversarial-ml especially the ones based on gradient techniques like GANs should not be used in the area of malware detection and protection. Some work covered in Sect. 4 highlighted the motivation that some DL-based models become resilient to noise when trained on synthetically generated adversarial samples. Sewak et al. explained that in endpoint protection, that the real threat is from malware that is compatible with the underlying host platform and could perform the desired malicious activities on that platform. Since synthetically generated perturbations from adversarial-ml-based systems like GAN [23] could not be compiled to host-compatible files, these mechanisms do not work for malware detection. Also, some research with GAN in security has pointed out that gradient-based adversarial samples do not work effectively in real life even if they could be made to evade another DL classifier [17]. Sewak et al. also argued that for malware generation only the techniques that preserve file functionality should be used as otherwise it is not guaranteed that the resulting file could behave as genuine malware. Because of these constraints there existed no work to generate a metamorphic malware, and this is the first work covered in literature to accomplish this.

Developing Malware Normalization Systems: In Sect. 5.2 we covered an obfuscated malware generation system as developed by Sewak et al. In this, the authors highlighted that since their main objective is not to generate a metamorphic malware but defences against the same, also they indicated that re-training the existing malware classifier with the generated malware data that could evade the classifier will not be optimal. Therefore, further, they created a malware normalization system that could provide defense against metamorphic malware that uses similar obfuscation techniques to evade detection [42].

A malware *normalization* system is a system that takes in an obfuscated executable file as input and uses de-obfuscation techniques to generate a common base form of the malware that is used to improve the detection rate of an existing malware detection system. All the different obfuscations of a given malware should be reverted to the same base variant for an existing malware that is trained on the malware's base variants. In this approach there is no need to re-train the existing malware classifier, thereby the malware's effectiveness against existing threats is not compromised by training it with adversarial sample data as pointed in [17].

Sewak et al. again used PPO to create this malware normalization system as well and evaluated it against obfuscated malware created from the Malicia dataset [28]. The results showed that **60%** of the previously un-detectable obfuscated metamorphic malware variants were now detected by the same malware classifier after normalizing with their system.

6   Conclusion

In this paper, we have presented the diverse and innovative applications of DRL in the field of cybersecurity threat detection and protection. With the increasing demand for more robust and capable defense systems, DRL has become a valuable tool in designing and enhancing the capabilities of modern NIDS and ATP systems. DRL is finding many unique applications in both intrusion and malware defense scenarios. It is enabling applications ranging from the ones that critically assist the development or selection of machine and deep learning algorithms to directly bolstering defences against advanced adversarial-ml attacks. DRL is also used in network anomaly detection as a replacement for a supervised learner, but the more empowering usage of DRL has been to form strategies for defense against modern and advanced adversarial attacks. DRL has also shown great promise in designing capable defences against advanced metamorphic malware. DRL itself is a trending research topic in AI and is continually being enhanced with more powerful and efficient algorithms and techniques. Therefore, we believe that it will empower many more unique and innovative applications of DRL in cybersecurity threat detection and protection, and therefore we believe that this is an interesting area for both cybersecurity and AI researchers to follow.

References

1. Abu Rajab, M., Zarfoss, J., Monrose, F., Terzis, A.: A multifaceted approach to understanding the botnet phenomenon. In: Proceedings of the 6th ACM SIG-COMM Conference on Internet Measurement, pp. 41–52 (2006)
2. Anderson, H.S., Kharkar, A., Filar, B., Roth, P.: Evading machine learning malware detection. Black Hat, pp. 1–6 (2017)
3. Apruzzese, G., Andreolini, M., Marchetti, M., Venturi, A., Colajanni, M.: Deep reinforcement adversarial learning against botnet evasion attacks. IEEE Trans. Netw. Serv. Manag. **17**(4), 1975–1987 (2020)
4. Arulkumaran, K., Deisenroth, M.P., Brundage, M., Bharath, A.A.: Deep reinforcement learning: a brief survey. IEEE Sig. Process. Mag. **34**(6), 26–38 (2017)
5. Athiwaratkun, B., Stokes, J.W.: Malware classification with LSTM and GRU language models and a character-level CNN. In: 2017 IEEE International Conference on Acoustics, Speech and Signal Processing (ICASSP), pp. 2482–2486 (2017)
6. Behera, C.K., Bhaskari, D.L.: Different obfuscation techniques for code protection. Procedia Comput. Sci. **70**, 757–763 (2015)
7. Bhuyan, M.H., Bhattacharyya, D.K., Kalita, J.K.: Network anomaly detection: methods, systems and tools. IEEE Commun. Surv. Tutor. **16**(1), 303–336 (2014)
8. Birman, Y., Hindi, S., Katz, G., Shabtai, A.: Cost-effective malware detection as a service over serverless cloud using deep reinforcement learning. In: 2020 20th IEEE/ACM International Symposium on Cluster, Cloud and Internet Computing (CCGRID), pp. 420–429 (2020)
9. Bridges, R.A., Glass-Vanderlan, T.R., Iannacone, M.D., Vincent, M.S., Chen, Q.: A survey of intrusion detection systems leveraging host data. ACM Comput. Surv. (CSUR) **52**(6), 1–35 (2019)
10. David, W.: NSL-KDD datasets (2019). https://www.kaggle.com/mrwellsdavid/unsw-nb15. Accessed 27 June 2021

11. Mohi-ud din, G.: NSL-KDD dataset (2017). https://www.unb.ca/cic/datasets/nsl. html. Accessed 27 June 2021
12. Fang, Z., Wang, J., Li, B., Wu, S., Zhou, Y., Huang, H.: Evading anti-malware engines with deep reinforcement learning. IEEE Access **7**, 48867–48879 (2019)
13. Firstbrook, P., Hallawell, A., Girard, J., MacDonald, N.: Magic quadrant for endpoint protection platforms. Gartner RAS Core Research Note G 208912 (2009)
14. Gülmez, H.G., Angın, P.: A study on the efficacy of deep reinforcement learning for intrusion detection. Sakarya Univ. J. Comput. Inf. Sci. **4**, 11–25 (2021)
15. Heady, R., Luger, G., Maccabe, A., Servilla, M.: The architecture of a network level intrusion detection system. Office of Scientific and Technical Information, U.S. Department of Energy, August 1990
16. Hsu, Y.F., Matsuoka, M.: A deep reinforcement learning approach for anomaly network intrusion detection system. In: 2020 IEEE 9th International Conference on Cloud Networking (CloudNet), pp. 1–6 (2020)
17. Hu, W., Tan, Y.: Generating adversarial malware examples for black-box attacks based on GAN. ArXiv abs/1702.05983 (2017)
18. Kienzle, D.M., Elder, M.C.: Recent worms: a survey and trends. In: Proceedings of the 2003 ACM Workshop on Rapid Malcode, WORM 2003, pp. 1–10. Association for Computing Machinery, New York (2003)
19. Lakshmi, V.: Beginning Security with Microsoft Technologies. Springer, Berkeley (2019). https://doi.org/10.1007/978-1-4842-4853-9
20. Li, Y., Liu, J., Li, Q., Xiao, L.: Mobile cloud offloading for malware detections with learning. In: 2015 IEEE Conference on Computer Communications Workshops (INFOCOM WKSHPS), pp. 197–201 (2015)
21. Li, Y.: Deep reinforcement learning: an overview. arXiv preprint arXiv:1701.07274 (2017)
22. Liao, H.J., Richard Lin, C.H., Lin, Y.C., Tung, K.Y.: Intrusion detection system: a comprehensive review. J. Netw. Comput. Appl. **36**(1), 16–24 (2013)
23. Lin, Z., Shi, Y., Xue, Z.: IDSGAN: generative adversarial networks for attack generation against intrusion detection. CoRR abs/1809.02077 (2018)
24. Liu, S.: Endpoint detection and response (EDR) and endpoint protection platform (EPP) market size worldwide from 2015 to 2020 (2020). https://www.statista.com/ statistics/799060/worldwideedr-epp-market-size/. Accessed 27 June 2021
25. Liu, Y., Dong, M., Ota, K., Li, J., Wu, J.: Deep reinforcement learning based smart mitigation of DDoS flooding in software-defined networks. In: 2018 IEEE 23rd International Workshop on Computer Aided Modeling and Design of Communication Links and Networks (CAMAD), pp. 1–6 (2018)
26. Lopez-Martin, M., Carro, B., Sanchez-Esguevillas, A.: Application of deep reinforcement learning to intrusion detection for supervised problems. Expert Syst. Appl. **141**, 112963 (2020)
27. Mnih, V., et al.: Human-level control through deep reinforcement learning. Nature **518**(7540), 529–533 (2015)
28. Nappa, A., Rafique, M.Z., Caballero, J.: The MALICIA dataset: identification and analysis of drive-by download operations. Int. J. Inf. Secur. **14**(1), 15–33 (2015). https://doi.org/10.1007/s10207-014-0248-7
29. Nguyen, T.T., Reddi, V.J.: Deep reinforcement learning for cyber security. arXiv preprint arXiv:1906.05799 (2019)
30. Pao, D., Lin, W., Liu, B.: A memory-efficient pipelined implementation of the ahocorasick string-matching algorithm. ACM Trans. Archit. Code Optim. (TACO) **7**(2), 1–27 (2010)

31. Rathore, H., Agarwal, S., Sahay, S.K., Sewak, M.: Malware detection using machine learning and deep learning. In: Mondal, A., Gupta, H., Srivastava, J., Reddy, P.K., Somayajulu, D.V.L.N. (eds.) BDA 2018. LNCS, vol. 11297, pp. 402–411. Springer, Cham (2018). https://doi.org/10.1007/978-3-030-04780-1_28

32. Rathore, H., Sahay, S.K., Chaturvedi, P., Sewak, M.: Android malicious application classification using clustering. In: Abraham, A., Cherukuri, A.K., Melin, P., Gandhi, N. (eds.) ISDA 2018 2018. AISC, vol. 941, pp. 659–667. Springer, Cham (2020). https://doi.org/10.1007/978-3-030-16660-1_64

33. Rathore, H., Sahay, S.K., Nikam, P., Sewak, M.: Robust Android malware detection system against adversarial attacks using Q-learning. Inf. Syst. Front. **23**, 867–882 (2021). https://doi.org/10.1007/s10796-020-10083-8

34. Rathore, H., Sahay, S.K., Rajvanshi, R., Sewak, M.: Identification of significant permissions for efficient Android malware detection. In: Gao, H., J. Durán Barroso, R., Shanchen, P., Li, R. (eds.) BROADNETS 2020. LNICST, vol. 355, pp. 33–52. Springer, Cham (2021). https://doi.org/10.1007/978-3-030-68737-3_3

35. Rathore, H., Sahay, S.K., Thukral, S., Sewak, M.: Detection of malicious Android applications: classical machine learning vs. deep neural network integrated with clustering. In: Gao, H., J. Durán Barroso, R., Shanchen, P., Li, R. (eds.) BROAD-NETS 2020. LNICST, vol. 355, pp. 109–128. Springer, Cham (2021). https://doi.org/10.1007/978-3-030-68737-3_7

36. Schulman, J., Levine, S., Abbeel, P., Jordan, M., Moritz, P.: Trust region policy optimization. In: International Conference on Machine Learning, pp. 1889–1897. PMLR (2015)

37. Schulman, J., Moritz, P., Levine, S., Jordan, M., Abbeel, P.: High-dimensional continuous control using generalized advantage estimation. arXiv preprint arXiv:1506.02438 (2015)

38. Schulman, J., Wolski, F., Dhariwal, P., Radford, A., Klimov, O.: Proximal policy optimization algorithms. CoRR abs/1707.06347 (2017)

39. Sethi, K., Sai Rupesh, E., Kumar, R., Bera, P., Venu Madhav, Y.: A context-aware robust intrusion detection system: a reinforcement learning-based approach. Int. J. Inf. Secur. **19**(6), 657–678 (2019). https://doi.org/10.1007/s10207-019-00482-7

40. Sewak, M.: Deep Reinforcement Learning - Frontiers of Artificial Intelligence. Springer, Singapore (2019). https://doi.org/10.1007/978-981-13-8285-7

41. Sewak, M., Sahay, S., Rathore, H.: Value-approximation based deep reinforcement learning techniques: an overview. In: 2020 IEEE 5th International Conference on Computing Communication and Automation (ICCCA), pp. 379–384 (2020)

42. Sewak, M., Sahay, S., Rathore, H.: DRLDO a novel DRL based de obfuscation system for defense against metamorphic malware. Def. Sci. J. **71**, 55–65 (2021)

43. Sewak, M., Sahay, S.K., Rathore, H.: DeepIntent: Implicitintent based Android IDS with E2E deep learning architecture. In: 2020 IEEE 31st Annual International Symposium on Personal, Indoor and Mobile Radio Communications, pp. 1–6. IEEE (2020)

44. Sewak, M., Sahay, S.K., Rathore, H.: DOOM: a novel adversarial-DRL-based op-code level metamorphic malware obfuscator for the enhancement of IDS. In: Ubi-Comp 2020 ACM International Joint Conference on Pervasive and Ubiquitous Computing, pp. 131–134. ACM (2020)

45. Sewak, M., Sahay, S.K., Rathore, H.: An overview of deep learning architecture of deep neural networks and autoencoders. J. Comput. Theor. Nanosci. **17**(1), 182–188 (2020)

46. Sewak, M., Sahay, S.K., Rathore, H.: Policy-approximation based deep reinforcement learning techniques: an overview. In: Joshi, A., Mahmud, M., Ragel, R.G., Thakur, N.V. (eds.) Information and Communication Technology for Competitive Strategies (ICTCS 2020). LNNS, vol. 191, pp. 493–507. Springer, Singapore (2022). https://doi.org/10.1007/978-981-16-0739-4_47
47. Suwannalai, E., Polprasert, C.: Network intrusion detection systems using adversarial reinforcement learning with deep Q-network. In: 2020 18th International Conference on ICT and Knowledge Engineering (ICT&KE), pp. 1–7. IEEE (2020)
48. Tehranipoor, M., Koushanfar, F.: A survey of hardware trojan taxonomy and detection. IEEE Des. Test Comput. **27**(1), 10–25 (2010)
49. Van Hasselt, H., Guez, A., Silver, D.: Deep reinforcement learning with double Q-learning. CoRR abs/1509.06461 (2015)
50. Wan, X., Sheng, G., Li, Y., Xiao, L., Du, X.: Reinforcement learning based mobile offloading for cloud-based malware detection. In: GLOBECOM 2017–2017 IEEE Global Communications Conference, pp. 1–6 (2017)
51. Wang, Y., Stokes, J.W., Marinescu, M.: Neural malware control with deep reinforcement learning. In: MILCOM 2019–2019 IEEE Military Communications Conference (MILCOM), pp. 1–8 (2019)
52. Wang, Z., Schaul, T., Hessel, M., Van Hasselt, H., Lanctot, M., De Freitas, N.: Dueling network architectures for deep reinforcement learning. In: Proceedings of the 33rd International Conference on International Conference on Machine Learning, ICML 2016, vol. 48, pp. 1995–2003. JMLR.org (2016)
53. Wu, D., Fang, B., Wang, J., Liu, Q., Cui, X.: Evading machine learning botnet detection models via deep reinforcement learning. In: ICC 2019–2019 IEEE International Conference on Communications (ICC), pp. 1–6 (2019)
54. You, I., Yim, K.: Malware obfuscation techniques: a brief survey. In: 2010 International Conference on Broadband, Wireless Computing, Communication and Applications, pp. 297–300 (2010)
55. Zahavy, T., Haroush, M., Merlis, N., Mankowitz, D.J., Mannor, S.: Learn what not to learn: action elimination with deep reinforcement learning. In: Advances in Neural Information Processing Systems, vol. 31, pp. 3562–3573 (2018)

A Framework for Syntactic and Semantic Quality Evaluation of Ontologies

Vivek Iyer$^{(\boxtimes)}$ [ID], Lalit Mohan Sanagavarapu [ID], and Y. Raghu Reddy [ID]

IIIT Hyderabad, Hyderabad, India
{vivek.iyer,lalit.mohan}@research.iiit.ac.in, raghu.reddy@iiit.ac.in

Abstract. The increasing focus on Web 3.0 is leading to automated creation and enrichment of ontologies and other linked datasets. Alongside automation, quality evaluation of enriched ontologies can impact software reliability and reuse. Current quality evaluation approaches oftentimes seek to evaluate ontologies in either syntactic (degree of following ontology development guidelines) or semantic (degree of semantic validity of enriched concepts/relations) aspects. This paper proposes an ontology quality evaluation framework consisting of: (a) SynEvaluator and (b) SemValidator for evaluating syntactic and semantic aspects of ontologies respectively. SynEvaluator allows dynamic task-specific creation and updation of syntactic rules at run-time without any need for programming. SemValidator uses Twitter-based expertise of validators for semantic evaluation. The efficacy and validity of the framework is shown empirically on multiple ontologies.

Keywords: Ontology quality evaluation · Syntactic evaluation · Semantic validation · Crowdsourcing · Twitter-based expertise

1 Introduction

The exponential increase in Internet users over the past decade has led to generation of large volume of data. Web 3.0, otherwise commonly referred to as Semantic web, seeks to represent internet data as knowledge through knowledge graphs, ontologies and other knowledge systems [4]. These representations enable knowledge integration, semantic ambiguity resolution, information extraction, decision making, reasoning and many other use cases relevant to the building of 'intelligent' software systems. Ontologies, in particular, store domain-specific knowledge, and represent this knowledge through concepts, relations, axioms and instances. They contain a formal structure and achieve a certain level of rigor due to the presence of rules and constraints. Ontologies are rarely static in nature. The range and the depth of the knowledge stored are enriched over time. This impacts a wide variety of software applications that utilize ontologies for reasoning, decision-making, question-answering, etc. Ontology enrichment is thus a crucial step in the ontology engineering process.

© Springer Nature Switzerland AG 2022
R. Krishnan et al. (Eds.): SKM 2021, CCIS 1549, pp. 73–93, 2022.
https://doi.org/10.1007/978-3-030-97532-6_5

Traditionally, ontologies are created and managed by knowledge engineers and domain experts resulting in high costs due to the expert human labour involved. Automated or semi-automated approaches to ontology enrichment are increasingly popular, driven by increased availability of domain-relevant internet data and improvements in natural language processing and machine learning models [36]. Research on ontology learning (both creation and enrichment) snowballed in the last two decades [15, 20, 36], with increased focus on fully automated Deep Learning based approaches [30]. Given the variety in ontology enrichment approaches, it is important to evaluate the quality of the enriched ontology.

```
:component_hasInstalled_Software rdf:type owl:ObjectProperty .
```

Fig. 1. Syntactic quality violation: no domain or range for property

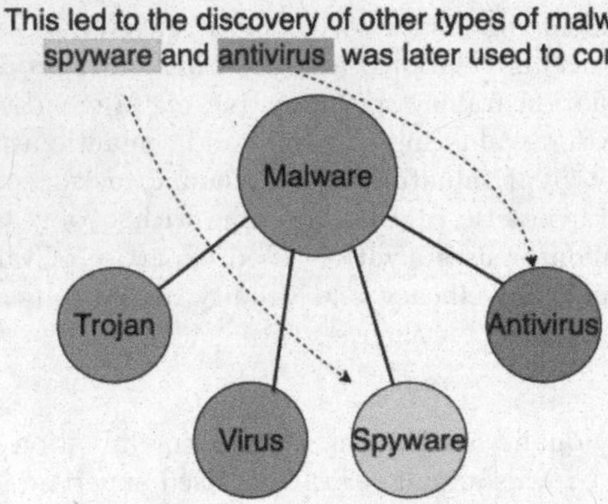

Fig. 2. Semantic violation: invalid enriched concept

Ontology evaluation approaches can broadly be divided into: manual, automated and semi-automated approaches. In general, ontology evaluation happens on one of two aspects: syntactic quality, or semantic quality. We define syntactic quality of an ontology as a measure of its adherence to ontology development guidelines or rules. For example, One such rule could necessitate presence of both domain and range elements in properties. Examples of other rules or guidelines could include explicit declaration of equivalent and inverse properties, presence of annotations [34], following of unique naming conventions [23], etc. Figure 1 shows, in Turtle syntax [3], a property without a defined range element-thus violating the rule that necessitates the presence of both domain and range elements. Semantic quality deals with validity of enriched concepts, relations and instances. Figure 2 shows an example ontology enriched with concepts extracted from a sentence to emphasize the need for evaluation of enriched ontologies.

The previously existing concepts are shown in blue, the valid enriched concepts in green and the invalid enriched ones in red. Ontology enrichment algorithms using Hearst patterns [14] could mistakenly detect 'antivirus' as a type of 'malware'. In such cases, before creating a final ontology, the enriched ontology needs to be validated for semantic quality, to accept or reject the enriched concepts, properties and instances.

A variety of metric-based methods were proposed to evaluate various syntactic quality-based characteristics of ontologies [9,19,32]. Publicly available tools were proposed that allow users to evaluate syntactical quality of ontologies using pre-defined metrics [18,22] or rules [28,31]. However, they offer limited customization and flexibility to the user for creating task-specific rules for evaluation, even more so for non-programmers. In regards to semantic evaluation, researchers have traditionally employed domain experts [21], while in this decade, crowdsourced validators [17,24] are being used for semantic ontology validation. This paper proposes a customizable and scalable framework that evaluates syntactic and semantic aspects of ontology quality using SynEvaluator and SemValidator respectively.

- *SynEvaluator*: a tool that uses a rule-creation framework for allowing users to non-programatically create rules during run-time and to set task-specific priorities for these rules.
- *SemValidator*: a tool that uses crowdsourcing for validation of semantic quality of enriched ontologies. In this paper, a Twitter-based expertise estimation algorithm is used to weight validators' decisions.

The source code for SynEvaluator and SemValidator is available on GitHub[1, 2]. They are also deployed on Heroku as web-applications[3, 4].

The rest of the paper is structured as follows: Sect. 2 describes related work in ontology quality evaluation. The proposed framework constituting of SynEvaluator and SemValidator is shown in Sect. 3. Section 4 details the experiments done to show the efficacy and accuracy of the framework, through these tools. SynEvaluator is tested for its utility and accuracy for implementing syntactical quality evaluation rules by comparing it against a popular syntactic quality evaluation tool, OOPS! [27]. The efficacy of *SemValidator* is shown by conducting crowdsourced survey involving 28 validators on two popular ontologies, Stanford Pizza [8] and Information Security ontology [10]. Accuracy of TweetExpert algorithm on responses to both of these ontologies using multiple ML regression algorithms is shown. Finally, Sect. 5 summarizes the contributions and suggests possible future directions of research.

---

[1] https://github.com/Remorax/SynEvaluator/.
[2] https://github.com/Remorax/SemValidator/.
[3] https://synevaluator.herokuapp.com/.
[4] http://semvalidator.herokuapp.com/.

2   Related Work

Ontology quality evaluation approaches can be broadly classified into a) syntactic and b) semantic quality evaluation approaches. Syntactic evaluation approaches primarily evaluate structural aspects of an ontology based on ontology development guidelines, common pitfalls, structural metrics etc. OntoClean [13], one of the earliest known works in this area, proposed a methodology for validating adequacy of relationships in an ontology based on notions drawn from philosophy such as essence, identity, and unity. Similarly, OntoQA [32] proposed ontology evaluation on the basis of schema metrics and instance metrics. They stated that 'goodness' or 'validity' of an ontology varies between different users and domains. Gangemi et al. [11] proposed structural, functional and usability-related measures using O^2 and oQual, a meta-ontology and an ontology model for ontology evaluation and validation. Burton et al. [5] proposed an ontology evaluation model based on semiotic theory. In order to apply the metrics proposed in these works, tools such as S-OntoEval [7] drawn from semiotic theory and AktiveRank [1] that ranked ontologies based on structural metrics like class match measure, density measure etc. were proposed. However, the tools proposed in these articles are either closed-source prototypes or theoretical frameworks and are not publicly available.

There are also a few publicly available closed-source ontology (syntactic) evaluation tools, such as OOPS! [28], DoORS [22] and OntoMetrics [18]. OntOlogy Pitfall Scanner (OOPS!) evaluates ontologies on the basis of established ontology quality rules related to human understanding, logical consistency, real world representation and modelling issues, and manually assigned priorities. DoORS, evaluates ontologies based on metrics drawn from Semiotic Theory while Onto-Metrics uses metrics proposed in OntoQA, [11]. These tools, however are not flexible or customizable, and evaluate ontologies using a fixed set of rules or metrics. Users are unable to create/update customized rules and set task-specific priorities, which can be crucial as requirements and application scenarios vary. The available open source implementations [33] require creation of new rules and priorities via programming which can be daunting for non-programmers.

Semantic evaluation approaches focus on semantic validity of concepts and relationships in an ontology. Traditionally, it has been formulated as a task requiring simple accept/reject decisions from domain experts [2]. In the past few years, a good number of crowdsourced ontology evaluation approaches have been proposed. Hanika et al. [35] have developed the UComp Protégé plugin to provide a platform for crowdsourced workers to validate classes, subclasses, properties and instances. Kiptoo et al. [16] use crowdsourcing for axiom and assertion verification in ontologies as well as for verification of subclass-superclass relations by Amazon Mechanical Turks [24]. Pittet et al. used crowdsourced workers to propose changes related to addition, deletion and substitution errors [25]. Zhang et al. [37] used crowdsourced workers to obtain written feedback (comments/suggestions/references) for making final validation decisions. Requiring complex tasks (such as making data quality decisions or requiring written feedback) from crowdsourced workers can be expensive and unscalable as the size of ontology and/or number of workers increases. Some approaches [17,25,35] used quality control mechanisms like majority voting that are debatable. Noy et al. [24] addressed this by using qualification questions and spam filtering techniques. While these mechanisms eliminate spammers, it may not be applicable where large number of workers have some degree of knowledge but only few are experts. Therefore, an assessment of domain expertise on a continuous scale would be useful as a quality control metric. Further, an integrated quality evaluation framework that seeks to evaluate ontologies on both syntactic and semantic aspects, and also addresses the above-mentioned problems would be useful for a holistic and integrated approach to quality evaluation of enriched ontologies.

3   Proposed Framework

In this paper, an ontology evaluation framework that combines automated syntactic evaluation and human-centric semantic evaluation is proposed. SynEvaluator aims at increasing user flexibility by allowing customized rule creation at runtime, as well as scalability (with respect to user base) by proposing an approach that removes the need for programming. SemValidator proposes a crowdsourcing based approach that uses the validators' Twitter profiles for quality control.

The framework's work flow is shown in Fig. 3. The input to quality evaluation process is an enriched ontology. The ontology may have been enriched with concepts, relations and instances using some automated and semi-automated algorithms. The ontology may contain syntactic quality errors (due to violation of ontology development guidelines) and/or semantic errors (due to wrongly enriched concepts). In the figure, for clarity, concepts and relationships with potential syntactic violations are bordered in yellow, an those that do not contain such violations are outlined in blue. Also, concepts that potentially contain semantic violations are highlighted in yellow colour and concepts that are semantically valid are highlighted in green.

An ontology engineer uploads an enriched ontology to SynEvaluator, and creates syntactic quality evaluation rules. The rules created using a theoretical rule creation framework are applied on the parsed ontology object through SynEvaluator's ontology evaluation module. This returns a list of detected violations and the elements causing these violations. Using these elements as suggestions, the ontology engineer can fix violations in a iterative manner. The iterations may be repeated as needed. Then, the ontology engineer can provide this ontology as input to SemValidator so that it can be validated for semantic quality. As part of semantic validation, the ontology is provided to crowdsourced validators who give their accept or reject validation decisions for each of the enriched concepts, relations and instances. Simultaneously, an estimate of the domain knowledge of each of these validators is calculated from their Twitter profile using the Tweet-Expert algorithm. These scores alluded to as 'TweetExpert scores', are used as a quality control mechanism to ensure that the decisions of crowdsourced validators are given weightages according to their knowledge of the ontology domain.

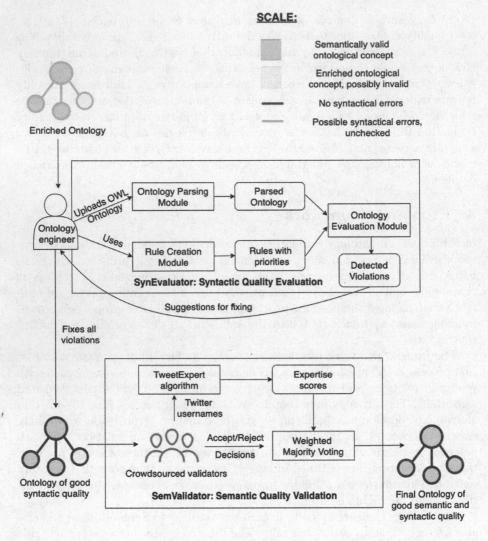

Fig. 3. Work flow for semantic and syntactic quality evaluation of ontologies. (Color figure online)

Finally, the output of this algorithm is used to take the final accept/reject decision for each enriched element, resulting in an ontology with both good syntactic and semantic quality.

3.1   Stage 1: SynEvaluator

In this section, the underlying terminology used in SynEvaluator and rule creation framework is illustrated with examples. Further, the implementation of SynEvaluator as a web application is detailed. Finally, the section ends with a discussion on potential benefits and limitations of SynEvaluator.

Defining the Rule Creation Framework. SynEvaluator allows users to create rules at run-time. The rules are constructed from individual components like "Subjects", "Clauses" or "Operator Expressions". The operational definitions of these and other relevant terms are:

- **Ontological Element**: Refers to any element that forms a constituent part of an ontology. It refers to any primary component (classes, individuals, properties), their related elements (subclasses, domains, ranges), annotations (labels, descriptions, comments) or attributes (ID, language, namespace).
- **Rule**: Refers to a sequence of one or more clauses, optionally connected by one or more operator expressions that returns either one or more ontological elements or a boolean value.
- **Clause**: Refers to a transformation applied on an ontological element(s) to return either one or more ontological elements or a boolean value.
- **Operator Expression**: An expression used to compare and/or connect non-empty sequences of clauses to return a boolean value.
- **Subject**: Refers to an ontological element (typically primary components such as classes, individuals and properties), that is subjected to transformations carried out through sequential clauses to form a rule.

```
<Rule> := <Subject> <Clause>* (<Operator Exp> <Clause>+)?

<Clause> := <Predicate> <Object>        # Extractive Clause
         := <Predicate> <Function>      # Functional Clause

<Operator Exp> := <Predicate> <Operator>
```

Fig. 4. Structure of supported expressions

Using these concepts, the expressions supported by SynEvaluator are formally defined as shown in Fig. 4. The notation used is similar to *RegEx* notation with * denoting zero to infinity, + denoting one to infinity, and ? denoting zero or one occurrences. A 'Subject' comprises the beginning and is always the first keyword in a rule in out proposed framework. It goes through a series of transformations as defined by sequences of clauses. Clauses can be of two types: a) Extractive Clauses and b) Functional Clauses. Extractive Clauses consist of (Predicate, Object) pairs that use the Predicate to execute a transformation on the return value from the previous clause using the Object as argument. More specifically, object specifies the type of element 'extracted' by the predicate, and elements satisfying this (Predicate, Object) pair are returned as output. Functional clauses, on the other hand, consist of (Predicate, Function) pairs that involve executing a function of type described by predicate on the return value from the previous clause. These clauses typically check for existence of a certain functional property and thus return a boolean value in response.

Currently, two kinds of functional properties are supported: i) ontological (or structural) properties, that execute ontology-level functions (such as uniqueness, validity, consistency etc.) on ontological elements, and ii) linguistic properties that linguistically analyze text (such as checking for polysemes, conjunctions etc.) returned from previous clauses. In case of 'False' value returned by a Functional Clause or an empty list (no matching elements) returned by an Extractive Clause, that particular ontological element is returned as an element containing a violation.

Extractive Clauses can also be chained together to form clause sequences. Since functional clauses return a boolean value, they cannot be chained further. Clause sequences can be compared through Operator Expressions. Operator Expressions essentially consist of a 'Predicate' indicating operator type, followed by an 'Operator' keyword. Operator Expressions comprise of two main categories of operators, namely: (a) Logical Operators and (b) Comparative Operators. Logical Operators like 'And', 'Or' and 'Not' are used to create logical combinations of clause sequences. Comparative Operators like 'Equality', 'Inverse' and 'Synonymy' are used to compare return values.

Table 1. Keywords for different expression types in the proposed framework

Subject	Extractive clause	Functional clause	Operator expression
	Predicate	Predicate	Predicate
Ontology Metadata	Has Related Element (1)	Has Ontological Property (1)	Uses Comparative Operator (1)
Ontological Element	Has Attribute (2)	Has Linguistic Property (2)	Uses Logical Operator (2)
Class	**Object**	**Function**	**Operator**
Instance	Domain (1)	ID Consistency (1)	Equality (1)
Property	Subclass (1)	Uniqueness (1)	Inverse (1)
Object Property	Disjoint Class (1)	Text Validity (1)	And (2)
Datatype Property	ID (2)	Contains Polysemes (2)	Or (2)
Symmetric Property	Language (2)	Contains Conjunctions (2)	Not (2)

Table 1 summarizes keywords supported by the proposed framework. Note that the table lists 8 Subject keywords, while for Extractive Clauses, Functional clauses and operator expressions it lists 2 predicates and 5 objects, functions and operators respectively. This is due to differing syntax followed by each expression type. Also, every predicate has a list of valid Objects/Functions/Operators. This is shown in the table through bracketed numbering. For example, the valid Predicates for 'Has Attribute' are 'ID' and 'Language'. The complete list of supported keywords is provided over here[5].

---

[5] https://bit.ly/3zfdI8f.

Examples of Created Rules. Figure 5 shows examples of 2 rules. In both examples 1 and 2, 'Property' is the 'Subject' of the rule. 'hasRelatedElement Domain', 'hasRelatedElement Range' and 'hasOntologicalProperty Uniqueness' are all clauses. In rule 1, the 'hasRelatedElement Domain' clause carries out a transformation that uses the 'hasRelatedElement' predicate to extract 'Domain' elements. A similar clause is used for extracting 'Range' elements. These two clauses (or clause sequences of length are combined using the operator expression 'usesLogicalOperator And'. This rule thus necessitates non-null values for both Domain and Range elements for each element of 'Subject', in this case, 'Property'. Properties that do not contain both elements are therefore returned as ontological elements containing violations.

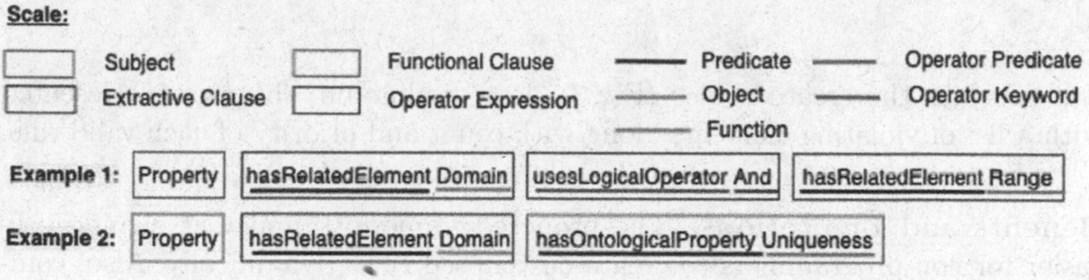

Scale:

☐ Subject	☐ Functional Clause	—— Predicate —— Operator Predicate
☐ Extractive Clause	☐ Operator Expression	—— Object —— Operator Keyword
		—— Function

Example 1: | Property | hasRelatedElement Domain | usesLogicalOperator And | hasRelatedElement Range |

Example 2: | Property | hasRelatedElement Domain | hasOntologicalProperty Uniqueness |

Fig. 5. Examples of rules implemented by SynEvaluator

Example 2 shows a rule where clauses have been chained together to constitute a clause sequence of length 2. This sequence consists of the extractive clause 'hasRelatedElement Domain' followed by functional clause 'hasOntologicalProperty Uniqueness'. The extractive clause essentially extracts Domain element(s) of each Property. Then, the functional clause applies 'Uniqueness' function on ontological elements returned by previous clause with function type defined by Predicate "hasOntologicalProperty". In case of non-existence of domain for a particular property or existence of multiple domains, this rule would return that property as containing a violation due to violation in first and second clauses respectively.

Proposing SynEvaluator: The Final Web Application. The rule creation framework proposed above is used to create a web application for use by the ontology engineer. The primary interface of this application, SynEvaluator, is shown in Fig. 6. It allows the users (ontology engineers) to use dropdown menus to create functional and extractive clauses, operator expressions and thus, rules, as well as set priorities for these rules. Users can choose between 'Low', 'Medium' and 'High' priorities based on the task-specific importance of the rule. Figure 8 shows, with the help of an activity diagram, how a user could create an appropriate rule using SynEvaluator. Finally, after uploading the enriched ontology and creating the rules, SynEvaluator parses the ontology using its parsing module

Fig. 6. The SynEvaluator interface. Subjects are highlighted in blue, Clauses in yellow, Operator Expressions in green and Rule Priorities in red. Among Clauses, Extractive Clauses are shown in solid lines while Functional Clauses are outlined with dotted lines. (Color figure online)

and executes the created rules (Fig. 3). Post evaluation, the user is presented with a list of violating elements along with count and priority of each valid rule.

Benefits and Limitations. The proposed framework makes it significantly easier for non-programmers to create customised rules dynamically. Also, compared to previous quality evaluation tools, due to the framework's ability to reuse keywords to create new rules, the developer effort required to hard-code rules is minimised. Another major benefit is that the proposed framework can potentially be used to query over entire OWL language. This can be done as any ontological element/attribute can be extracted using extractive clauses and the appropriate function executed on them. Lastly, due to functional clauses, it is possible to execute ontological or ontology-level functions like normal query languages and use linguistic analysis on text. This is particularly useful in quality evaluation while applying appropriateness checks on IDs or labels.

Example 1: Element hasDescriptiveElement Comment usesLogicalOperator Or hasDescriptiveElement Description

Example 2: Class hasAttribute ID usesComparativeOperator Dissimilarity hasRelatedElement EquivalentClass hasAttribute ID

Example 3: Element usesLogicalOperator Not hasDescriptiveElement Label hasLinguisticProperty ContainsConjunctions

Example 4: Element usesLogicalOperator Not hasDescriptiveElement Label hasLinguisticProperty ContainsPolysemes

Fig. 7. More examples of rules supported by SynEvaluator

In Fig. 5 (Example 1), it can be seen that properties with missing domain or range, a common quality violation, could be detected through a combination of logical operators and extractive clauses. Another common violation is related to the absence of annotations (comments, descriptions, etc.) for an ontological element [34]. This can be converted into a rule, once again through Extractive Clauses as shown in Fig. 7 (Example 1). A third quality violation would be when similar (or synonymous) classes are incorrectly defined as equivalent classes [23]. This can be defined as in Fig. 7 (Example 2), where the comparative operator 'Dissimilarity' is used to test for semantic similarity through cosine similarity of label embeddings. As mentioned previously, it is also possible to perform linguistic tests unlike other query languages. A basic example of this is detection of conjunctions in a label as shown in Fig. 7 (Example 3). This is useful to identify quality violations where different concepts are merged in the same class using conjunctions [28]. A more advanced example of a linguistic test would be a rule detecting polysemous elements (Fig. 7, Example 4). This is useful in detecting violating elements that have labels denoting differing conceptual ideas in differing senses. SynEvaluator implements this check through the use of WordNet's synsets to find out how many senses a word can have. Once these rules are created, the ontology engineer can add domain/range elements; annotations; remove synonymous equivalent classes and fix classes with conjunctions and polysemes as appropriate. SynEvaluator can thus help in fixing structural and linguistic quality violations.

The current version of SynEvaluator has a few limitations. It is currently only possible to chain clauses together or use operators to compare chained clauses. As a result, it is not possible to create rules with multiple lines. One major consequence of this is that variable assignment is not supported, and it is not possible to create a variable in one line and refer to it in another, as part of the same rule. Aggregation operators, such as 'Count' or 'Sum', are currently not supported either. Finally, it is not possible to create rules that require reasoning. The described limitations shall be addressed in future iterations of SynEvaluator. In spite of the limitations, the current framework (as shown in Experiments section) is still able to support creation of the majority of quality evaluation rules.

3.2   Stage 2: SemValidator

SemValidator uses a crowdsourced approach to semantically evaluate ontologies. The key feature of SemValidator is that it does not require ontology engineers, domain experts or knowledge of OWL language for validation. This is useful in a crowdsourced setting, where validators may have varying degrees of expertise and knowledge. If further necessitates the use of appropriate quality control mechanisms. To ensure quality, SemValidator uses TweetExpert algorithm to calculate expertise score of a crowdsourced validator, which is then used to weigh their decisions. This section describes the approach used by TweetExpert and justifies the choices made. This is then followed by a discussion on the assumptions made by TweetExpert and the feasibility of the assumptions in the context of crowdsourcing. The section finally ends with a description of the implementation of SemValidator and how it can be used by crowdsourced validators.

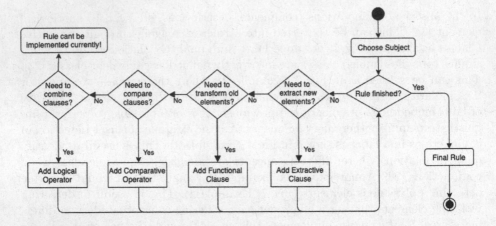

Fig. 8. Activity diagram for creating a rule in SynEvaluator

TweetExpert Algorithm. TweetExpert algorithm takes Twitter usernames of validators as input. For each of the validators, it calculates two scores: a) a 'TweetSim' score and b) a 'FriendSim' score. A 'TweetSim' score is intended to assess the similarity of the validator's tweets to the domain of the ontology while 'FriendSim' estimates the domain similarity of the validator's friends (pages they are following). To calculate the 'TweetSim' score, the validator's 'n' most recent tweets are extracted from their profile and their semantic similarity with the domain keyword is computed using the Universal Sentence Encoder (USE) [6]. Here the 'domain keyword' is manually chosen as the word most relevant to the domain of the ontology. For instance, "Pizza" for Stanford Pizza ontology [8] and "Information Security" for the ISO 27001 based "Information Security" ontology [10]. The current implementation uses only one keyword, but it is possible to compute similarity scores with multiple keywords and average these scores for greater accuracy. The similarities are sorted in decreasing order. Out of n similarities, the top-K similarities are chosen. These top-K similarities are then averaged to yield 'TweetSim' score. A similar approach is used to calculate 'FriendSim' score. The 'm' most recent friends are extracted to calculate their 'TweetSim' scores. After sorting in decreasing order, the top-K most similar scores are averaged to yield 'FriendSim' score. The reason behind extracting the most recent tweets and friends is to get a better estimate of the validator's current knowledge and interests. On the other hand, a top-K average helps in both filtering out occasional out-of-domain tweets from domain experts and smoothening out the effects of coincidental in-domain outliers from non-experts. The value of K is thus appropriately empirically chosen such that it is large enough to not include in-domain outliers from laymen, but small enough to exclude any out-of-domain tweets from experts. The pseudocode for TweetExpert is shown in Algorithm 1.

Finally, the calculated 'TweetSim' and 'FriendSim' scores are input to a pre-trained Machine Learning regression algorithm that predicts the final

---

Algorithm 1: TweetExpert algorithm

Result: TweetExpert score

Function `calculate_tweet_similarity(`*username*`):`
>   user_tweets := extract_tweets(username)
>   tweet_similarities := calculate_USE_similarity(user_tweets, domain_name)
>   best_tweet_similarities := get_top_K_tweets(tweet_similarities)
>   tweet_similarity_score = average(best_tweet_similarities)
>   **return** tweet_similarity_score

Function `calculate_friend_similarity(`*username*`):`
>   user_friends := extract_friends(username)
>   user_friends_scores := **foreach** $friend \in user\_friends$ **do**
>   calculate_tweet_similarity(friend)
>   best_friend_scores := get_top_K'_friends(user_friends_scores)
>   friend_similarity_score = average(best_friend_scores)
>   **return** friend_similarity_score

tweet_sim := calculate_tweet_relevance(username)
friend_sim := calculate_friend_relevance(username)
score := ML_predict_score(tweet_sim, friend_sim)

TweetExpert score using the two scores as feature vectors. The current implementation uses Epsilon-Support Vector Regression (SVR), since it was experimentally found to yield best results (shown in Experiments section). However, the system uses strategy software design pattern [29] which enables easy interchange of regression algorithms. The TweetExpert score is calculated for each of the validators by repeating the process described above. The final decision is taken using a weighted majority voting algorithm with the TweetExpert scores being used as weights. The TweetExpert scores provide a way to estimate a confidence value for the decisions input by each validator. This is particularly crucial as a quality control metric in non-probabilistic sampling techniques like crowdsourcing where number of validators can grow exponentially in count and diversity.

Assumptions. SemValidator makes reasonably grounded assumptions to establish efficacy and suitability in a crowdsourced setting. For example, about 49% of crowdsourced workers whose primary source of income is Amazon Mechanical Turk, a popular crowdsourcing platform, are in the 18–29 age range[6]. As of February 2021, about 42% of Americans in the 18–29 age range use Twitter, with this age group being the most active demographic on Twitter[7]. It is also assumed that in order for expertise estimation to work, Twitter users tweet reasonably frequently. The average number of tweets per day per user, according

---

[6] https://pewrsr.ch/3vX5q2G.
[7] https://bit.ly/3z5IDn9.

to a 2016 study[8], is 4.422, which translates to over 1600 tweets a year. This is typically sufficient since $K \sim$50–100. Finally, SemValidator assumes workers have public Twitter profiles, which would enable tweets and friends of a worker to be extracted. This assumption is predicated upon a recent 2019 survey[9] that showed 87% of Twitter users in USA have public accounts. Also, as part of future work, SemValidator would allow login through Facebook and Linkedin as well and a similar algorithm for expertise estimation could be used. This is expected to further increase the applicability of this expertise-based approach for crowdsourcing.

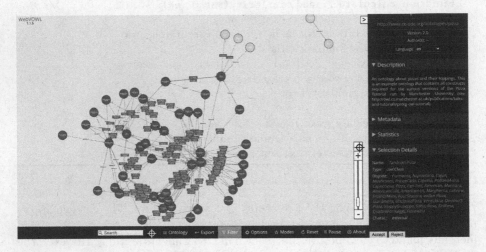

Fig. 9. The main validation interface of SemValidator. The Stanford Pizza ontology has been uploaded on SemValidator, with its concepts in blue and the enriched concepts in green. One of the enriched concepts, "Tandoori Pizza" has been selected, with options to "Accept" and "Reject" it. (Color figure online)

Proposing SemValidator: The Final Validation Workbench. The proposed workflow is used to develop a validation workbench for crowdsourced workers that allows for accepting or rejecting enriched concepts, relations and instances in an enriched ontology. The main validation interface of this workbench, called SemValidator, is shown in Fig. 9. This application integrates Twitter authentication and uses the TweetExpert algorithm for calculating validator expertise. SemValidator allows for two types of users: (a) the administrator and (b) the validator. The administrator, typically the ontology engineer, can upload/delete ontologies to be validated and also access decisions made by validators. When the validator selects an ontology to validate, the ontology is served

---

[8] https://bit.ly/3fSjWmA.

[9] https://bit.ly/3pmMc3O.

using the WebVOWL ontology visualization software. The enriched concepts and instances are highlighted in green, and on selection, enable the validators to select accept/reject decisions accordingly. Enriched relations, also in green, may also be accepted/rejected independent of the concepts they relate. The validators' decisions are recorded by SemValidator and logged to a database. The administrator can download this database after the crowdsourcing survey is completed, evaluate validator expertise using their Twitter usernames and then make final accept/reject decisions.

The syntactic and semantic evaluation aspects of the framework may be used independently of each other. However, utilizing the framework in an integrated manner as shown in Fig. 3 is expected to give best results. This way, syntactical violations can be detected easily and in an automated and customizable manner, while semantic violations can now be detected more accurately by crowdsourced validators. The resulting ontology has enhanced syntactic and semantic ontological quality and is now fit for reuse.

4   Experiments

Stanford Pizza and ISO-IEC 27001 Information Security ontologies are evaluated using the proposed framework to demonstrate ontology quality evaluation. Since the focus of this work is on enriched ontologies, these are manually enriched with concepts, properties and instances before quality evaluation. The RDF triples used to enrich Pizza and Information Security ontologies are provided over here[10]. Only 5 triples were chosen for this iteration, considering that ontology enrichment is as an iterative process and the count of triples per iteration is expected to be of this order. For Pizza, the domain-specific webpages used for extraction consisted of culinary articles[11] and food travel blogs[12]. For Information Security they consisted of informative articles and product pages by Cisco[13], Barracuda[14] and SearchSecurity[15]. Please note that some relevant data in this section is shown through external links due to space constraints.

4.1   Syntactic Quality Evaluation Using SynEvaluator

This section attempts to evaluate the applicability and accuracy of SynEvaluator in creating rules and detecting violations respectively. It is hypothesized that SynEvaluator's reusable theoretical framework for priority-specific rule creation increases its applicability for diverse range of tasks, but without compromising on violation-detection accuracy. To prove these claims, SynEvaluator is compared against OOPS! [27], a popular, publicly available SOTA tool that allows

---

[10] https://bit.ly/3z5lGR1.
[11] https://bit.ly/3yYGGZP.
[12] https://bit.ly/3iiEtCm.
[13] https://bit.ly/3wXRHZj.
[14] https://bit.ly/34PIUN9.
[15] https://bit.ly/3wXRJQV.

qualitative rule evaluation using rules. Moreover, OOPS! compiles 41 most commonly observed pitfalls drawn from several popular works on ontology quality evaluation [12,23,34] and the ones described in the OOPS! catalogue [26] are chosen as rules for implementation. This allows appropriate assessment of applicability for rule creation, while also allowing accuracy evaluation by comparing SynEvaluator's detected violations to that of OOPS! Note that while SynEvaluator's suitability for rule creation is being assessed here by comparing with rule-based evaluation approaches, it cannot be compared yet with other contemporary works focusing on metric-based evaluation. This is being planned as part of future work by introducing metric-to-rule conversion, which would allow metrics to be framed as rules. One possible way this could be done is by adding conditions, such as comparison operators, after metrics to form rules.

Table 2. No of pitfalls implemented by SynEvaluator (SE) vs OOPS!

SE	OOPS!	
	Implemented	Not implemented
Implemented	29	4
Not implemented	1	7

SynEvaluator's framework can be used to successfully formulate 30 of the 41 pitfalls compiled in the catalogue, compared to OOPS! which can automate 33. As shown in Table 2, the majority of pitfalls (29 of 41) can be successfully implemented by both OOPS! and SynEvaluator. 7 cannot be implemented by either of them, and this involves rules that require human knowledge and reasoning (such as overspecialization of ontology hierarchy, usage of wrong relations, etc.). 1 of the pitfalls (involving linguistic polysemy detection) could be implemented by SynEvaluator but not by OOPS!. There are 4 pitfalls implemented by OOPS! which SynEvaluator cannot check. This includes rules that check for undeclared disjoint concepts, undeclared transitive properties, equivalent classes, etc. Supporting such rules involves a higher degree of ontological reasoning that SynEvaluator is incapable of. Nevertheless, SynEvaluator's ability to implement vast majority of quality evaluation rules off-the-shelf in a customizable manner increases confidence in its applicability for future evaluation tasks that may involve more rules.

For comparing accuracy of violation detection, SynEvaluator's reported violations are compared with OOPS! [27]. Given the absence of ground truth and the widespread popularity of OOPS!, it is assumed that OOPS! uses valid, non-erroneous rule checks for the implemented pitfalls. It can be observed that the violations reported by SynEvaluator match those of OOPS! in all pitfalls except for P22. OOPS! mentions that these could be due to inconsistent naming conventions, however SynEvaluator is unable to detect any such errors in the ontologies. This may be a result of the incorrect naming checks currently used. But for the other pitfalls, both tools returning the same number of violations suggests that for the implemented framework, SynEvaluator is accurate in evaluating rules and detecting pitfalls.

4.2   Semantic Quality Validation Using SemValidator

SemValidator uses a crowdsourced survey to semantically validate the enriched Pizza and Information Security ontologies. Crowdsourced validators were invited by tweeting a description of the task along with the link to the SemValidator application. Among the 31 validators that participated in the survey, 3 had private Twitter accounts so their responses were discarded. The 28 validators with public accounts included 5 validators with a background in Cybersecurity, 4 in Artificial Intelligence, 5 in Software Engineering, 4 in Healthcare, 3 in Food domain (such as chefs and culinary experts), 3 in Literature, 2 in Politics and 1 each in Fashion and Pure Science. These diverse bunch of validators were asked to self-identify their domain of expertise for statistical purposes before participating in the survey. To preserve validator anonymity, the anonymized results of the survey are provided here[16]. After completion of the survey for both ontologies, 'TweetSim' and 'FriendSim' scores were calculated for all 28 validators using the TweetExpert algorithm, described previously. TweetExpert took 15 seconds to execute for our values of $K = 20$ and $K' = 5$ per validator profile. Finally, TweetExpert score was calculated by experimenting with 4 standard regression algorithms: Linear Regression, Random Forest Regression, K-Nearest Neighbours (KNN) Regression and Epsilon-Support Vector Regression (SVR). A standard majority voting where all decisions have equal weightage is considered as a naive baseline.

The input features for each algorithm were 'TweetSim' and 'FriendSim' scores of a validator and the label was the ratio of correct answers (to total answers) given by them. This was done to ensure validators with more correct answers received higher 'TweetExpert' scores using similarity scores as feature vectors. Since a gold standard for the correct answers did not exist, CISOs were asked to manually validate the enriched triples from the information security domain, while the authors themselves validated the triples from the pizza domain. To determine the best among the 4 regression algorithms for score prediction, 7-fold cross validation was carried out. The 28 responses (now reduced to feature vectors and labels) available for both ontologies were divided into 7 folds of 4 responses each. 5 folds were used for training, 1 for validation and 1 for testing. For each chosen test fold, immediately succeeding fold was chosen as the validation set and all the other folds were used for training.

Different sets of hyperparameters were considered for each regression algorithm[17]. The best set of hyperparameters for each algorithm was determined by selecting the algorithm with highest accuracy on the validation set, calculated by determining the proportion of correctly answered questions to the total number of questions. The predicted answer to a question is determined by using weighted

---

[16] https://bit.ly/3pvzbFh.
[17] https://bit.ly/3wUa9SA.

majority voting algorithm on the predicted expertise scores in the validation set. The higher the number of correct answers, the closer the predicted scores are to their actual value. The same procedure was followed for calculating the accuracy on the test folds. Accuracy obtained on test and validation sets for each of these algorithms is shown in Table 3 for both ontologies. Epsilon Support Vector Regression was found to yield best results on both datasets.

To determine whether training score prediction algorithms requires feature vectors from the same domain, an SVR model is trained on a more generic dataset, i.e. the Pizza dataset and tested on Information Security, a niche dataset. The model hyperparameters are chosen as the ones that performed best on the Information Security dataset earlier. Varying percentages of the Pizza dataset are used to construct training subsets, to observe variation in test accuracy with subset size. To ensure randomness while choosing these subsets, 10 experimental trials were conducted where the dataset is shuffled before each trial and trained on the first $x\%$ of samples, where x is the percentage of the training dataset chosen. The results are shown in Table 4. The accuracy monotonically increases with increase in size of training subset. The results suggest that a model pre-trained to predict the expertise score on one domain could be reused multiple times in different domains, even if they are niche.

Table 3. Mean validation and test accuracy scores on Pizza and Security datasets

Algorithm	Pizza		Security	
	Val	Test	Val	Test
Majority Voting	71.43	71.43	51.43	51.43
Linear Regression	85.71	83.57	68.57	71.43
Random Forest	80.0	81.43	68.57	74.28
KNN	85.71	80.0	77.14	77.14
SVR	**88.57**	**85.71**	**80.0**	**80.0**

Table 4. Mean accuracy scores on test dataset (Information Security) with variation in % of training dataset (Pizza).

Dataset%	10%	25%	50%	75%	100%
Accuracy	70%	76%	86%	92%	100%

Table 3 shows that the best-performing algorithm (TweetExpert with SVR followed by weighted majority voting) significantly outperforms naive majority voting. It can be observed that naive majority voting gives particularly bad results for Information Security, a relatively niche domain, than Pizza, a domain known more to laymen as well. When replacing naive majority voting with TweetExpert + SVR, a drastic increase in performance in Information

Security (55.55%) vs Pizza (20%) can be observed. Even the worst performing regression algorithm gives an increase of 38.8% and 14% respectively. As a result, it can be inferred that estimating expertise using TweetExpert can be particularly useful for quality control in niche domains.

5 Conclusion and Future Work

Ontology evaluation is a critical stage of any ontology engineering process. In this paper, SynEvaluator and SemValidator are proposed for syntactic and semantic evaluation of an enriched ontology respectively. Although the work focuses on an enriched ontology, it can be easily extended for evaluation of any generic ontology.

SynEvaluator automatically evaluates ontologies using customised rules created dynamically at runtime, and improves on previous quality evaluation approaches in a variety of ways. Firstly, it offers greater flexibility to the user in terms of creating, updating and deleting custom rules as well as setting priorities. Secondly, it proposes rule creation by the usage of a novel theoretical framework that factors rules into sequences of 'clauses' and 'operator expressions'. This facilitates creation of an interactive interface that makes it easier for non-programmers to dynamically create rules. In addition, chaining together independent keywords can facilitate creation of a large number of rules without requiring additional developer programming. SemValidator improves on previously proposed crowdsourced ontology validation approaches by incorporating a Twitter-based quality control mechanism. The TweetExpert algorithm is proposed for calculating the expertise score of a validator using the tweets and friends extracted from their Twitter profile as input.

The efficacy of SynEvalautor was shown by implementing rules to detect pitfalls and the accuracy of the detected violations was compared with publicly available OOPS! tool. Semantic quality evaluation using SemValidator is performed on both Pizza and Information security ontologies with the help of a crowdsourced survey of 28 validators. The experimental results showed a significantly higher than naive majority voting.

The experimental results are encouraging but also can be used as an aid to further extend the research work. For example, SynEvaluator can be expanded to support additional, more complex operations such as using parantheses, arithmetic operators, variable assignment etc. Although the TweetExpert algorithm used by SemValidator currently calculates expertise using only tweets and friends as feature vectors, it could be extended to use additional information such as Twitter lists, followers, tweet metadata, etc.

References

1. Alani, H., Brewster, C., Shadbolt, N.: Ranking ontologies with AKTiveRank. In: Cruz, I., et al. (eds.) ISWC 2006. LNCS, vol. 4273, pp. 1–15. Springer, Heidelberg (2006). https://doi.org/10.1007/11926078_1
2. Amardeilh, F., Laublet, P., Minel, J.L.: Document annotation and ontology population from linguistic extractions. In: Proceedings of the 3rd International Conference on Knowledge Capture, pp. 161–168 (2005)
3. Beckett, D., Berners-Lee, T., Prud'hommeaux, E., Carothers, G.: RDF 1.1 turtle. In: World Wide Web Consortium, pp. 18–31 (2014)
4. Berners-Lee, T., Hendler, J., Lassila, O.: The semantic web. Sci. Am. **284**(5), 34–43 (2001)
5. Burton-Jones, A., Storey, V.C., Sugumaran, V., Ahluwalia, P.: A semiotic metrics suite for assessing the quality of ontologies. Data Knowl. Eng. **55**(1), 84–102 (2005)
6. Cer, D., et al.: Universal Sentence Encoder. arXiv preprint arXiv:1803.11175 (2018)
7. Dividino, R.Q., Romanelli, M., Sonntag, D., et al.: Semiotic-based ontology evaluation tool (S-OntoEval). In: LREC (2008)
8. Drummond, N.: Stanford pizza ontology. https://protege.stanford.edu/ontologies/pizza/pizza.owl. Accessed 28 Mar 2021
9. Duque-Ramos, A., et al.: Evaluation of the OQuaRE framework for ontology quality. Expert Syst. Appl. **40**, 2696–2703 (2013)
10. Fenz, S., Goluch, G., Ekelhart, A., Riedl, B., Weippl, E.: Information security fortification by ontological mapping of the ISO/IEC 27001 standard. In: 13th Pacific Rim International Symposium on Dependable Computing (PRDC 2007), pp. 381–388. IEEE (2007)
11. Gangemi, A., Catenacci, C., Ciaramita, M., Lehmann, J.: A theoretical framework for ontology evaluation and validation. In: SWAP, vol. 166, p. 16 (2005)
12. Gómez-Pérez, A.: Evaluation of taxonomic knowledge in ontologies and knowledge bases (1999)
13. Guarino, N., Welty, C.: Evaluating ontological decisions with OntoClean. Commun. ACM **45**(2), 61–65 (2002)
14. Hearst, M.A.: Automatic acquisition of hyponyms from large text corpora. In: Proceedings of the 14th Conference on Computational Linguistics, vol. 2, pp. 539–545. Association for Computational Linguistics (1992)
15. Iyer, V., Mohan, L., Bhatia, M., Reddy, Y.R.: A survey on ontology enrichment from text. In: Proceedings of the 16th International Conference on Natural Language Processing, pp. 95–104. NLP Association of India, International Institute of Information Technology, Hyderabad, India, December 2019. https://aclanthology.org/2019.icon-1.11
16. Kiptoo, C.C.: Ontology enhancement using crowdsourcing: a conceptual architecture. Int. J. Crowd Sci. (2020)
17. Kontokostas, D., Zaveri, A., Auer, S., Lehmann, J.: TripleCheckMate: a tool for crowdsourcing the quality assessment of linked data. In: Klinov, P., Mouromtsev, D. (eds.) KESW 2013. CCIS, vol. 394, pp. 265–272. Springer, Heidelberg (2013). https://doi.org/10.1007/978-3-642-41360-5_22
18. Lantow, B.: OntoMetrics: putting metrics into use for ontology evaluation. In: KEOD, pp. 186–191 (2016)
19. Lozano-Tello, A., Gómez-Pérez, A.: OntoMetric: a method to choose the appropriate ontology. J. Database Manag. **2**, 1–18 (2004)

20. Maedche, A., Staab, S.: Ontology learning for the semantic web. Intell. Syst. **16**(2), 72–79 (2001)
21. Makki, J., Alquier, A.M., Prince, V.: An NLP-based ontology population for a risk management generic structure. In: Proceedings of the 5th International Conference on Soft Computing as Transdisciplinary Science and Technology, pp. 350–355 (2008)
22. McDaniel, M., Storey, V.C., Sugumaran, V.: Assessing the quality of domain ontologies: metrics and an automated ranking system. Data Knowl. Eng. **115**, 32–47 (2018)
23. Noy, N.F., McGuinness, D.L., et al.: Ontology development 101: a guide to creating your first ontology (2001)
24. Noy, N.F., Mortensen, J., Musen, M.A., Alexander, P.R.: Mechanical Turk as an ontology engineer? using microtasks as a component of an ontology-engineering workflow. In: Proceedings of the 5th Annual ACM Web Science Conference, pp. 262–271 (2013)
25. Pittet, P., Barthélémy, J.: Exploiting users' feedbacks: towards a task-based evaluation of application ontologies throughout their lifecycle. In: International Conference on Knowledge Engineering and Ontology Development, vol. 2 (2015)
26. Poveda, M.: Catalogue of common pitfalls. http://oops.linkeddata.es/catalogue. jsp. Accessed 28 Mar 2021
27. Poveda-Villalón, M., Gómez-Pérez, A., Suárez-Figueroa, M.C.: OOPS!: a pitfall-based system for ontology diagnosis. In: Innovations, Developments, and Applications of Semantic Web and Information Systems, pp. 120–148. IGI Global (2018)
28. Poveda-Villalón, M., Suárez-Figueroa, M.C., Gómez-Pérez, A.: Validating ontologies with OOPS! In: ten Teije, A., et al. (eds.) EKAW 2012. LNCS (LNAI), vol. 7603, pp. 267–281. Springer, Heidelberg (2012). https://doi.org/10.1007/978-3-642-33876-2_24
29. Richard, E., Ralph, H., Johnson, R., et al.: Design patterns: elements of reusable object-oriented software (1995)
30. Sanagavarapu, L.M., Iyer, V., Reddy, Y.R.: OntoEnricher: a deep learning approach for ontology enrichment from unstructured text. arXiv preprint arXiv:2102.04081 (2021)
31. Schober, D., Tudose, I., Svatek, V., Boeker, M.: Ontocheck: verifying ontology naming conventions and metadata completeness in protégé 4. J. Biomed. Semant. **3**, 1–10 (2012)
32. Tartir, S., Arpinar, I.B., Sheth, A.P.: Ontological evaluation and validation. In: Poli, R., Healy, M., Kameas, A. (eds.) Theory and Applications of Ontology: Computer Applications. Springer, Dordrecht (2010). https://doi.org/10.1007/978-90-481-8847-5_5
33. Tibaut, A.: Ontology Evaluation. https://github.com/atibaut/ontology-evaluation. Accessed 15 Mar 2021
34. Vrandečić, D.: Ontology evaluation. In: Staab, S., Studer, R. (eds.) Handbook on Ontologies. IHIS, pp. 293–313. Springer, Heidelberg (2009). https://doi.org/10.1007/978-3-540-92673-3_13
35. Wohlgenannt, G., Sabou, M., Hanika, F.: Crowd-based ontology engineering with the ucomp protégé plugin. Semant. Web **7**(4), 379–398 (2016)
36. Wong, W., Liu, W., Bennamoun, M.: Ontology learning from text: a look back and into the future. ACM Comput. Surv. (CSUR) **44**(4), 1–36 (2012)
37. Zhang, Y., Saberi, M., Chang, E.: Semantic-based lightweight ontology learning framework: a case study of intrusion detection ontology. In: Proceedings of the International Conference on Web Intelligence, pp. 1171–1177 (2017)

Deep Learning for Security

Attribute-Based Access Control Policy Review in Permissioned Blockchain

Sherifdeen Lawal[✉] and Ram Krishnan[✉]

University of Texas at San Antonio, San Antonio, TX 78249, USA
{sherifdeen.lawal,ram.krishnan}@utsa.edu

Abstract. Permissioned blockchain is of a great deal to enterprise uses cases. There is a need to support access control policy review for legal and security reasons in some use cases. Specifying and maintaining a complex access policy for a permissioned blockchain may be well managed using attributes. The ABAC policy approaches offer a solution to a peculiar set of challenges for distributed system access control, like the blockchain. There are studies on leveraging Smart Contracts in implementing blockchain-based ABAC policy. However, most of these contributions implement an Attribute-Based Access Control policy expressed in a logical format. We proposed the ABAC enumerated policy format as an access control mechanism for the permissioned blockchain, Hyperledger Fabric network. We also proposed an algorithm for a set of policy review problems and implemented the algorithm for a blockchain-based policy specification.

Keywords: Attribute based access control · Policy review · Authorization · Revocation · Policy machine · Authorization graph

1 Introduction

The two general classes of a blockchain network are permissionless (public) and pemissioned (private) blockchain, from the context of network entity identity. The participants in a public blockchain network are anonymous. A federated or centralized authority grants access to the participants of a permissioned blockchain. The permission blockchain serves enterprise use cases where there is a need to verify the identity of their customers, such as financial transaction that requires the Know-Your-Customer (KYC) and Anti-Money Laundering (AML) regulations. This work aims at the study of revocation and authorization policy review in the Hyperledger Fabric blockchain network. Hyperledger Fabric is a pluggable, modularized, and open-source architecture for commercial-grade permissioned distributed ledger technology (DLT) platform.

The blockchain is not an exemption to the particular set of challenges for distributed system access control. It requires a unique set of concepts and considerations different from traditional systems. An important requirement is that distributed applications on multiple coordinated systems have permission to access

© Springer Nature Switzerland AG 2022
R. Krishnan et al. (Eds.): SKM 2021, CCIS 1549, pp. 97–109, 2022.
https://doi.org/10.1007/978-3-030-97532-6_6

the data for processing and controlling the access to the distributed processes and data from their local users. The Attribute-Based Access Control (ABAC) offers a solution to the discussed problem of access policy on the blockchain network. It uses dynamic attribute values for privilege assignment in a distributed system that requires federated or autonomous control. Applications in Hyperledger Fabric interact with the blockchain network by submitting a request to operate on the ledger. A logic-based ABAC policy controls the access of these applications on the Fabric network.

The access control model of a blockchain network is critical. Nevertheless, the ability to create and modify policy specifications without unintended consequence is of equal importance. The policy review in ABAC models that express policy using logic-based formula has the NP-complete time complexity. For instance, the evaluations for a given user attribute to access a particular resource. The work in [10] shows the lack of scalability by the logic-based ABAC model like the XACML in policy evaluation. An empirical study by Mell et al. demonstrates that the enumerated-based policy ABAC model of the NIST Next Generation Access Control (NGAC) is scalable [11].

This work proposes a modularized ABAC architecture of the Policy Machine as an on-chain mechanism to control access to the blockchain ledger. The Policy Machine is the foundation for the NIST Next Generation Access Control (NGAC) [8,9]. This work implemented the Policy Machine standard architectural components on the Hyperledger Fabric network. We applied our proposed algorithm to the authorization and revocation policy review problem of the Policy Machine. Through a set of Smart Contracts (chaincode), our implementation stores access policy information to the blockchain ledger. The protected resource ledger is a different ledger from the access policy information ledger. A low-level Hyperledger Fabric API enables the communication between the Smart Contracts deployed for the two types of blockchain ledgers.

In summary, the contributions of this paper include:

1. the NIST NGAC system architecture implemented for a blockchain network.
2. a proposed algorithm for the policy review of revocation and constrained authorization in a blockchain-based Policy Machine system.

The reminder of this paper is structured as follows. In Sect. 2, we touch on related work on this subject. Section 3 provides overview of the Hyperledger Fabric and Policy Machine framework. Section 4 details on policy review problem in Policy Machine. Section 5 describes the policy review algorithm to revoke and grant (with constraint) access. An implementation of policy machine in Hyperledger Fabric and evaluation of our policy review algorithm is in Sect. 6, and Sect. 7 concludes this work.

2   Related Work

In this section, we touch on previous research contributions that implement ABAC on a blockchain network. We also discuss the few contributions to ABAC policy reviews in general. There is a handful of work on blockchain as an Attribute-Based Access Control system for different domains. Pinno et al. [1], Ding et al. [3], and Dukkipati et al. [4] study the implementation of blockchain-based ABAC in IoT systems. Zhang and Posland studied the blockchain authorization approach for Electronic Medical Records (EMRs) [5]. A granular authorization scheme for blocks and attribute values query was at the core of their research. Also, they lower the computational overhead for access decisions by eliminating the use of Public Key Infrastructure (PKI).

Few research works are out there on blockchain attribute-based access control for the general-purpose use case [2, 6, 7]. Previous studies [2, 7] utilized the XACML to express access policies. We applied the Policy Machine, the NIST implementation of the attribute-based access control framework, an open-source project. The only generic implementation of attribute-based access control on Hyperledger Fabric blockchain network deployed ABAC components as smart contracts to control access to an off-chain system [2]. In contrast, we implemented Smart Contracts for access control to the blockchain ledger. This work includes the capability for review of authorization and revocation.

Mell et al. improve the efficiency of the existing functions that answer users' capability and object access entry queries [11]. Their contribution reduced the computational overhead of capability and access entry queries using an optimized graph search algorithm. We proposed an algorithm for the policy review questions not addressed by the NIST Policy Machine specification or any previous research work.

The analysis of ABAC policies through the category-based metamodel [12] addresses a similar set of policy review questions in the NIST Policy Machine specification. The policy review algorithm we proposed answers question not covered by the NIST Policy Machine or any previous research work.

3   Background

3.1   Hyperledger Fabric

Hyperledger Fabric core building blocks are the distributed ledger, different types of nodes, chaincode, channel, and Membership Service Provider (MSP).

Hyperledger Fabric blockchain ledgers are deployed on peer nodes to store assets. An asset is a representation of valuable items digitally stored on the blockchain network. Participants on the blockchain network can trade (transfer) assets. Hyperledger Fabric ledger has two components. The first component is the blockchain ledger that is an immutable sequence of transaction blocks. The second component is the state database that contains the current value of the key-value pairs created, modified, or deleted by transaction requests in the blockchain network. Blockchain transaction occurs when a client application invokes the programmable business logic (smart contract/chaincode) to read or write from the ledger.

The Hyperledger Fabric has three types of nodes - client, peer, and orderer nodes. The client node has an application that provides an interface for users to invoke smart contracts by sending a transaction proposal to a peer node. The peer nodes are where the shared ledger resides and their installed chaincode mediated end-user read/write operations to the distributed ledger. The orderer nodes perform the ordering of transactions on a first-come-first-serve basis for the blockchain network. It distributes the ordered blocks to peer nodes. Hyperledger Fabric allows the integration of other implementation of the orderer service apart from the out-of-the-box Kafka and Raft varieties.

A smart contract is a code packaged as a chaincode in Hyperledger Fabric. It manages access and modifications to a set of key-value pairs in the state database when invoked by client applications external to the blockchain network. A channel is an isolated overlay of the blockchain network on the Hyperledger Fabric network that provides data privacy and confidentiality. Each channel has a ledger shared across the peers on the channel, and only participants authenticated to the specific channel can transact on such channel. The Membership Service Provider (MSP) governs the validity of credentials for a group of participants on the network. Transaction authentication and validation respectively by client and peer node requires identity credentials. There's a need to install chaincode on a channel before end-user invocation to read and write to the ledger through an application or client node CLI.

3.2   Policy Machine Basic Elements and Relations

Policy specification in Policy Machine has an annotated Directed Acyclic Graph (DAG) representation. The node of the Policy Machine authorization graph is the of Policy Elements (PE). The policy elements are the finite sets of Users (U), Objects (O), User Attributes (UA), Object Attributes (OA), and Policy Classes (PC). An assignment relations in Fig. 1 are unlabeled DAG edges between the ordered pair of a user to user attribute node, object to object attribute node, an attribute to an attribute of the same type, and user or object attribute node to the policy class node. Any outward unlabeled edge (assignment relation) from a source policy element must terminate at a policy class of an authorization graph.

An association relation in Fig. 1 is an annotated edge between user attributes and user attributes or object attributes. For example, the association edge (*Group Head, aars$_i$, Retail & Foreign Serv*) specifies that individuals with a sequence of assignments to the *Group Head* can execute the actions enabled through administrative access right set *aars$_j$* on *Retail & Foreign Serv* and the policy element *Retail & Foreign Serv* contains. The association relation is partitioned into two as administrative (a-association) and resource (r-association) association.

An association is a relation represented by labeled (annotated) downward-arcing edge from a user attribute node to an attribute (user attribute or object attribute node). For example, in Fig. 1, the association triple (*Group Head, aars$_i$, Retail & Foreign Serv*) implies that a user who has a path to *Group Head* is authorized to perform operations enabled by *aars$_i$* on *Retail & Foreign Serv* and policy element that has a sequence of assignment relation to *Retail & Foreign Serv*. An association grants access through a set of resource access rights (i.e., r-association in the legend) or a set of administrative access rights (i.e., a-association in the legend). The policy elements and the relations constitute the authorization graph.

4 Policy Review Problem in Policy Machine

The Policy Machine authorization graph can grant access by creating assignment and/or association relations. Likewise, the deletion of assignment and/or association relations may revoke access. Given the hierarchical structure of the Policy Machine, for a lot of scenarios, we can grant or deny access in various ways. However, a subset of the possible ways of allowing or denying access may contradict another policy. Also, some of the approaches of granting or denying access may have unintended authorization or revocation. The proposed algorithm of this paper generates a comprehensive list with the combination of relations to delete or create for revoking or authorizing access requests, respectively. The algorithm result provides the Policy Machine administrator guidance on the approach for access authorization or revocation.

We demonstrated in the coming example how the number of approaches to grant access explodes and how utilizing constraints can limit the authorization approaches.

Example: Figure 1 shows the authorization graph for a financial institution with the policy class called *BankOp Access*. The task 'trans-T' requires two related ordered administrative operations with the permissions granted through access rights $aars_q$ and $aars_p$ on Wire Trans Serv and ATM & POS Serv, respectively. Two employees (*Alice* and *Bob*) of the financial institution each have a different subset of authorities granted to *Cathy* to complete the task 'trans-T'.

In another task, 'T-1' an officer in this financial institution with the attributes *ATM Custodian* and *Trans Serv Supervisor* needs to assign a member of the *Backup Officer* role to *ATM Custodian* for the completion of the task 'T-1'. *Cathy* has no permission to assign a *Backup Officer* to the *ATM Custodian* role in the current transition state of the authorization graph of Fig. 1. Let's assume the employees (i.e., *Jane* and *Paul*) in this example with permissions enabled by the administrative access right set, $aars_i$, can authorize *Cathy*'s requested access. Here are approaches that will allow the assignment of a *Backup Officer* to the *ATM Custodian* role by *Cathy*:

1. *Creating association:* Using an association only and assuming a label (access right) $aars_k$ grants the permission *Cathy* is seeking, an association relation from *ATM Custodian*, or *Trans Serv Supervisor*, or *Op Officers* to *Backup Officer*, or *Op Officers* will authorize *Cathy*'s request. There are six possible relations to allow *Cathy*'s request using association relation.

2. *Creating user attribute assignment:* Users with permissions from the access right set $aars_i$ can create an assignment to authorize *Cathy*'s request. This assignment is from user attribute nodes that are descendants of the user

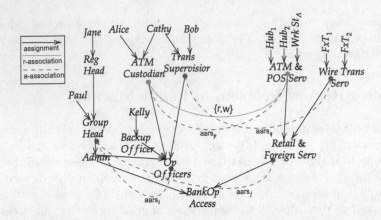

Fig. 1. Policy machine authorization graph

node, *Cathy*, to the ancestor user attribute nodes of *Group Head* and *Group Head*. For this approach of authorization, the user attribute assignments that conform with the DAG definition of the authorization graph are the relations from *ATM Custodian* or *Trans Serv Supervisor* to *Group Head* or *Regional Head*.

3. *Creating user assignment:* Any user with the permissions from the access right set $aars_i$ can use the user assignment operation to create an assignment of the *Cathy* user node to either of the user attribute nodes *Group Head* or *Regional Head*.

This illusive example above considers only single operation approaches to authorize *Cathy*'s request, to keep it simple. Overall, there are twelve different approaches of creating assignment or association relation to allow *Cathy* to complete task 'T-1'. The only caveat is that only two of these twelves ways of granting access to *Cathy* do not violate the constraint on the task 'trans-T'. Authorization of *Cathy*'s request through the approaches enumerated in (1) and (2) leaves the room for *Alice* and *Bob* to collude on the sensitive task 'trans-T'.

In addition, this example is by no means a comparison of the more complicated issues in an enterprise scenario. Note that the structure of the Policy Machine authorization graph permits granting access using any non-redundant combination of the three operations. For instance, using the preceding example, permissions enabled by the access right set $aars_i$ allows creating two assignment operations to authorize *Cathy*'s request. The sequence of operation may be a user assignment of the user node *Cathy* to user attribute node *Backup Officer* and the *Backup Officer* to a user attribute node granted the permissions of the access right set $aars_i$.

Observation

A Principal Authority (PA) is a mandatory preexisting user in the Policy Machine, also called the root user. The PA is responsible for the creation and control of the Policy Machine policies in their entirety. S/he fundamentally holds the universal authority to perform all the actions within the Policy Machine framework.

Apart from the permissions for creating and deleting policy classes and attribute assignments to policy classes, the PA may delegate access rights to a domain or sub-ordinate administrators. Note that the deployed system represented by the authorization graph of Fig. 1 does not include the Principle Authority. The Principal Authority of the authorization graph created the policy elements and relations as shown in the figure. Authorities delegated to the Group Head user attribute will suffice for creating new policy elements and assignment and association relations.

5 Policy Review Algorithm

We now provide our graph algorithm to answer these two questions on a given request (*user, op, resource*).

1. If a *user* is allowed to perform *op* on *resource*, what are the approaches to deny the *user* access to perform *op* on the protected *resource*?
2. If a *user* is not authorized to perform *op* operation on a *resource*, What are the approaches to grant the *op* on protected *resource* to the *user*?

5.1 Derived Functions

To generate approaches to revoke or authorize a given request in a policy graph, we utilize the following derived functions in creating groups of attributes in the preceding subsection. A combination of elements from these groups of attributes enables the creation of relation(s) as an approach to authorizing a denied access. Similarly, the deletion of the relation(s) created through elements of attribute groups is an approach to revoke authorized access.

- `tail` : ASSOCIATION $\longrightarrow$ UA: is a function that maps an edge, association relation, $(ua_i, ars_j, at_k) \in$ ASSOCIATION to the (user attribute) node $ua_i \in$ UA it originates.
- `head` : ASSOCIATION $\longrightarrow$ AT: is a function that maps an edge, association relation, $(ua_i, ars_j, at_k) \in$ ASSOCIATION to the (user/object attribute) node $at_k \in$ AT it terminates. Where AT = UA $\cup$ OA
- `anc`: PE $\longrightarrow 2^{\text{PE}}$: is the mapping from a policy element to the set of policy elements that is an ancestor to the policy element.
- `des`: PE $\longrightarrow 2^{\text{PE}}$: is the mapping from a policy element to the set of policy elements that is a descendant to the policy element.
- $\text{PE}_{i_{\text{func}}} = \{\text{node} \mid (\exists pe_j \in \text{PE}_i)[\text{node} \in \text{func}(pe_j)]\}$: is the set of all policy elements returned by `func` for the set PE_i, where `func` is `anc` or `des`.

5.2   Groups of Attribute Enabling Authorization and Revocation

The following defined sets of (user and object) attribute groups form the basis of our algorithm for the policy review of access authorization and revocation. We derived the attribute groups considering the resource a user wants to perform an action on is of type user or object. When the resource in question is a user or user attribute, the following user attribute groups create relations that authorize and revoke access requests.

- $UA_1 = \{\text{ua} \mid \text{ua} = \texttt{tail}((ua_i, ars_j, at_k)) \vee \text{ua} \in \texttt{anc}(\texttt{tail}((ua_i, ars_j, at_k)))\}$
- $UA_2 = \{\text{ua} \mid \text{ua} \in \texttt{anc}(\texttt{head}((ua_i, ars_j, at_k))) \wedge \text{ua} \in \texttt{des}(user)\}$
- $UA_3 = \{\text{ua} \mid \text{ua} \in \texttt{anc}(\texttt{head}((ua_i, ars_j, at_k)))$, $\text{ua} \notin UA_{2_{anc}}$, $\text{ua} \notin UA_2$, $\text{ua} \notin UA_{1_{des}}$, $\text{ua} \notin UA_1\}$
- $UA_4 = \{\text{ua} \mid \text{ua} \in \texttt{des}(user) \wedge \texttt{des}(resource) \}$

Where (ua_i, ars_j, at_k) is an association relation for authorizing $user$ to operate on $resource$

Assuming we want to grant or deny access to an object or object attribute. Combining the sets UA_1, UA_2, UA_3, above and the following object attribute groups enable the creation of relations that authorize or revoke access.

- $OA_1 = \{oa \mid oa \in \texttt{anc}(\texttt{head}((ua_p, ars_q, ao_r))), oa \notin \texttt{des}(resource), oa \neq resource\}$
- $OA_2 = \{oa \mid (oa \in \texttt{des}(resource) \wedge oa \notin OA_{1_{des}}) \vee oa = resource\}$
- $OA_3 = \{oa \mid (oa \in \texttt{anc}(\texttt{head}((ua_p, ars_q, ao_r))), oa \in \texttt{des}(resource), oa \in OA_{2_{des}}) \vee oa = \texttt{head}((ua_p, ars_q, ao_r)) \}$

This scenario requires two association relations. The association (ua_i, ars_j, at_k) grants authority to create or delete the relation(s) from attribute(s) of the user to whom we want to authorize/deny access. The second association (ua_p, ars_q, ao_r) allows the creation or deletion of relation(s) to the requested resource (object or object attribute).

5.3   Revocation and Constrained Authorization Methodology

Our policy review algorithm generates approaches to revoke and authorize access to Policy Machine protected resource. The relation(s) created or removed amongst group attributes (authorization/revocation enablers) provides approaches to allow and revoke access.

As input, the algorithm takes a request ($user$, op, $resource$), a graph associated with the request, and a record ($authmode$) with fields of key-value pair. Firstly, if there is an association relation (policy) that grants the user the authority to perform op on the resource, the algorithm generates approaches to revoke the access. Otherwise, it produces possible relation(s) that allow the user access to perform op on the resource. The key-value pairs from the input record allow a policy administrator to specify modes of authorization. The algorithm can generate all possible approaches with/without constraint to authorize a request. A key

Table 1. Scope of authorization/revocation on attribute groups

Attribute groups	Pattern of relations(s)	Authorization effect
UA_1	Assignment: to	No effect
UA_2	Assignment: from	Access granted
	Association: from	or inherited
UA_3	Assignment: from and to	Access granted
	Association: from	or inherited
UA_4	Association: to	No effect
OA_1	Association: to	No effect
OA_2	Association: to	No effect
	Assignment: from	Access entry granted
OA_3	Association: to	No effect

isGeneric with a boolean value of true generates all approaches without restriction, while the value of false produces constrained authorization approaches. When *isGeneric* is true the two other key-value pair in the record becomes null. Another key is the *denySet*, and the value is a set that authorization granted or inherited by its elements is constrained. Its value is a user attribute set.

Let's examine the scope of access granted through the revocation/ authorization enablers attribute sets. While authorizing a request, access is granted or inherited by some attribute groups. The table summarizes the pattern of relation(s) created using these attribute groups and the change in capability or access entry of these attributes after an authorization.

The column pattern of relation created (i.e., <relation/edge type> : <direction>) in the table describe the type of edge(s) we can create from or to elements of a given access enabling attribute set. As an example when the resource is a user or user attribute, a possible approach to authorize access is creating an edge (assignment) from ua_2 to ua_1 or creating an assignment from ua_2 to ua_3 and creating an association from ua_3 to ua_4, where $ua_i \in UA_i$. The third column of the table signifies the change in capability or access entry of a user or an object attribute respectively. Authorizing a request elevate the capability of the user attributes UA_2 and UA_3, and access entry of object attribute OA_3. A policy administrator can constrain the authorization of a request through these attributes with elevated capability or access entry.

For example, if the key *denySet* has a value UA_2, the algorithm excludes all relations(s) that authorize access through the user attribute set UA_2. An attribute set with elevated capability or access entry that is not the value of the *denySet* key is also constrained through the third key *limitto*. The value for the key *limitto* specifies the number of elements used to generate approaches to authorize access. Its value is a user attribute set if the resource is a user or user attribute and an object attribute set for an object or object attribute resource.

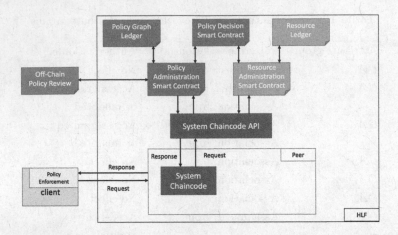

Fig. 2. Blockchain access control system architecture for policy machine.

Assuming request = (user, op, resource), Graph = (PE, ASSIGN, ASSOCIA-TION), $authmode = \{isGeneric : false, denySet : UA_2, limitto : 1\}$ are input parameters for the algorithm, the output is a set of constrained approaches of authorizing *user* request. It excludes authorization approaches using elements in the user attribute set UA_2. The value of *limitto* permits creating authorization approaches using one element of UA_3 or OA_3 if the resource is a user or an object type, respectively.

6   System Implementation and Evaluation

In this section, we discuss the implementation of the policy machine reference architecture in hyperledger fabric. We used Hyperledger Caliper and simulated policy graph to measure the performance of our policy review algorithm.

6.1   Blockchain Implementation of Policy Machine

Section 3 discussed the sets of policy elements and relations of the Policy Machine referenced in this work. The functional architectural components (see Fig. 2) of the Policy Machine we implemented as smart contracts in the Hyperledger Fabric network are the Policy Administration Point (PAP), Policy Decision Point (PDP), Resource Access Point (RAP). Also, the two databases of the Policy Machine standard architectural components, Policy Information Point and Resource Repository were implemented as the Policy Information Ledger and Resource Ledger respectively. The Policy Administration Smart Contract is an access mediator and manages the create, read, update and delete requests to the Policy Information Ledger. Administrative and resource users' requests are separately received by the Policy Administration and Resource Access Smart Contracts. The Policy Administration and Resource Access Smart Contracts forwards intercepted access requests to the Policy Decision Smart Contract that has the logic for allowed and denied access requests.

The client modes are the Policy Enforcement Point (PEP) that imposed the access decision returned by the Policy Decision Smart Contract and responds to the user with the proper result. The Event Process Point (EPP) in the Policy Machine triggers obligations, which is outside the scope of this work. As documented in the Hyperledger Fabric developer guide, an iterative process like the policy review degrades the performance of the blockchain network. We implemented an interface for the policy review as an off-chain component.

We leverage the invokeChain Application Programming Interface (API) for the request and response between Smart Contracts (chaincode) for the different ledgers. Assuming the Smart Contracts deployed belong to the same channel, as an example. An application user receives access decisions through the Resource Access Smart Contract. This Smart Contract makes a local call through the invokeChaincode API to the Policy Decision Smart Contract for access request decisions. This implementation considers only chaincode invocation from another chaincode when on the same channel. Recall that the Policy Information Ledger preserves the abstract representation of the policy element and relations for the Resource Ledger. To maintain consistency between the two ledgers, the Policy Decision Smart Contract needs read and write access to the two ledgers. In a network configuration that the Policy Decision Smart Contract is on a different channel with the two ledgers, any (delete/create) modification request will not reflect in the blockchain ledgers.

6.2   Performance Evaluation

We present the details of our experiments carried out for the system evaluation. The experiments were in two steps, an on-chain that reads the Policy Information Ledger and an off-chain policy review analysis. An iterative process in the policy review algorithm will degrade the blockchain network performance if deployed to the network. We used a virtual machine configured with 2 CPUs, 10 GB memory, an Ubuntu Linux OS 16.04 LTS, and Hyperledger Fabric version 2.2. Our Fabric network for this experiment has a single Raft orderer node, two peer nodes on the same channel, and a LevelDB database.

We created a policy graph generator script that simulates the creation of policy elements to the Policy Information Ledger. The policy graph comprises a policy class, 300 user and object attributes, and 200 users and objects. The Hyperledger Caliper version 0.4.2 enables us to generate workloads for the read policy graph transaction into our configured Fabric network. Hyperledger Caliper is a performance benchmark framework that provides different blockchains a suite of performance evaluation outcomes. To test the performance of our algorithm another script reads the policy graph ledger, simulates requests for authorization and revocation, and sets values for authorization mode record. The graph in Fig. 3 shows the average latency for reading the policy graph using the Caliper. Also, on the same graph, the average response time to generate revocation and

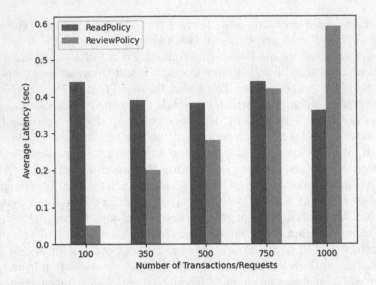

Fig. 3. Average latency for number of transactions and access requests

constrained authorization approaches for the request sizes are shown. The *policyRead* average latency varies in the range of 0.36 to 0.44 s for the number of transactions. The average response time of the *policyReview* increases as the number of requests for revocation and constrained authorization increases.

7   Conclusion

The Policy Machine is a promising alternative for logically expressed attribute-based policies with the prohibitive computational overhead in the policy review. It is feasible to perform policy reviews or queries using Policy Machine implemented access control for a permissioned blockchain. Apart from Policy Machine implemented in Hyperledger Fabric, we implemented our proposed algorithm that reviews authorization and revocation of access policy. Through the illustrative example, our proposed algorithm can help an administrator from granting access inadvertently. Our experimental results presented the evaluation of reading the Policy Information Ledger on the Hyperledger Fabric network and the response time for a policy review of various request sizes.

Acknowledgements. This work is partially supported by NSF grants HRD-1736209 and CNS-1553696.

References

1. Pinno, O., Gregio, A., De Bona, L.: ControlChain: a new stage on the IoT access control authorization. Concurr. Comput. **32**(12) (2020)

2. Rouhani, S., Belchior, R., Cruz, R., Deters, R.: Distributed attribute-based access control system using permissioned blockchain. World Wide Web (Bussum) **24**, 1617–1644 (2021)
3. Ding, S., Cao, J., Li, C., Fan, K., Li, H.: A novel attribute-based access control scheme using blockchain for IoT. IEEE Access **7**, 38431–38441 (2019)
4. Dukkipati, C., Zhang, Y., Cheng, L.: Decentralized, blockchain based access control framework for the heterogeneous Internet of Things. In: Proceedings of the Third ACM Workshop on Attribute-Based Access Control, pp. 6–69 (2018)
5. Zhang, X., Poslad, S.: Blockchain support for flexible queries with granular access control to electronic medicalrecords (EMR). IEEE International Conference on Communications (ICC) 2018, pp. 1–6 (2018)
6. Guo, H., Meamari, E., Shen, C.: Multi-authority attribute-based access control with smart contract. In: Proceedings of the 2019 International Conference on Blockchain Technology, pp. 6–11 (2019)
7. Di Francesco Maesa, D., Mori, P., Ricci, L.: A blockchain based approach for the definition of auditable access control systems. Comput. Secur. **84**, 93–119 (2019)
8. Ferraiolo, D., Gavrila, S., Jansen, W.: Policy machine: features, architecture, and specification. National Institute of Standards and Technology Internal Report 7987(2014)
9. Ferraiolo, D., Atluri, V., Gavrila, S.: The policy machine: a novel architecture and framework for access control policy specification and enforcement. J. Syst. Archit. **57**(4), 412–424 (2011)
10. Biswas, P., Sandhu, R., Krishnan, R.: Label-based access control: an ABAC model with enumerated authorization policy. In: Proceedings of the 2016 ACM International Workshop on Attribute Based Access Control. ACM Press (2016)
11. Mell, P. James, S., Harang, R., Gavrila, S.: Restricting insider access through efficient implementation of multi-policy access control systems. In: Proceedings of the 8th ACM CCS International Workshop on Managing Insider Security Threats (MIST 2016). ACM, New York, pp. 13–22 (2016)
12. Fernandez, M., Mackie, I., Thuraisingham, B.: Specification and analysis of ABAC policies via the category-based metamodel. In: Proceedings of the Ninth ACM Conference on Data and Application Security and Privacy (CODASPY 2019). Association for Computing Machinery, New York, pp. 173–184 (2019)

Learning Password Modification Patterns with Recurrent Neural Networks

Alex Nosenko, Yuan Cheng(✉) , and Haiquan Chen

California State University, Sacramento, CA 95819, USA
{anosenko,yuan.cheng,haiquan.chen}@csus.edu

Abstract. The majority of online services continue their reliance on text-based passwords as the primary means of user authentication. With a growing number of these services and the limited creativity and memory to come up with new memorable passwords, users tend to reuse their passwords across multiple platforms. These factors, combined with the increasing amount of leaked passwords, make passwords vulnerable to cross-site guessing attacks. Over the years, several popular methods have been proposed to predict subsequently used passwords, such as dictionary attacks, rule-based approaches, neural networks, and combinations of the above. In this paper, we work with a dataset of 28.8 million users and their 61.5 million passwords, where there is at least one pair of passwords available for each user. We exploit the correlation between the similarity and predictability of these subsequent passwords. We build on the idea of a rule-based approach but delegate rule derivation, classification, and prediction to a Recurrent Neural Network (RNN). We limit the number of guessing attempts to ten yet get an astonishingly high prediction accuracy of up to 83% in under five attempts in several categories, which is twice as much as any other known models or algorithms. It makes our model an effective solution for real-time password guessing against online services without getting spotted or locked out. To the best of our knowledge, this study is the first attempt of its kind using RNN.

Keywords: Authentication · Passwords · Recurrent neural networks

1 Introduction

Passwords remain the first and sometimes the only line of defense for most online services. Having a strong, unique password is extremely important to keep users' data safe. The government agencies, especially those storing users' personally identifiable information (PII), medical and legal records, follow the password guidance of the National Institute of Standards and Technology (NIST). Different online services have independent definitions of secure passwords. They also enforce different password composition, expiration, and reuse policies. This puts a lot of responsibility on users to create and maintain a large number of passwords. To cope with this burden, a user can either use a password manager, create and remember a unique password for each account, or create a very

© Springer Nature Switzerland AG 2022
R. Krishnan et al. (Eds.): SKM 2021, CCIS 1549, pp. 110–129, 2022.
https://doi.org/10.1007/978-3-030-97532-6_7

strong but memorable password that follows all the guidelines and use it across all platforms. According to a survey by a cybersecurity company NordPass, 50% of the respondents in the UK find it extremely difficult to remember unique passwords for multiple accounts [21]. The problem worsens when a user is required to change passwords due to password expiration or known security breaches. Based on numerous studies, the majority of people reuse their passwords by modifying them slightly every time a new password is required [5,9,20,28]. Since most of these studies were conducted in academic institutions and involved participants with higher education levels and better security awareness, the situation for the rest of the Internet community is probably even worse.

The habit of password reuse is detrimental to account security due to the increasing threat of *cross-site password guessing attacks*. In this form of attack, an attacker leverages previously leaked password datasets to guess passwords potentially used by the same user at different sites [4]. With an abundance of password leaks and data breaches, there is a large pool of publicly available passwords for a swarm of users. Attackers have various tools at their disposal, such as dictionary-based attacks, rule-based attacks, and machine learning models for effective and automated guessing. Suppose each online service allows up to three attempts to enter a password before locking down the account and consider that each user has registered on at least five popular online services. An attacker thus has at least 15 attempts to guess a password before being spotted or flagged. The traditional brute-force attack and dictionary attack will not be effective in this setting due to the rate limit. However, rule-based and neural network-based predictions can still yield a high probability of successful guesses with rate-limiting enforced [11,14,16,17].

In this paper, we leverage the rule-based approach and automate the guessing process using a neural network model to derive modification patterns, complete the classification, and generate a password guess. We resort to neural networks, which outperform traditional classifiers like Naïve Bayes and k-nearest neighbors (KNN) used in prior research [28] to solve the classification problem. We use a character-based bidirectional long short-term memory (BiLSTM) model to generate passwords for each modification category. We then build an experimental model that can make predictions without knowing the modification patterns. We use the character-based LSTM encoder-decoder model as it is commonly used when one sequence of characters (e.g., the original password) needs to be transformed into another sequence of characters (e.g., a subsequent password). This model delivers outstanding prediction results for a significant amount of password pairs.

The main contributions of our study can be summarized as follows:

- We created a neural network-based classifier for password modification category prediction.
- We built an LSTM based model for password generation for each category.
- We designed an LSTM based model that predicts a subsequent password based on the original password with up to 83% accuracy in under five attempts.

- We quantified the vulnerability of password reuse based on Levenshtein distance, Jaro-Winkler distance, and modification patterns.
- We made recommendations for online services to enhance their password security.

The remainder of this paper is organized as follows. We discuss the related work in Sect. 2. We describe the original dataset, the pre-processing steps, and the resulting datasets in Sect. 3. Section 4 elaborates the prediction process and the model architecture. Section 5 presents our results and compares them with the results from the existing models. Section 6 talks about the security recommendations and key takeaways of this research. We conclude this study and identify some future directions for this line of research in Sect. 7.

2   Related Work

The problem of password guessing is not new. And over time, there has been an abundance of methods proposed to solve it. Among the most prominent guessing approaches are dictionary-based attacks, rule-based attacks, and neural network-based attacks. While some methods train and test their prediction models on the same dataset, other methods extract rules from one dataset and try to guess passwords from another dataset. The first type of method is referred to as the *single-site password guessing attack*, where attackers crack passwords from a single password leak. The second type is known as the *cross-site password guessing attack*, which exploits leaked passwords from multiple online services. Our research falls into the second type, where we aim to guess users' subsequent passwords from their known passwords from the same or a different site.

Next, we will provide an overview of different password guessing methods, including the most recent advance of using neural networks for this purpose.

2.1   Dictionary Attacks

Dictionary attacks depend upon the assumption that a password is either a word that belongs to a pre-compiled word list or dictionary [9], a valid, complete word (used in vocabulary attacks) or a valid passphrase (used by Markov model-based methods). The first two attacks may need many attempts to make a correct guess, require constant maintenance of dictionaries, and cost a tremendous amount of time and resources. Markov model-based methods, on the other hand, enable efficient password and passphrase cracking by only generating and testing linguistically likely passwords [19] or linguistically correct phrases [24]. These methods are commonly used for single-site password guessing attacks but can also instigate cross-site attacks with slight modifications. Unfortunately, most of the passwords in our dataset do not fall under the category of valid dictionary words or linguistically correct phrases. Thus, these methods are of limited use in solving our problem.

2.2   Rule-Based Attacks

Rule-based attacks rely on password creation and reuse patterns extracted from previously leaked datasets or user surveys and are widely used for cross-site attacks. Researchers conducted statistical analyses of leaked password datasets and discovered that most users stick to simple and easily memorable patterns [4,28–30,33]. Based on the patterns, researchers were able to build algorithms and prediction trees that indicate the most probable modification categories and the most likely transformations. These data-driven algorithms aim to minimize the number of guesses and maximize prediction accuracy. Among the several rule-based mechanisms is Probabilistic Context-Free Grammar (PCFG). This method analyzes leaked datasets and existing wordlists to create grammars for generating word-mangling rules [30]. The next generation of rule-based guessing mechanisms is based on PCFG but leverages previously used passwords as an additional input to help predict subsequent passwords. This targeted prediction algorithm is known as TarGuess-II [29]. Zhang et al. developed a generic algorithmic framework for searching out possible transformations that convert a user's previous passwords to future ones [33]. Their optimal search strategy successfully cracked an average of 13% of the accounts in the experiment within five online guesses and 18% within ten attempts. Wang et al. introduced the next iteration of rule-based predictors by breaking a process into two steps [28]. The first step uses a Naïve Bayes classifier to guess a modification category, and the second step applies the rule-based mechanism to guess the actual password. This approach shows significant improvements in prediction, but the accuracy within ten attempts is still below 30%.

2.3   Neural Network-Based Guessing

This relatively new neural network-based approach was surfaced in 2016 with a premise that Recurrent Neural Networks (RNNs) can predict the next symbol in a character string if provided with enough training data [17]. It presented promising results in single-site and cross-site attacks and was used in combination with rule-based attacks [16] and Markov model [14]. It helped overcome several previous limitations, such as the utilization of fixed-length context, by using long short-term memory (LSTM) network. LSTM is a subset of RNNs and can store features discovered over a longer period of time [22]. Generative Adversarial Networks (GANs), a subset of neural networks, were used as a specific training approach for neural network models to eliminate the need for learning modification patterns on a single-site attack [11]. Despite showing good prediction rates, most of these studies did not limit the number of guessing attempts and ran models until they exhausted every possibility. This assumption makes these models impractical in online password guessing in the real world.

Our research is based on the understanding of password modification patterns. We specifically focus on the subsequent password guessing problem, that is, guessing future passwords from preceding ones. We propose an RNN-based approach, which focuses on lowering the number of attempts used for cross-site password guessing. We generate two models, one with rules provided and the other one that derives the rules itself, and explore the prediction accuracy of the two models in under ten attempts.

3   Dataset

The dataset was provided by Wang et al. [28], which consists of 61,552,446 individual passwords that belong to 28,836,775 users from 107 online services over eight years. The dataset has been sanitized and anonymized to protect personally identifiable information. Every user in the dataset has at least two passwords; thus, we can form at least one pair of subsequently used passwords. Although some users have more than two passwords, we only choose two passwords (i.e., one pair) for each user for simplicity.

We then pre-process the dataset to eliminate pairs of identical passwords and those that appear more than once. The resulting dataset contains 17,133,333 unique pairs. This process helps us identify a set of the most common passwords for further analysis. Among the most popular passwords are "123456," "password," "qwerty," "111111," "123123," "dragon," "monkey," "shadow," and "love."

When looking at the length of the passwords, we discover that 99% of the passwords are 5–17 characters long, which seems to be consistent with the common password requirements enforced by online services as well as the general human memory capacity [25]. The passwords that are longer than 17 characters (hard to memorize) or shorter than 5 (not acceptable by most online services), as well as the passwords that contain non-ASCII characters, are considered outliers and are thus removed from further consideration.

We analyze the distribution of passwords based on two metrics, Levenshtein distance and Jaro-Winkler distance.

The Levenshtein distance is the number of edits (e.g., substitution, insertion, or deletion) needed to transform one string into another. For example, transforming "rain" to "shine" requires three steps, consisting of two substitutions and one insertion: "rain" → "sain" → "shin" → "shine." These operations could have been done in other orders, but at least three steps are needed [10]. In our dataset, the Levenshtein distance between passwords ranges from 0 to 17, as shown in Fig. 1. And the majority of password pairs have a Levenshtein distance in the range from 1 to 11. The Levenshtein distance can help set up password reuse rules that are easy for users to understand (e.g., make sure the subsequent password is different from the original by three characters). However, it suffers from a major limitation. For example, the Levenshtein distance between the words "password" and "password12345678" is 8, which is relatively high, although both words exhibit an easy-to-guess pattern.

We then resort to the Jaro-Winkler distance for a more meaningful measure. The Jaro-Winkler distance considers the substitution of two close characters less important than the substitution of two characters that are far from each other [7]. It computes the string similarity by returning a value that lies in the

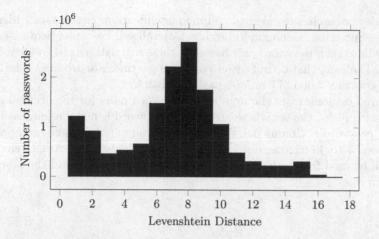

Fig. 1. Password distribution by Levenshtein distance

interval of [0.0, 1.0]. For instance, the Jaro-Winkler distance between the words "password" and "password12345678" is 91.7%. Figure 2 shows the distribution of password pairs in the dataset based on the Jaro-Winkler distance. The majority of the password pairs fall in between 0.4 and 0.99.

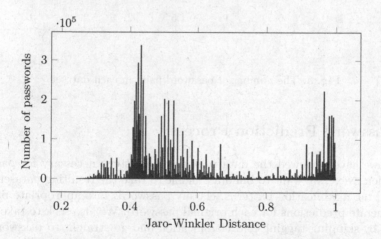

Fig. 2. Password distribution by Jaro-Winkler distance

The passwords that exhibit the highest similarity will have the smallest Levenshtein distance and the highest Jaro-Winkler distance and will be the best candidates for performing cross-site guessing attacks. We use the NLTK Python library for the Levenshtein distance and the StrsimPy library for the Jaro-Winkler distance to implement both metrics.

In prior research, several most common modification patterns were identified, including Substring, Common Substring, Capitalized, Leet, and Sequential Keys [28]. We label each password pair based on these five patterns to create a labeled dataset. The pairs that do not fit into any of these rules are dropped. The labeled dataset contains 3,006,871 unique password pairs.

Figure 3 demonstrates the number of password pairs for the original dataset ("All passwords"), the set where an original password is not the same as its subsequent password ("Unique pairs"), the set of unique pairs where each password is between 5 to 17 characters long and contains only valid ASCII characters that will be used for most of this research ("Working set"), and the labeled set ("Known rules").

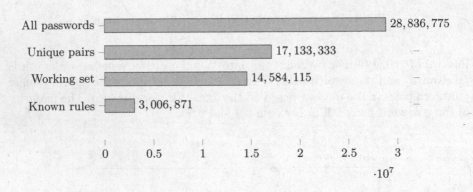

Fig. 3. The number of password pairs in each dataset

4 Password Prediction Process

So far, we have reviewed the data pre-processing steps necessary for password prediction. Next, we want to build a pipeline to take the resulting dataset, identify and tag modification patterns, classify passwords into appropriate buckets, and generate predictions for each original password. We also seek to take a step further by skipping tagging and classification and go straight to password prediction. We will refer to this process as *direct password prediction*. This approach will be especially beneficial when users combine multiple modification patterns or no rules can be identified. To the best of our knowledge, this approach has not been used for launching a single-user cross-site password guessing attack yet.

The prediction pipeline consists of four steps. During the first step, common modification patterns are defined, and each password pair is analyzed and labeled with a corresponding category. We use a neural network model to assign each original password into a single modification category during the second step.

This process is known as the single-label prediction problem. During the third step, we build a second model to learn about possible modifications within each category. With 90% accuracy on the test data, the model can understand and generate all possible modifications for each category. Both models are then combined, and the resulting pipeline is assembled in the last step. Our approach can take just one original password as an input, classify it into a modification category, and generate password guesses. We will now review each step in further detail.

4.1   Tagging

Before tagging password pairs, let us first introduce the common password modification patterns we borrowed from [28]. Leet refers to any transformation of alphanumeric characters to visually similar symbols and vice versa. The Substring category includes password pairs where one password is a substring of the other. Adding symbols to the head or tail of a string is the most common modification of this category. Capitalization is where one or more symbols are in uppercase. The Common Substring category contains password pairs that share common letter combinations. The Sequential Keys category consists of passwords that contain alphabetically ordered letters (e.g., "abcd"), sequential numbers (e.g., "1234"), and adjacent keys on the keyboard (e.g., "qwert," "asdfg," etc.). We define a function to identify which pattern each password pair fits in and tag each pair with a corresponding modification pattern category. After the tagging is completed, we drop the passwords that do not match any rules or contain non-ASCII symbols. The resulting dataset has 3,006,871 pairs of passwords. Figure 4 shows the distribution of each password modification category in the tagged dataset. The most common patterns found in the dataset are Substring and Common Substring. Together they cover 2,674,521 password pairs, which are around 89% of the dataset. These password pairs provide sufficient training data for our proposed model. The other three categories represent about 10% of the dataset. Except for the Sequential Keys category, we still collect enough training data from the categories of Capitalization and Leet.

4.2   Classification

Conventional classifiers have been used to solve the classification problem as they are easy to use and do not require heavy data pre-processing. However, neural networks have proven to deliver better prediction rates, especially on larger datasets [23].

We build a 4-layer LSTM classifier using the Keras Python library, as shown in Fig. 5. The Input Layer takes a single sequence of characters with the same length as the longest password in the dataset, which is 17 characters long. The One-Hot Encoder processes every password as a sequence of characters and transforms those sequences into a one-hot numeric array. It assigns the value of 1 if the character is present in a given word or 0 if otherwise. The encoding is passed to the LSTM units. We use a character-level Bidirectional LSTM (BiLSTM) Layer,

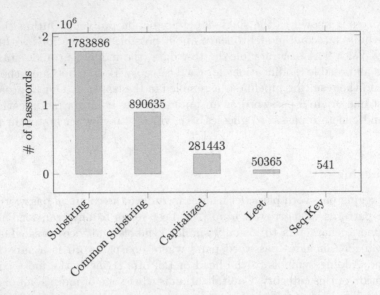

Fig. 4. Category distribution of the tagged dataset

which is an extension of traditional LSTMs and can improve the model performance on sequence classification problems. The BiLSTM Layer runs inputs in two directions, one from the past to the future and the other from the future to the past. Unlike unidirectional LSTM, BiLSTM uses two hidden states and can preserve information from both past and future at any point in time. Because of these qualities, BiLSTM can better understand the context around each character in the sequence [31]. The output of the BiLSTM cells is fed to a dense Activation Layer. The Activation Layer contains an activation function, which defines how the weighted sum of the input is transformed into an output. To ensure that a model learns features and does not converge prematurely, we use the Adam optimizer with a small learning rate [12]. This optimizer is used to update network weights during each training iteration.

As a result of this step, we build a neural network classifier to predict password modification patterns.

4.3   Password Generation

In this step, we train a 7-layer character-level BiLSTM model to generate passwords within each modification category. The model shown in Fig. 6 has two input streams. The left stream includes Input Layer #1, the One-Hot encoder, and the BiLSTM layer. These three layers act similarly to what is described in Sect. 4.2. The right input stream includes Input Layer #2 and a Repeat Vector Layer, which are both used to add a list of modification patterns to the model as each prediction is generated within a single category. The Concatenation Layer combines the outputs of both streams and feeds the combined outputs into the

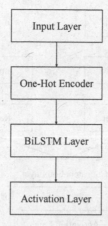

Fig. 5. Classification model architecture

Activation Layer. The Activation Layer acts the same as described in Sect. 4.2. The resulting model can generate password guesses for each modification category with high accuracy.

To generate password guesses for all categories, we put the classification model and the password generation model together into one prediction pipeline, namely Pipeline Prediction Mechanism (PPM). As an original password enters the pipeline, the first model predicts the modification category. Then, the predicted category, along with the original password, is fed into the second model, which generates password candidates and chooses the top 10 candidates with the highest probability. Once the prediction is completed, we verify if a password is guessed correctly.

4.4   Direct Password Prediction

To the best of our knowledge, RNN has never been used to solve cross-site password guessing for the same user before. This problem, however, is similar to the problem of machine translation. In both problems, the source may vary in length and character dictionary. The model architecture consists of at least two LSTM layers, encoder and decoder. The encoder takes the input sequence and summarizes the information into a context vector or hidden states of LSTM [3]. The outputs are not important and thus are dropped, but the hidden states are saved. This context vector encapsulates the information for all input elements and will be used by the decoder to generate predictions. The decoder is also an LSTM layer that takes the encoder output as an initial state and produces an output sequence. We use the Softmax layer from the Keras library as an Activation Layer in our model. The Softmax function is based on normalized

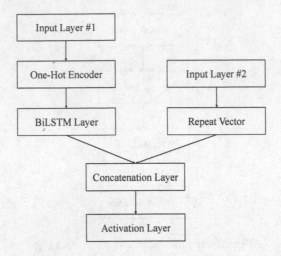

Fig. 6. Password generation model

exponential function and is used as the last layer on a neural network to normalize the output to a probability distribution over predicted output classes [13]. In our model, it will determine the output modified password.

Since a model can generate multiple predictions with different degrees of confidence, we need an algorithm to choose the top 10 most probable outputs. We use the Beam search algorithm, one of the most widely used for sequence-to-sequence machine translation problems [32], to help us identify the most probable predictions. Direct password prediction proves to be the most promising approach as it eliminates the need for constant rule derivation and distribution analysis and eases dataset pre-processing. The resulting model, namely Direct Prediction Mechanism (DPM), is rule-independent and delivers high prediction rates.

4.5   Prediction on a Reversed Dataset

To increase the number of password pairs, Wang et al. [28] switched source and target passwords and attempted a prediction of original passwords based on the subsequent ones. We decide to replicate the same experiment providing a model with modified passwords as a source and asking it to predict the original passwords. This adds additional 3.1M password pairs to our experiment. No changes to the model are necessary to run this experiment, which exhibits another advantage of using neural networks to solve the password guessing problem. We realize that predicting the original password can be easier for the DPM model since most users tend to use simpler passwords to begin with and add complexity (e.g., Leet, Capitalization, String, etc.) as they change them. Additionally, we try to reverse the order of characters in the original password before passing it to the model for prediction. This approach was used by Sutskever et al. [26], where the authors reversed the word order in the source sentence before passing it to an RNN model, which ultimately yields better prediction results.

5   Experimental Results

5.1   Hardware Requirements

Most of this project was executed on Google Colab Pro, which is a cloud-based Jupyter notebook environment. The hosted runtime environment uses Tesla P100-PCIE-16 GB GPU, Intel(R) Xeon(R) CPU @ 2.20 GHz processor, 25 GB of RAM, and 109 GB of disk space. The most hardware demanding parts of the experiment were dataset pre-processing, model training, and direct password prediction. Direct password prediction was the most computationally expensive. Based on Google Colab measurements, it took 13 GB of RAM to train a model on 400k records and 20 GB for 500k records. Even though it might sound like a significant amount of resources, it is not unreachable for a sophisticated attacker. Better hardware resources will yield better performance results since we can train the model on a larger dataset and make faster predictions with higher accuracy.

5.2   Results

We first compared the results of an LSTM classifier and a Naïve Bayes classifier. Table 1 shows that the LSTM based model delivers better results than the Naïve Bayes classifier, especially in underrepresented categories, such as Leet and Common Substring.

Table 1. LSTM model vs. Naïve Bayes classifier

		Precision	Recall	F1-score
LSTM	Capitalized	0.65	0.58	0.61
	Common substring	0.58	0.31	0.4
	Leet	0.49	0.23	0.31
	Seq-Key	0	0	0
	Substring	0.73	0.91	0.81
Naïve Bayes	Capitalized	0.6	0.39	0.48
	Common substring	0.38	0.05	0.08
	Leet	0.14	0.01	0.01
	Seq-Key	0	0	0
	Substring	0.66	0.9	0.79

LSTM outperforms traditional classifiers because it captures and preserves the sequential order (i.e., the order in which the characters appear in a password), while the classical models do not. For example, "abac" is different than "aabc" for LSTM, while it is the same for a classical model as it only considers the frequency of the featured characters 'a,' 'b,' 'c,' which are the same for both strings.

We then evaluated the performance of our password generation model. Since our approach is novel, we do not have an exact baseline to make a one-to-one comparison with the existing work. The closest studies are the ones that estimate how many guesses are needed to predict a password correctly [4,28, 29]. All of these papers published their prediction rates within the first ten attempts. Therefore, we use ten attempts as part of the experiment parameters. We compared the results of our Pipeline Prediction Mechanism (PPM) and Direct Prediction Mechanism (DPM) with three existing algorithms from [28] (referred to as "Domino" hereafter), [29] (referred to as "TarGuess-II" hereafter), and [4] (referred to as "Tangled" hereafter).

On average, both of our models exhibited a 5% improvement of overall prediction rates comparing to "Domino" and three times more accurate predictions than TarGuess-II and "Tangled" as shown in Fig. 7. Although the improvement does not seem drastic, if we can predict 5% more passwords out of 6 million, that is around 300,000 more compromised accounts.

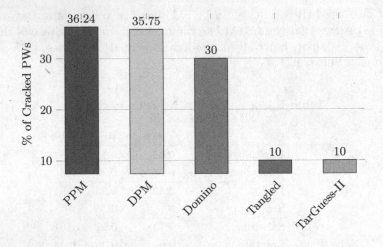

Fig. 7. Model comparison at ten attempts

A larger difference in prediction rates between "Domino," PPM, and DPM can be observed in the first four attempts, as shown in Fig. 8, where our model is 100% more effective. This is especially surprising considering that DPM was only provided with the original password and no other prior information. It can also be observed that the DPM model makes most of the predictions during the first few attempts, and then its confidence decreases as well as the number of predicted passwords (see Fig. 9). On the other hand, traditional approaches exhaust all possible combinations and thus predict more as they try more. This reveals a fundamental difference between our method and those traditional ones.

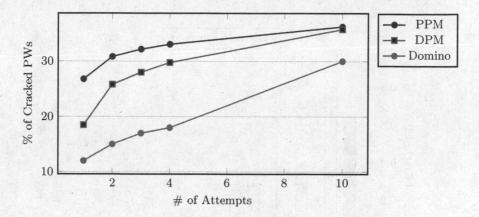

Fig. 8. Model comparison under ten attempts

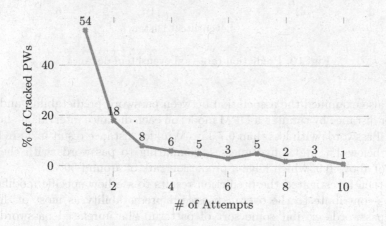

Fig. 9. DPM prediction rate for each attempt

Next, we zoomed in on the results of the DPM predictions to quantify for the first time the correlation between password predictability and Levenshtein distance for subsequent passwords. The prediction rates, as shown in Fig. 10, are broken down by the Levenshtein distance on the x-axis (x-coordinates correspond to the distance values 1, 2, 3, 4, 5, and 6, respectfully). The y-axis refers to the percentage of guessed passwords. We found that it is 6–8 times harder to predict a subsequent password when the Levenshtein distance is 4 compared to the same task when the distance is 1. Changing only one character in subsequent passwords does almost nothing to improve the overall password strength since the prediction rate is as high as 83%. In other words, almost 8 out of 10 subsequent passwords can be predicted regardless of modification patterns if the two passwords only differ in one character.

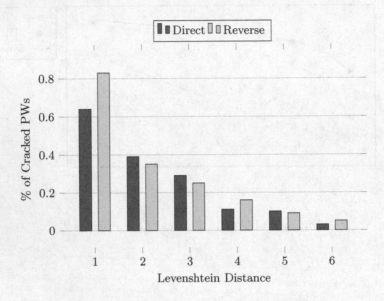

Fig. 10. Prediction rate vs. Levenshtein distance

We also examined the association between password predictability and Jaro-Winkler distance by running a DPM model on each distance interval, as shown in Fig. 11. Passwords with less than 0.7 Jaro-Winkler distance result in a prediction rate of below 1% under five guesses, comparing to passwords with the same metric of above 0.9, which have a prediction rate of around 50%.

We then investigated the prediction results to see how specific modification patterns contribute to the overall password predictability as most of the predicted passwords exhibit some sort of pattern. The unrelated password pairs that do not have any syntactic or semantic similarity proved to be the hardest to predict. Figure 12 shows that Capitalization along with having a subsequent password being a substring or containing a substring of the original are the easiest categories to break and are at least 20%–50% less secure. Considering how easy it is for a user to remember a password with a few added characters or some capitalization changes, it is as easy for the model to guess it. Since Substring is the most represented category in the original dataset, it is not surprising to see that DPM is well trained in this category and is thus able to make a successful guess around 50% of the time, as shown in Fig. 12. However, the interesting fact is that Capitalization represents only around 9% of the dataset, yet a model successfully predicts around 64.5% of those passwords. It is also worth noticing

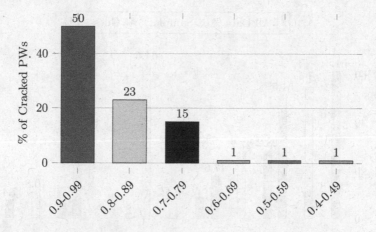

Fig. 11. Prediction rate vs. Jaro-Winkler distance

that DPM is able to predict around 7.4% or 25,000 of passwords that do not follow any known modification patterns.

Overall, both models demonstrated great prediction rates, beating the close competitors 2:1 in scenarios where only a small number of guessing attempts is allowed. Our models adopt a more fine-grained prediction approach and are capable of predicting 83% of passwords in certain common modification categories. With more data available, the performance of our models improves. But our models can also work well on a smaller training set (e.g., 50k size).

6 Discussion

Predicting slightly modified subsequent passwords is getting easier. With more data breaches occurring each year, there is an abundance of leaked passwords, including subsequent passwords for the same users. This allows us to extract more fine-grained modification patterns and train more robust prediction models. Our experiment showed that having the original password alone is enough to predict a subsequent password with a high probability in just a few attempts. With most online services allowing up to ten attempts [1], an attacker can use the proposed mechanisms and models to generate subsequent passwords and try to compromise an account without raising the alarm. With the availability of more powerful computational resources and companies delaying the public release of data breach details, an attacker can re-train the models to account for newly acquired data and enhance the chance of success.

The length and complexity requirements recommended by the NIST guideline [2] are outdated in practice today. Having a long password that consists of various symbols might add extra security only when it comes to single-site dictionary attacks and eavesdropping [8]. Making slight modifications based on an original password provides little to no additional security in cross-site attacks. It may even give users a false sense of security as these changes seem to align with

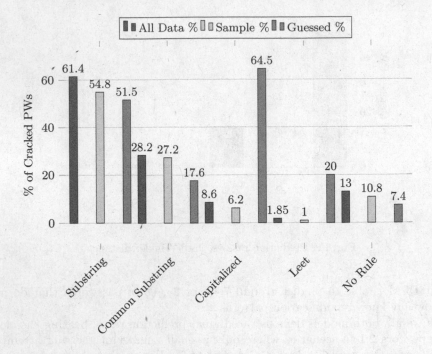

Fig. 12. Prediction within each category

the characteristics of "strong passwords" defined by the guideline. Our studies showed that we need to consider the similarity between an original password and its successors as a new requirement in a future edition of user authentication guidelines. The less similarity there is between subsequent passwords, the more secure user data is [18]. Even with sufficient training data, neural network-based guessing algorithms require much more attempts to crack passwords that are distant in terms of similarity metrics. For example, we observed that passwords that are four edits away are at least three times harder to break than those with just one modification away. Having completely unrelated passwords can mitigate cross-site attacks in the presence of a password breach.

Updating user authentication guidelines also helps standardize web frameworks and development tools include libraries that support similarity-based proactive password checking. A proactive password checker can prevent users from choosing an easy-to-guess subsequent password, especially when it is similar to the used ones. This process, however, should not have a detrimental effect on user experience and may include a system to suggest a secure password if a user struggles to come up with one.

The use of passwords alone should be re-considered by service providers in favor of two-factor authentication, biometrics, and other alternative means. Users' creativity, memory capacity, or the level of education in computer security should not be the decisive factors of data security. Most survey participants involved in the password guessing studies represent a younger and higher educated cohort compared to the general population [4,27]. The safe guess would be that a general population would have even more insecure password habits. It is hard to change users' habits as we consistently see users reusing the same passwords or modifying them slightly. As users entrust their data and private information to more and more online services, these services should step up and carry more responsibilities to ensure that users' negligence or lack of education does not jeopardize the safety of their data.

Password managers are considered by many as an appealing substitute for alleviating password fatigue. However, password managers usually require a local or cloud-based password storage, and the access to such storage relies on a master password. An insecure implementation or a lost master password adds a single point of failure to authentication. Prior studies showed that most popular password managers in use suffered from various kinds of vulnerabilities [6,15]. The widespread adoption of password managers will not overshadow the efforts on making passwords stronger. In fact, the advances in both directions complement each other.

7   Conclusion and Future Work

In this research, we investigated the problem of subsequent password prediction. We built a password prediction pipeline to automate password categorization and password generation using Recurrent Neural Networks. The prediction results were superior to the ones delivered by traditional classification and guessing algorithms. The performance boost was especially significant when we limit the number of guessing attempts to five. We combined the understanding of rule-based prediction algorithms and the power of LSTM neural networks to solve the problem of cross-site prediction for passwords created by the same user. It is a relatively new approach and perhaps one of the very first attempts to use Recurrent Neural Networks for this specific task. We were able to quantify the correlation between the similarity, modification patterns, and predictability of subsequent passwords. In addition, we demonstrated the ease of prediction and high accuracy of the most common modification strategies, such as adding head or tail symbols to the original password or capitalization. We showcased that such a prediction process could be facilitated by affordable hardware or online computing resources, such as Google Colab, due to the low complexity and shallow nature of the RNN model used. The efficiency of prediction allows it to run on platforms where five or fewer attempts are allowed before an account gets locked. We also discussed the concrete steps the online services should take to improve the security of the authentication process.

In the future, we would like to apply the model to a single-site attack scenario to see how well it can perform compared to the other models. We would also like to investigate password pairs that are not syntactically but semantically similar (e.g., synonyms, associated words). The prediction of these passwords was out of the scope of this research. We may also improve the password prediction by training the model on a synthetic balanced dataset that contains various under-represented modification patterns found in this research (e.g., common names).

Lastly, we would like to build a neural network model to classify the passwords that involve more than one type of modification pattern (e.g., Capitalization and Leet, Substring and Leet, etc.).

References

1. Brostoff, S., Sasse, M.A.: "Ten strikes and you're out": increasing the number of login attempts can improve password usability. In: CHI 2003 Workshop on Human-Computer Interaction and Security Systems (2003)
2. Burr, W., Dodson, D., Perlner, R., Gupta, S., Nabbus, E.: NIST SP800-63-2: Electronic Authentication Guideline. Tech. rep, National Institute of Standards and Technology, Reston, VA (2013)
3. Cho, K., Van Merriënboer, B., Bahdanau, D., Bengio, Y.: On the properties of neural machine translation: encoder-decoder approaches. arXiv preprint arXiv:1409.1259 (2014)
4. Das, A., Bonneau, J., Caesar, M., Borisov, N., Wang, X.: The tangled web of password reuse. In: NDSS. vol. 14, pp. 23–26 (2014)
5. Florencio, D., Herley, C.: A large-scale study of web password habits. In: 16th International Conference on World Wide Web, pp. 657–666 (2007)
6. Gasti, P., Rasmussen, K.B.: On the security of password manager database formats. In: Foresti, S., Yung, M., Martinelli, F. (eds.) ESORICS 2012. LNCS, vol. 7459, pp. 770–787. Springer, Heidelberg (2012). https://doi.org/10.1007/978-3-642-33167-1_44
7. Gomaa, W.H., Fahmy, A.A., et al.: A survey of text similarity approaches. Int. J. Comput. Appl. **68**(13), 13–18 (2013)
8. Grassi, P.A., Garcia, M.E., Fenton, J.L.: DRAFT NIST SP800-63-3 digital identity guidelines. Tech. rep, National Institute of Standards and Technology, Los Altos (2017)
9. Haque, S.T., Wright, M., Scielzo, S.: A study of user password strategy for multiple accounts. In: Third ACM Conference on Data and Application Security and Privacy, pp. 173–176 (2013)
10. Hardeniya, N.: NLTK Essentials. Packt Publishing Ltd., Birmingham (2015)
11. Hitaj, B., Gasti, P., Ateniese, G., Perez-Cruz, F.: PassGAN: a deep learning approach for password guessing. In: Deng, R.H., Gauthier-Umaña, V., Ochoa, M., Yung, M. (eds.) ACNS 2019. LNCS, vol. 11464, pp. 217–237. Springer, Cham (2019). https://doi.org/10.1007/978-3-030-21568-2_11
12. Kingma, D.P., Ba, J.: Adam: a method for stochastic optimization. arXiv preprint hyperimagehttp://arxiv.org/abs/1412.6980arXiv:1412.6980 (2014)
13. Kouretas, I., Paliouras, V.: Simplified hardware implementation of the softmax activation function. In: 2019 8th International Conference on Modern Circuits and Systems Technologies (MOCAST), pp. 1–4. IEEE (2019)
14. Li, H., Chen, M., Yan, S., Jia, C., Li, Z.: Password guessing via neural language modeling. In: Chen, X., Huang, X., Zhang, J. (eds.) ML4CS 2019. LNCS, vol. 11806, pp. 78–93. Springer, Cham (2019). https://doi.org/10.1007/978-3-030-30619-9_7
15. Li, Z., He, W., Akhawe, D., Song, D.: The emperor's new password manager: Security analysis of web-based password managers. In: 23rd USENIX Security Symposium. pp. 465–479 (2014)

16. Liu, Y., et al.: GENPass: a general deep learning model for password guessing with PCFG rules and adversarial generation. In: 2018 IEEE International Conference on Communications (ICC), pp. 1–6. IEEE (2018)

17. Melicher, W., et al.: Fast, lean, and accurate: modeling password guessability using neural networks. In: 25th USENIX Security Symposium, pp. 175–191 (2016)

18. Murray, H., Malone, D.: Exploring the impact of password dataset distribution on guessing. In: 2018 16th Annual Conference on Privacy, Security and Trust (PST), pp. 1–8. IEEE (2018)

19. Narayanan, A., Shmatikov, V.: Fast dictionary attacks on passwords using time-space tradeoff. In: 12th ACM Conference on Computer and Communications Security, pp. 364–372 (2005)

20. Notoatmodjo, G., Thomborson, C.: Passwords and perceptions. In: Seventh Australasian Conference on Information Security, vol. 98, pp. 71–78. Citeseer (2009)

21. Rawlings, R.: Password habits in the US and the UK: This is what we found (2020). https://nordpass.com/blog/password-habits-statistics/

22. Schmidhuber, J., Hochreiter, S.: Long short-term memory. Neural Comput. **9**(8), 1735–1780 (1997)

23. Schumacher, M., Roßner, R., Vach, W.: Neural networks and logistic regression: Part i. Comput. Stat. Data Anal. **21**(6), 661–682 (1996)

24. Sparell, P., Simovits, M.: Linguistic cracking of passphrases using Markov chains. IACR Cryptol. ePrint Arch. **2016**, 246 (2016)

25. Stobert, E., Biddle, R.: The password life cycle: user behaviour in managing passwords. In: 10th Symposium on Usable Privacy and Security (SOUPS), pp. 243–255 (2014)

26. Sutskever, I., Vinyals, O., Le, Q.V.: Sequence to sequence learning with neural networks. arXiv preprint arXiv:1409.3215 (2014)

27. von Zezschwitz, E., De Luca, A., Hussmann, H.: Survival of the shortest: a retrospective analysis of influencing factors on password composition. In: Kotzé, P., Marsden, G., Lindgaard, G., Wesson, J., Winckler, M. (eds.) INTERACT 2013. LNCS, vol. 8119, pp. 460–467. Springer, Heidelberg (2013). https://doi.org/10.1007/978-3-642-40477-1_28

28. Wang, C., Jan, S.T., Hu, H., Bossart, D., Wang, G.: The next domino to fall: empirical analysis of user passwords across online services. In: Eighth ACM Conference on Data and Application Security and Privacy, pp. 196–203 (2018)

29. Wang, D., Zhang, Z., Wang, P., Yan, J., Huang, X.: Targeted online password guessing: an underestimated threat. In: 2016 ACM Conference on Computer and Communications Security, pp. 1242–1254 (2016)

30. Weir, M., Aggarwal, S., De Medeiros, B., Glodek, B.: Password cracking using probabilistic context-free grammars. In: 2009 30th IEEE Symposium on Security and Privacy, pp. 391–405. IEEE (2009)

31. Xu, G., Meng, Y., Qiu, X., Yu, Z., Wu, X.: Sentiment analysis of comment texts based on BiLSTM. IEEE Access **7**, 51522–51532 (2019)

32. Yoo, J.Y., Morris, J.X., Lifland, E., Qi, Y.: Searching for a search method: benchmarking search algorithms for generating NLP adversarial examples. arXiv preprint arXiv:2009.06368 (2020)

33. Zhang, Y., Monrose, F., Reiter, M.K.: The security of modern password expiration: an algorithmic framework and empirical analysis. In: 17th ACM Conference on Computer and Communications Security, pp. 176–186 (2010)

Analyzing CNN Models' Sensitivity to the Ordering of Non-natural Data

Randy Klepetko[✉] and Ram Krishnan

Department of Electrical and Computer Engineering,
University of Texas at San Antonio, San Antonio, TX, USA
randy.klepetko@my.utsa.edu, ram.krishnan@utsa.edu

Abstract. Convolutional Neural Networks (CNN) have revolutionized image recognition technology, and has found uses in various non-image related fields. When dealing with non-natural data, where the ordering of various parts of a data sample is not dictated by nature, it is known that a model trained on certain orderings of the data performs better than models trained on other orderings. Understanding how to best order the training data for improving CNN performance is not well-studied. In this paper, we investigate this problem by examining several different CNN models. We define a functional algorithm for ordering, show that order importance in CNNs is model dependent and that depending on the model, statistical relationships are an important tool in establishing order with better performance.

Keywords: Convolutional Neural Networks · Data preparation ·
Security · Malware detection · Cloud IaaS · Deep learning

1 Introduction

Recent explosion in CNN architectures has pushed computer image recognition [8] to an art form. It has provides a variety of options depending on the need [5]. They are also used in non-image related fields, so understanding how they work with images should help us leverage their use in these other areas.

It has been shown that entropy can be used to both increase detail [24] and reduce noise [2]. By examining the entropy of an image, for example, the dog in Fig. 1a, and comparing the activation values found by analyzing it with a shallow CNN, Fig. 1b, we can see it identifying patterns in entropy. We hypothesize that these new CNN models are finding novel ways of making identifiable information out of these patterns of entropy.

Exploration has been made in using CNN in fields other than image classification. Text [14], sound samples [4], and medical diagnostics of DNA [20] are examples of how this technology has other uses. Oftentimes these sources of data have a naturally defined order such as the acoustical waves in a sound or DNA in

This work is partially supported by NSF grants HRD-1736209 and CNS-1553696.

R. Krishnan et al. (Eds.): SKM 2021, CCIS 1549, pp. 130–148, 2022.
https://doi.org/10.1007/978-3-030-97532-6_8

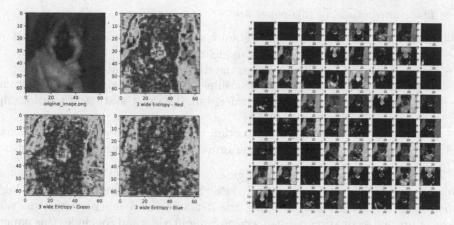

(a) Image with a 3 wide Entropy of Primary   (b) CNN Level-2 Activations of Image
Colors

Fig. 1. Image processed by CNN

a sequence. But many times these data sources do not have a naturally defined order, for example, a series of sensors on an automated vehicle [22]. In most *"non-natural"* cases, the researcher defaults the matrix order to a structural relationship between features usually established by an arbitrary specification. We use the term *"non-natural"* as a definition of ordering sources that were not defined in nature. This is opposed to *"unnatural"* which leads to the idea that they were ordered by something super-natural.

Our previous research showed that if high accuracy and precision are desired, using a non-natural structural order is not preferred when training a shallow convolution neural network model. We found that using statistical relationships as a basis for order does improve performance. We hypothesize that this holds true for the other styles of CNN architectures.

A particular subset of non-natural data that has gained interest is in detecting security issues. For example, raw IP traffic [16,23], computer process metrics [1], and industrial sensors [10] are examples where researchers are evaluating the use of CNN in security-related fields. The ability for a CNN to examine a large number of features from which extract the important subsets is what make CNN successful. Properly compiling various sources of data in a structure for a deep learning algorithm to analyze should be of concern when using CNNs.

Security can have many forms of data, all from a single source, for example, computer metrics [1]. Some are integers, others floats, include strings, all with various ranges. In a different scenario, a researcher could include audio, video, and or bio-metric packages to augment and enrich the source. We hypothesize that how the data is structured and prepared is imperative to use CNN successfully.

The contributions of this paper are:

- Show that ordering of rows and columns has a major impact on the performance of CNN, but how much is model dependent.
- Define a methodology for ordering the data by statistical relationships.
- Show that using statistical relationships to define matrix order is a strong predictor of a good performing order, but the exact statistical relationship can depend on the model of CNN.
- Increase the state of malware detection technology by providing data preparation tools that improve CNN performance when analyzing security data.

The remainder of the paper is organized as follows: Sect. 2 discusses related work using CNN with non-natural data. Section 3 outlines the methodology including, a description of ordering the data. Section 4 describes the analysis procedure and evaluation results. Section 5 summarizes and concludes this paper.

2   Related Work

2.1   Convolutional Neural Networks and Non-natural Data

As we understand the CNN capabilities, its use cases continue to expand. In this section, we examine the use of CNN by other researchers using non-naturally ordered data sets.

Lihao and Yanni analyze the quality of rubber tire treads in [15] using the parameters measured during the manufacturing process. With four levels to the procedure and eleven metrics sampled at each level, this provided a 4×11 matrix. After vectorizing these parameters, filtering for noise, they then feed them to a CNN, achieving a 94% accuracy. The order of the grid construction wasn't discussed.

Using a one dimensional CNN as a feature extractor for other machine learning algorithms (k-Nearest Neighbor with k = 1, Support Vector Machine, and Random Forest), Golinko et al. in [6], examine with non-natural "Generic" data if the ordering of the source data for the CNN has a performance impact on the final classifying algorithm. Using statistical correlation as a method for identifying relationships of adjacent data they show that not pre-ordering the data for CNN feature extraction is detrimental. They show using correlation as an ordering offers improvement in most cases, especially for kNN and SVN, improving accuracy from 76% with no feature extraction to 82% if the features were ordered by correlation prior to CNN feature extraction.

In [22] Park, et al. used information from robotic sensors and actuators to design a robot collision detection system using 66 features. They tested both a Support Vector Machine Regression and a one-dimensional CNN and were able to show that the CNN would perform better if it trained with enough data, but the SVMR performed better with less training. The construction of vector order wasn't discussed.

With connected and automated vehicles, Van Wyk, et al. [22] used cross-related sensor data (local speed, GPS location, and accelerometer) fed through an analyzer to identify whenever any of the sensors behaved anomalously. They tested different analyzers using a Kalman Filter, CNN, and a CNN-KF hybrid. Each had its unique benefits. Order of the grid constructing wasn't discussed, but trivial with three sensors over time.

2.2 Convolutional Neural Networks and Security

In security-based applications, CNNs have found value. Their ability to extract features out of a large data pool enables the algorithm's non-linear space to find patterns instead of statically looking for distinct signatures, allowing the dynamic/online detection of zero-day attacks. These data sources are often non-natural.

After minor pre-processing of raw IP traffic packets which included stripping the physical protocol layer, Zhang et al. [23], then they analyzed the resulting grids using CNN, LSTM, and a hybrid of the two, for both binary classification (benign/maleficent) and multi-classification (benign + 10 maleficent types). He shows they all achieve quite remarkable, near-perfect results. Differences being for binary classification the hybrid is slightly better than a CNN, which is better than LSTM. With multi-classification, CNN may have some minor advantage in precision over the hybrid, but LSTM is behind both. Data order was defined per the packet specification by the order of packets received.

Using process metrics as they are reported from hypervisors in a cloud environment Abdelsalem et al. in [1], places them in a grid-like structure looking for malware as it is injected into the virtual machines. Per time segment this produces a set of 35 metrics that are captured for each process running on the VM. They are compiled into a process row metric column matrix, which is supplied to a Lenet-5 [17] CNN. Using the order as found in the logs and specifications, they achieved an 89% accuracy. Using the same data set and ordering scheme, McDole et al. [18] follow up with research analyzing different CNN architectures. With ResNet [7] and DenseNet [11] he showed that Dense-121 performed the best at 92%, but Lenet-5 trained in an order of magnitude less time and detected in one-third. Kimmell et al. [13] includes the use of other deep learning models, Recurrent Neural Networks, by testing the validity using Long Short Term Memories and Bi-Direction LSTMs. In it, they explore if the order has an effect on training and discover that it does affect performance metrics for both models. For example, a precision of 99.95% with one random order and 98.46% with another.

Our previous research expands on the techniques discussed by Abdelsalem et al. [1] by exploring the relationship between ordering of the rows, columns, and CNN performance. We identify several structural relationships on which to base our ordering scheme, we include the use of a statistical relationship as an option for ordering the metric columns, and we compare those against a background of random orderings. We found that by establishing order using statistical correlation as a basis, we increased overall performance and achieved a 99% accuracy in detecting injected malware. We also show that using structural relationships as an ordering appears to have no more advantage than a random

Table 1. Virtual machine process metrics

Metric category	Description
Status	Process status, Current working directory
CPU information	CPU usage, CPU user space, CPU system/kernel space, CPU children user space, CPU children system space
Context switches	Voluntary context switches, Involuntary context switches
IO counters	Read requests, Write requests, Read bytes, Write bytes, Read chars, Write chars
Memory information	Swap memory, Proportional set size (PSS), Resident set size (RSS), Unique set size (USS), Virtual memory size (VMS), Dirty pages, Physical memory, Text resident set (TRS), Library memory, Shared memory
Threads	Used threads
File descriptors	Opened file descriptors
Network information	Received bytes, Sent bytes
Group information	Group ID real, Group ID saved, Group ID effective

order, but statistical relationships offer some insight. Based on this related work, our research goals are:

- Further explore finding a preferred or even an optimum order for any data that is supplied to a specific CNN model for analysis.
- Improve dynamic malware detection by choosing the proper CNN model and pre-processing the data with regards to row and column ordering.
- Explore the use of this data set with later models of CNN architecture.

3   Methodology

3.1   Dataset - Metric by Process Grids

The source of the data are samples taken from virtual machines in a cloud IaaS environment. These virtual machines are arrayed as a LAMP stack hosted web-site. The application server is injected with malware halfway through the experiment. Each sample is for a specific process running on the VM kernel and contains a series of M number of metrics per process (Table 1) during a segment in time. Stacking P number of processes that are captured during a single slice of time results in the matrix:

$$\mathbf{X}_t = \begin{bmatrix} & m_1 & m_2 & \dots & m_M \\ p_1 & x_{m_1 p_1} & x_{m_2 p_1} & \dots & x_{m_M p_1} \\ p_2 & x_{m_1 p_2} & x_{m_2 p_2} & \dots & x_{m_M p_2} \\ \vdots & \vdots & \vdots & \ddots & \vdots \\ p_P & x_{m_1 p_P} & x_{m_2 p_P} & \dots & x_{m_M p_P} \end{bmatrix}$$

For our experiments, the 35 metrics expanded through one hot encoding to $M = 75$ metric columns and we made available room in the matrix for as many as $P <= 150$ process rows. The 29+ million process samples were organized around 114 experiments (infections), and consisted of 31,064 matrices, about half of which are considered infected. The experiments were split between 80% training, 20% validation, and 20% testing. The entire grid set for each experiment was included in the group it was assigned, so no experiment was split between training, validation, and testing.

3.2   Row and Column Ordering Algorithms

This paper is to demonstrate if row/column ordering effects performance of different CNN models. Our initial method was to randomly sort the rows and columns. We choose ten rows and column orders which combined give us 100 unique ordering to use as a backdrop for comparison.

In our previous work we explored the use of structural relationships as one method for establishing an order. We found several relationships as determined by specification, log location, process number, parent/child and sibling status, related virtual machines, and naming convention. In these cases we found on average they performed no better than the random option if not worse. Since these ordering methods were previously defined we include them in our processing and as part of the general backdrop along with the random 100. We do not examine them specifically in the evaluation section of this paper.

Perhaps images provide us some insight on how to best order our matrices. CNN's are used to identify objects. What makes up an object in an image? Statistically, an object is a set of highly related pixels. All of the pixels will have a similar shade. Pixels outside the object boundaries usually have few patterns that match inside an object. This edge can be found using the statistical correlation relationship minimum. It is this fact that led to many advances in image compression techniques [12, 17, 21].

Table 2. Metric and process correlation functions

Metric statistical correlation function	
$\rho_{m_i m_j} = \dfrac{E(x_{m_i} x_{m_j}) - E(x_{m_i}) E(x_{m_j})}{\sqrt{E(x_{m_i}^2) - E(x_{m_i})^2} \cdot \sqrt{E(x_{m_j}^2) - E(x_{m_j})^2}}$	(1)
Process statistical correlation function	
$\rho_{m_k p_i p_j} = \dfrac{E(x_{m_k p_i} x_{m_k p_j}) - E(x_{m_k p_i}) E(x_{m_k p_j})}{\sqrt{E(x_{m_k p_i}^2) - E(x_{m_k p_i})^2} \cdot \sqrt{E(x_{m_k p_j}^2) - E(x_{m_k p_j})^2}}$	(2)

We hypothesize that we should create *artificial objects* by grouping the rows and columns to increase the average statistical relationship between neighboring features while decreasing the overall entropy of the image. In our previous paper, we found a relationship, statistical correlation $\rho_{m_i m_j}$ as shown in Table 2, between metric columns m_i and m_j for all processes, comparing results from a LENET-5 style CNN with *relu*, we found that ordering based on statistical correlation improved performance. We attempted to disperse the *artificial objects* by minimizing the correlation between columns and it had a negative impact on performance. We include these column orderings in our evaluation details using other CNN models. This consists of three relationship functions, metric correlation (Table 2), the absolute value of the correlation $\rho_{ABSm_im_j} = |\rho_{m_im_j}|$ to increase object edge creation, and anti-correlation, $\rho_{ANTIm_im_j} = 1 - |\rho_{m_im_j}|$, to test a counter hypothesis dispersing the objects and increase the entropy.

In our previous work, we struggled to derive a statistical relationship for the process rows. Since there could be as many as 150 processes statistically related over the 35 metrics, each sample unique per process, our initial queries became infeasible. They suffered from a *vanishing correlation* when a large set of samples that are not related to the feature are included in the calculations. For this research, we pared down the queries so only related a pair of processes p_i and p_j over a single metric m_k were calculated at a time. We reduced the data set for this specific relation value to only include samples when these two processes were running on the same machine at the same time. This reduced the query time from what was months, to all process pairs around a single metric, $\rho_{m_kp_ip_j}\forall i,j$, in roughly 24 h. We then incremented through each metric. Once these calculations were finished, we had a full set of process pair correlation values per metric, $\rho_{m_kp_ip_j}\forall i,j,k$.

Summing the correlations for a single pair we had a statistical relationship value between the processes $\rho_{SUMp_ip_j}$:

$$\rho_{SUMp_ip_j} = \sum_{k=1}^{M}(\rho_{m_kp_ip_j}) \tag{3}$$

Since we processed the row relationship values per metric before we summed them, we purposely chose which order of metric to derive these relationship values. We already had a relative importance order in our metric correlations from our previous research (Eq. 1 above). By summing all of the columns correlations for a single metric:

$$\rho_{TOTm_i} = \sum_{j=1}^{M}(\rho_{m_im_j}) \tag{4}$$

This is the *total metric correlation* on which to order their importance, largest to smallest. We also do the same for process rows, resulting in *total process correlation*:

$$\rho_{TOTp_i} = \sum_{j=1}^{P}(\rho_{SUMp_ip_j}) \tag{5}$$

Along with our fully correlated rows ordered derived from Eq. 3, we took the opportunity to tests some other options derived from this function. Like metric columns, we test similar relationship ideas with both the absolute values of the correlations, $\rho_{ABSp_ip_j} = \sum_{j=1}^{M} |\rho_{m_kp_ip_j}|$ and anti-correlations $\rho_{ANTIp_ip_j} = \sum_{j=1}^{M}(1 - |\rho_{m_kp_ip_j}|)$.

With this statistical relationship value, we rank the importance of each metric column and process row with each other. We built a methodology to construct the order. The process is generic and modular with regards to the data source ,f_i row or column, and the function used to derive the statistical relationship value $\rho_{f_if_j}$. The ordering methodology uses the steps in Algorithm 1.

Algorithm 1: Derive Statistical Relationship Order

For features along an axis, f_i, define a function, $\rho_{f_if_j}\forall i,j$;
From $\rho_{f_if_j}$ define $\rho_{TOTf_i}\forall i$;
Create a selection pool of features $P \ni f_i$;
while $P \neq \varnothing$ **do**
  Create an empty bidirectional queue Q for features f_i;
  Find $max(\rho_{TOTf_i})\forall f_i \in P$;
  Place the corresponding feature $f_{max(\rho)}$ onto Q;
  Remove $f_{max(\rho)}$ from P;
  Create two pointers left, L, and right, R; $L, R \in Q$;
  Point L and R towards $f_{max(\rho)}$ in Q;
  while $P \neq \varnothing$ and not(**STOP**) **do**
    if $\exists\rho_{f_Lf_i}\forall f_i \in P$ or $\exists\rho_{f_Rf_i}\forall f_i \in P$ **then**
      Find $max(\rho_{f_Lf_i}, \rho_{f_Rf_i})\forall f_i \in P$;
      Place the feature $f_{max(\rho)}$ next to f_L or f_R on Q;
      Remove $f_{max(\rho)}$ from P;
      Move the pointer, L or R, to the new feature $f_{max(\rho)}$ in Q;
    else
      Stack current queue Q into a final ordered axis V;
      STOP
    end
  end
end
Result: A vector V of features f_i that are ordered by the relationship
       function, $\rho_{f_if_j}$
Derive Statistical Relationship Order

Occasionally, there are ties. This was especially true for the anti-correlated function. Many pairs of processes rows had no correlation between them. We would settle ties by examining the next set of neighbors to see which set increased the relative total relationship value of the entire grid.

After compiling the statistically related orders with the previously defined order sets, we have a total of 252 distinct grid orders to compare. A visual example of the grids in different ordering sets is shown in Fig. 2 and Fig. 3.

We show two slices, one benign and another infected, using different row and column ordering schemes. It includes a 3-square pixel entropy filter plot to highlight possible patterns the CNN may be detecting. One order set, Fig. 2, has both rows and columns correlated while the other, Fig. 3, has them anti-correlated. You can see how we construct objects using the correlated order while dispersing them into tiny objects using the anti-correlated order.

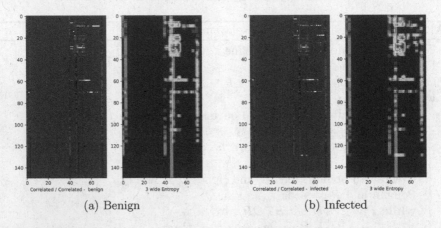

(a) Benign   (b) Infected

Fig. 2. Visual plot of correlated samples with 3 wide entropy

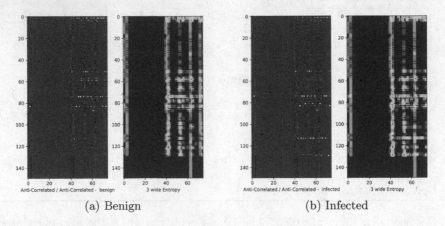

(a) Benign   (b) Infected

Fig. 3. Visual plot of anti-correlated samples with 3 wide entropy

4   Evaluation

4.1   Test Beds

We run our pre-processing and analysis using two desktops with the following specifications:

Desktop-1

- Central Processor Unit: Intel©Core^{TM}i7-8700 CPU @ 3.2 GHz × 12
- Memory: 15.6 GB
- Graphical Processor Unit: GeForce^{TM}GTX 1070i/PCIe/SSE2
- OS: 64-bit Ubuntu©20.04.2 LTS (Gnome 3.36.8)
- CUDA^{TM}: 11.1
- Python: 3.6

Desktop-2

- Central Processor Unit: Intel©Core^{TM}i7-9700K CPU @ 3.6 GHz × 8
- Memory: 15.5 GB
- Graphical Processor Unit: NVIDIA GK210GL (Tesla K80)
- OS: 64-bit Ubuntu©20.10 LTS (Gnome 3.38.3)
- CUDA^{TM}: 11.2
- Python: 3.6

We used Tensorflow^{TM}v2 with Tensorboard^{TM}, the underlying engine, to perform the CNN analysis. Comparing between these machines, we found that the Tesla could handle larger CNN models with two cores and more GPU memory, while the GeForce machine would process about 30% faster with the later CUDA capable features.

4.2   CNN Models - Chosen Through Experimentation

Our previous research examined the use of a shallow CNN model, Lenet-5 with *relu* as an activation function. In this research, we wanted to see if our statistical relationship hypothesis would hold with other forms of CNN. We initially experimented with Resnet-50 and found that the training times took longer per epoch and more epochs than Lenet-5. Lenet-5 would usually saturate training in 20 epochs, but Resnet-50 would take as long as 50. We shifted to ©Auto-Keras and by 20 epochs it would settle on a plain CNN with a couple of dense layers but fail to produce any meaningful performance.

We then took a modularly broad but targeted approach by re-coding our test ground to use the recently released ©Keras application set of deep learning models. Using a limited set of ordered experiments, we test model training saturation. Because of our methodology, using the same data set for the different models was simply changing the model name within the script. Our post calculation analysis found that five models would saturate training much quicker than the others, within three epochs, so we chose to compare those in order of their release date:

- Inception-V3 [19].
- ResNet-18 [7].
- Xception [3].
- MobileNet [9].
- DenseNet121 [11].

To help in our analysis, we examined the model summary so we could identify the parameters count and see if there might be some relationship between that and order performance via the architecture design. These details are found in Table 3.

Table 3. Model parameter count and process times

CNN architecture	Parameter count		Desktop-2 median 3-epoch train time (min)
	Functional layers	Dense layers	
Inception-V3	21,802,208	12,290	2:45
ResNet-18	11,186,698	162	11:43
Xception	20,860,904	61,442	6:03
MobileNet	3,230,338	6	1:20
DenseNet-121	7,031,232	16,386	3:54

4.3   Result Plots

Since malware infections are rare compared to normal machine activity, we decided to compare the precision/recall curves. We start by showing the results for the Inception V3 model. In Fig. 4, we see all of the PR curves as the light background with the dark lines representing a subset of PR curves that are generated running the model over a particular order set. Note that these plots are scaled in to 50%–100%. Here we see Inception prefers correlated columns and ABS-correlated rows, while and correlated rows offer another well performing alternative, but anti-correlated rows should be avoided.

We follow with the results from ResNet-18 in Fig. 5. Note that these plots are at 0–100% scale. It's obvious by the wide varieties in PR curves that this model is very susceptible to minor changes in order. For this model anti-correlated rows and columns perform better than average, while the other orderings have only minor variation around the poor average.

Our next model is Xception, and the results are found in Fig. 6. Note that this model seems order ambivalent with near perfect results every time, but we see that the statistically related order performs well if not better than average. Only the ABS-correlated columns fell below average, but this was by only 0.0007 AUC. It appears the best performance is found using correlated rows and anti-correlated columns.

We included MobileNet as a small format option with it's intention to be used in mobile devices. You can find the results in Fig. 7. Like ResNet-18, MobileNet

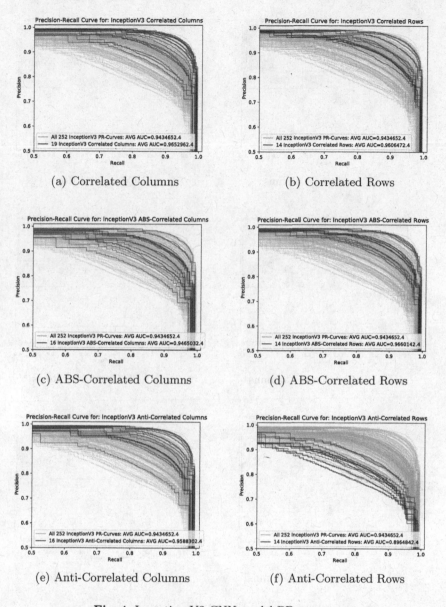

Fig. 4. Inception V3 CNN model PR curves

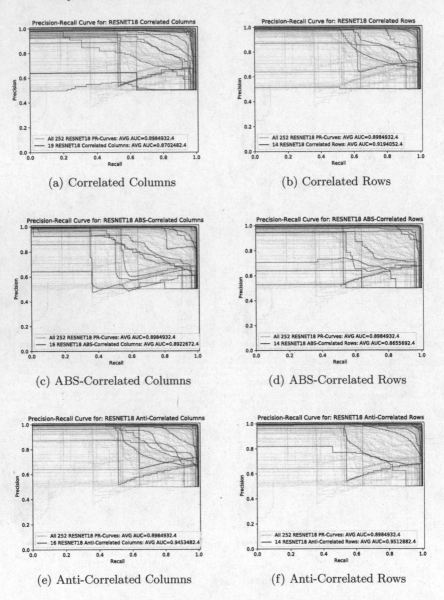

(a) Correlated Columns

(b) Correlated Rows

(c) ABS-Correlated Columns

(d) ABS-Correlated Rows

(e) Anti-Correlated Columns

(f) Anti-Correlated Rows

Fig. 5. ResNet-18 CNN model PR curves

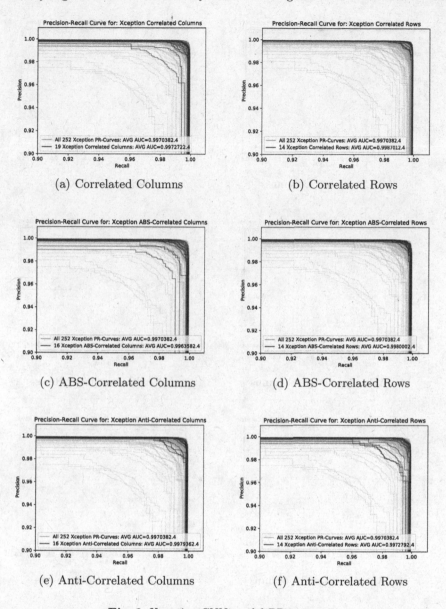

Fig. 6. Xception CNN model PR curves

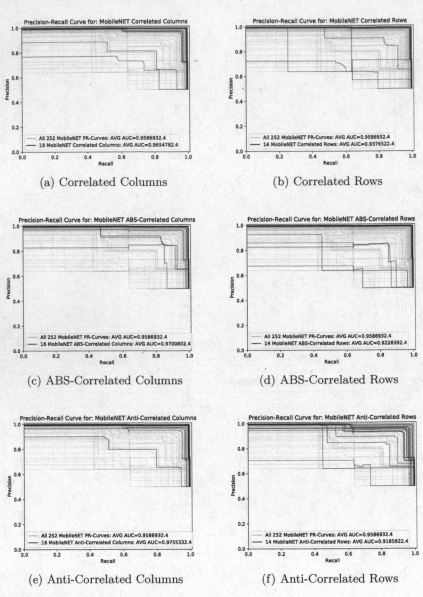

(a) Correlated Columns

(b) Correlated Rows

(c) ABS-Correlated Columns

(d) ABS-Correlated Rows

(e) Anti-Correlated Columns

(f) Anti-Correlated Rows

Fig. 7. MobileNet CNN model PR curves

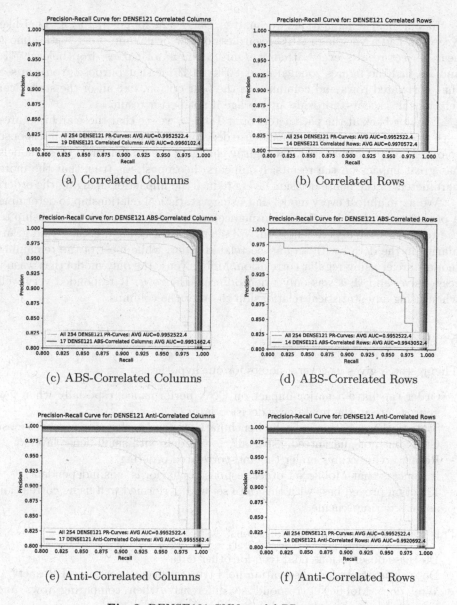

(a) Correlated Columns   (b) Correlated Rows

(c) ABS-Correlated Columns   (d) ABS-Correlated Rows

(e) Anti-Correlated Columns   (f) Anti-Correlated Rows

Fig. 8. DENSE121 CNN model PR curves

seems to be very reactive when there are changes in the order. We have these plots at full zoom, 0–100%, to observe all of the curves. Unlike ResNet-18 (0.898 AUC), it appears to respond better on average (0.958 AUC). It also appears that it loves any statistical relationship in column order, but choosing a random order is better than anything we analyze for row order.

In our final examination, we analyze Dense-121 found in Fig. 8. This like Xception had a vary high AUC regardless of row or column order, with almost near-perfect results every attempt. Only a couple of curves drop below 97%, and we had the figures zoomed in at 80%–100% for that purpose. You can see that correlated rows and columns are the best option, but all of the statistical relationships seem to provide an average if not better result.

Looking back at the parameter count Table 3, we see that those architectures with fewer parameters in the final dense decision layers were fragile with response to order and performance. Even slightly changing the grid order in these models has great impact on the results. It appears the opposite is true, that the more parameters in the dense decision layers reduce the impact of changing the order.

We see in almost every model that using a statistical relationship to determine a proper order does improve performance, but identifying which relationship to use requires some experimentation. We see that ResNet architectures find granularity in the detail with an anti-correlated order, while most of the remaining models prefer using regular correlation. MobileNet is the only model that wasn't responsive, and that was only when ordering the rows. It responded very well when using any statistical relationship to order the columns.

5   Conclusion

This research gives us several points for our hypothesis.

- Order can have a major impact on CNN performance, especially when few neurons are in the final dense decision layer.
- Statistical correlation is a solid benchmark for good performing order for most CNN, but not guaranteed, especially for models with small dense layers.
- Resnet architectures prefer the anti-correlated ordering.
- It appears that MobileNet order response behavior is axis independent.
- Xception proved best with this data set and performed well using correlation as an ordering scheme.

This leads us to several open questions:

- Do these observations hold true for other data?
- Does anti-correlation observation hold true for deeper versions of Resnet?
- Why does MobileNet respond so differently when comparing rows and columns? Is it the axis size difference?
- Can we leverage our understanding of entropy to further improve CNN performance?

It's these questions that lead us into our next topic.

5.1   Future Work

To further our understanding on how order has an affect on CNN performance, we plan on continuing our research by:

– Examine the use of this technique using other security data sets, the CIC-IDS-2017 in particular.
– See if this technique holds true for non-security related data sets, especially in industrial and medical fields.
– Identify if there are other statistical relationships that could improve the performance of the CNN using data preparation alone.

References

1. Abdelsalem, M., Krishnan, R., Huang, Y., Sandu, R.: Malware detection in cloud infrastrueture using convolutional neural networks. In: IEEE 11th International Conference on Cloud Computing (2018)
2. Avula, S.B., Badri, S.J., Reddy P, G.: A novel forest fire detection system using fuzzy entropy optimized thresholding and STN-based CNN. In: 2020 International Conference on COMmunication Systems NETworkS (COMSNETS), pp. 750–755 (2020). https://doi.org/10.1109/COMSNETS48256.2020.9027347
3. Chollet, F.: Xception: Deep learning with depthwise separable convolutions (2017)
4. Deng, L., Hinton, G., Kingsbury, B.: New types of deep neural network learning for speech recognition and related applications: an overview. In: 2013 IEEE International Conference on Acoustics, Speech and Signal Processing, pp. 8599–8603 May (2013). https://doi.org/10.1109/ICASSP.2013.6639344
5. Elhassouny, A., Smarandache, F.: Trends in deep convolutional neural networks architectures: a review. In: 2019 International Conference of Computer Science and Renewable Energies (ICCSRE), pp. 1–8 (2019). https://doi.org/10.1109/ICCSRE.2019.8807741
6. Golinko, E., Sonderman, T., Zhu, X.: Learning convolutional neural networks from ordered features of generic data. In: 2018 17th IEEE International Conference on Machine Learning and Applications (ICMLA), pp. 897–900, December 2018. https://doi.org/10.1109/ICMLA.2018.00145
7. He, K., Zhang, X., Ren, S., Sun, J.: Deep residual learning for image recognition. CoRR abs/1512.03385 http://arxiv.org/abs/1512.03385 (2015)
8. He, K., Zhang, X., Ren, S., Sun, J.: Delving deep into rectifiers: surpassing human-level performance on imagenet classification. In: The IEEE International Conference on Computer Vision (ICCV), December 2015
9. Howard, A.G., et al.: Mobilenets: efficient convolutional neural networks for mobile vision applications (2017)
10. Hu, Y., Zhang, D., Cao, G., Pan, Q.: Network data analysis and anomaly detection using CNN technique for industrial control systems security. In: 2019 IEEE International Conference on Systems, Man and Cybernetics (SMC), pp. 593–597 (2019). https://doi.org/10.1109/SMC.2019.8913895
11. Huang, G., Liu, Z., Weinberger, K.Q.: Densely connected convolutional networks. CoRR abs/1608.06993 http://arxiv.org/abs/1608.06993 (2016)
12. Jiang, W., Bruton, L.: Lossless color image compression using chromatic correlation. In: Proceedings DCC 1999 Data Compression Conference (Cat. No. PR00096), pp. 533 (1999). https://doi.org/10.1109/DCC.1999.785690
13. Kimmel, J.C., Mcdole, A.D., Abdelsalam, M., Gupta, M., Sandhu, R.: Recurrent neural networks based online behavioural malware detection techniques for cloud infrastructure. IEEE Access 9, 68066–68080 (2021). https://doi.org/10.1109/ACCESS.2021.3077498

14. Lee, J.Y., Dernoncourt, F.: Sequential short-text classification with recurrent and convolutional neural networks. CoRR abs/1603.03827 http://arxiv.org/abs/1603.03827 (2016)

15. Lihao, W., Yanni, D.: A fault diagnosis method of tread production line based on convolutional neural network. In: 2018 IEEE 9th International Conference on Software Engineering and Service Science (ICSESS), pp. 987–990, November 2018. https://doi.org/10.1109/ICSESS.2018.8663824

16. Liu, C., Dai, L., Cui, W., Lin, T.: A byte-level CNN method to detect DNS tunnels. In: 2019 IEEE 38th International Performance Computing and Communications Conference (IPCCC), pp. 1–8 (2019). https://doi.org/10.1109/IPCCC47392.2019.8958714

17. Liu, G., Zhao, F.: An efficient compression algorithm for hyperspectral images based on correlation coefficients adaptive three dimensional wavelet zerotree coding. In: 2007 IEEE International Conference on Image Processing, vol. 2, pp. II - 341-II - 344 (2007). https://doi.org/10.1109/ICIP.2007.4379162

18. McDole, A., Abdelsalam, M., Gupta, M., Mittal, S.: Analyzing CNN based behavioural malware detection techniques on cloud IaaS. In: Zhang, Q., Wang, Y., Zhang, L.-J. (eds.) CLOUD 2020. LNCS, vol. 12403, pp. 64–79. Springer, Cham (2020). https://doi.org/10.1007/978-3-030-59635-4_5

19. Milton-Barker, A.: Inception v3 deep convolutional architecture for classifying acute (2019). https://software.intel.com/content/www/us/en/develop/articles/inception-v3-deep-convolutional-architecture-for-classifying-acute-myeloidlymphoblastic.html

20. Mobadersany, P., et al.: Predicting cancer outcomes from histology and genomics using convolutional networks. Proc. Nat. Acad. Sci. **115**(13), E2970–E2979 (2018). https://doi.org/10.1073/pnas.1717139115, https://www.pnas.org/content/115/13/E2970

21. Wang, Q., Shen, Y.: A jpeg2000 and nonlinear correlation measurement based method to enhance hyperspectral image compression. In: 2005 IEEE Instrumentationand Measurement Technology Conference Proceedings, vol. 3, pp. 2009–2011 (2005). https://doi.org/10.1109/IMTC.2005.1604524

22. van Wyk, F., Wang, Y., Khojandi, A., Masoud, N.: Real-time sensor anomaly detection and identification in automated vehicles. IEEE Trans. Intell. Transp. Syst. **21**(3), 1264–1276 (2020). https://doi.org/10.1109/TITS.2019.2906038

23. Zhang, Y., Chen, X., Jin, L., Wang, X., Guo, D.: Network intrusion detection: based on deep hierarchical network and original flow data. IEEE Access **7**, 37004–37016 (2019). https://doi.org/10.1109/ACCESS.2019.2905041

24. Zhao, X., Gao, L., Chen, Z., Zhang, B., Liao, W., Yang, X.: An entropy and MRF model-based CNN for large-scale landsat image classification. IEEE Geosci. Remote Sens. Lett. **16**(7), 1145–1149 (2019). https://doi.org/10.1109/LGRS.2019.2890996

Web and Social Network

Dealing with Complexity for Immune-Inspired Anomaly Detection in Cyber Physical Systems

Lenhard Reuter[1,3], Maria Leitner[2,3]([✉]), Paul Smith[3],
and Manuel Koschuch[1]

[1] University of Applied Sciences FH Campus Wien, Vienna, Austria
lenhard.reuter@stud.fh-campuswien.ac.at,
manuel.koschuch@fh-campuswien.ac.at
[2] Faculty of Computer Science, University of Vienna, Vienna, Austria
maria.leitner@univie.ac.at
[3] Center for Digital Safety & Security, AIT Austrian Institute of Technology GmbH,
Seibersdorf, Austria
{lenhard.reuter.fl,maria.leitner,paul.smith}@ait.ac.at

Abstract. With digitization, critical infrastructures face a higher risk of security incidents and attacks on cyber-physical systems (CPS). In the past 50 years, research and practice have developed various approaches to monitor and detect attacks such as with anomaly detection. While many approaches focuses on artificial neural networks, bio-inspired approaches utilize nature as reference. For example, artificial immune systems (AIS) refer to principles of the natural immune system. In this paper, we investigate the Negative Selection Algorithm (NSA), an algorithm from the domain of AIS for anomaly detection in CPS. Particularly in CPS, datasets can become quite complex and can require a number of detectors for the analysis. Therefore, we will investigate how AIS can be extended to handle and manage complex datasets of CPS. We propose two models that use Principal Component Analysis (PCA) and Autoencoder (AE) to enable dimensionality reduction. Using these models, we are able to show that it is possible to apply the NSA approach to such datasets. Our results indicate that the use of PCA and AE is beneficial for both a better representation of the data and therefore significantly relevant for an improvement of the detection rate, and provides in addition the possibility to add further features to support the identification of anomalies. As the NSA approach allows for distributed computation, it might be possible to allow faster or distributed detection; the extent to which this is possible remains to be investigated and therefore represents future work.

Keywords: Anomaly detection · Negative selection algorithm · Cyber physical system · Principal component analysis · Autoencoder

© Springer Nature Switzerland AG 2022
R. Krishnan et al. (Eds.): SKM 2021, CCIS 1549, pp. 151–170, 2022.
https://doi.org/10.1007/978-3-030-97532-6_9

1   Introduction

In recent years, control systems of critical infrastructures are being increasingly digitized [25], which not only improves their accuracy, enables easier monitoring and delivers general economic advantages, but also increases their attack surface and thus leads to a substantially increased risk of cyber-physical attacks. Adversaries from within the cyber world become capable of penetrating the boundary to the physical world by executing cyber attacks. Digital attacks with the goal and potential to cause physical damage undoubtedly pose serious threats, especially when considering scenarios in critical infrastructures such as water supplies, hospitals or power plants. In general, an upward trend of this type of attack can be observed, both in relative frequency and in severity [30]. This demands a solution for anomaly detection in such systems in order to identify attacks reliably on time.

Anomaly detection in complex systems is a fundamental computational challenge. Nature is generally regarded as a rich source of inspiration for new successful technologies and mechanisms that can be transferred to engineering, which is also the case when it comes to mastering increasingly complex computational challenges. These so-called *bio-inspired* algorithms use nature as a model to derive metaphors that are subsequently manifested as algorithms. This has led to the development of genetic algorithms [11] (GA) that borrow from evolutionary theory, Artificial Neural Networks [4] (ANN) mimicking the functioning of the human brain, and Artificial Immune Systems [5] (AIS) using the principles of the Natural Immune System (NIS). The latter seems predestined for the task of anomaly detection, since it corresponds exactly to its main purpose: *recognizing malicious invaders whilst distinguishing them from endogenous cells in order to prevent autoimmune diseases.*

An algorithm inspired by the NIS, the Negative Selection Algorithm (NSA), has already been applied to the challenge of anomaly detection in the past [6, 10,19,22,23]. However, the NSA approach faces a number of challenges that make it difficult to apply. Its runtime complexity is often exponential due to its means of generating detectors and often generates enormous numbers of detectors that consequently require a long detection time and impedes its application. These limitations are caused mainly by the complexity (i.e. dimensionality) of the source dataset, which has to be addressed in order to be able to use NSA with data such as that of industrial control systems.

However, the NSA approach has some advantages that makes its shortcoming worth addressing: Unlike other machine learning methods, NSA does not produce a model in the strict sense, instead the entire detection mechanism is based on a set of individual detectors – an iterable list of elements that can be checked one by one, which is a prime example of distributed computation. Such lists can be easily distributed to arbitrary nodes for further computation. As the number of these nodes increases, the required detection time decreases proportionally. Even if a small communication overhead must be taken into account. Another favorable factor in this context is that these lists are independent of their generation, which enables a refinement of the basis detection system during operation without interfering with the actual detection procedure. This further allows it to be responsive to newly developing benign states, gradually improving its approximation of the benign states.

In this paper, we applied the Antigen Space Triangulation Coverage (ASTC) algorithm [7], a relatively new approach to compute the required detectors. With the goal of using this NSA detection mechanism for CPS, the corresponding approach must be capable of handling the complexity of a data set that typically arises from CPS. Previous work and our experiments, which are described herein, suggest that ASTC is not well-suited to anomaly detection for data sets with high dimensionality.

Our contribution therefore primarily focused on how these limitations resulting from the complexity of the data sets can be mitigated. We have extended the original ASTC approach by preprocessing methods for dimension reduction. We used both a linear reduction approach, that of Principal Component Analysis (PCA), and a non-linear approach, through the use of a special type of neural network, an autoencoder (AE), and evaluated and compared their results.

The main results show that these augmentations are beneficial for both their performance and its applicability to complex datasets, i.e. with high dimensionality, which allowed in further consequence the use of additional feature engineering, improving the identification of anomalies by mapping temporal dependencies. Both proposed models can be used as base models for further work on anomaly detection in CPS.

This paper is structured as follows: Sect. 2 describes background on the negative selection algorithm and related work. Section 3 specifies the approach of the anomaly detection. In particular, the dataset, the data pre-processing, implementation, analysis of the ASTC algorithm, proposed models with dimensionality reduction and evaluation. Section 4 concludes the paper.

2   Preliminaries

This section summarizes the negative selection algorithm in Sect. 2.1 and related work in Sect. 2.2.

2.1   Negative Selection

The immune system uses lymphocytes, which represent immune detector cells, to identify invaders or foreign cells, so-called pathogens. A very important concept in this context is that of *affinity,* which plays a decisive role in a so-called *recognition event.* A recognition event in the NIS is based on chemical bonds between the receptors on the surface of lymphocytes (detector cells within the white blood cells) and the molecular structures, so-called *epitopes* of pathogens (see Fig. 1). Both, receptors and epitopes are complex electrically charged 3-dimensional structures. These bonds are formed by opposing electrical charges, the more complementary the structures are, the more likely they are to bind. The strength of this binding is referred to as affinity. When a certain threshold

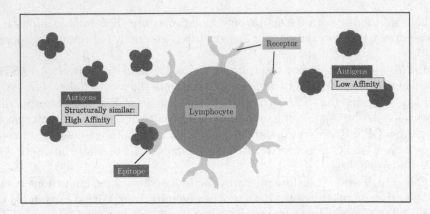

Fig. 1. Affinity in nature (authors own illustration, based on Fig. 2 in [15])

of bound receptors is exceeded, i.e. when the affinity is sufficiently high, the respective lymphocytes are activated [15].

The NIS attempts to detect a broad spectrum of pathogens by means of a somatic hypermutation during the affinity maturation of the lymphocytes. During this process, new combinations of existing receptor components are assembled more or less randomly in order to be able to react on never encountered threats. The strength of the randomness depends on the respective affinity to known pathogens; the stronger the affinity, the lower the mutation.

Also part of this maturation process is censoring, in which immature detector cells are confronted with the body's own, the so-called *self*-cells. If binding occurs during this exposure, the affected cells are eliminated. This process is known as clonal deletion or *negative selection* [15].

Negative Selection Algorithm (NSA). In the computational variant of negative selection, the affinity is determined by so-called matching rules. In the course of time, different methods have been developed, whereby the general principle is: a matching rule M determines the proximity between a recognizing element d and an element e to be recognized [17].

While earlier approaches worked primarily on binary data and could thus use matching rules such as *Hamming distance, r-contiguous-bits* (RCB) [31], or *r-chunk-bits* [32] rule, for data in real-valued space, referred to as *Euclidean space,* over the real numbers $\mathbb{R}^n$ in n dimensions, the idea of actual close proximity is usually used as a matching rule, where an element e and detector d match, if their *Euclidean distance,* the length of the direct connection, does not exceed a certain threshold [16].

NSA Outline. In its most basic design, a general-purpose NSA procedure can be described in 3 steps [12,13]:

1. Define a *self*-set as a collection S in a feature space U that represents the states to be monitored.

2. Generate a set D of detectors to cover the complementary space of the self-set. Candidate detectors are confronted with the instances of the self-set S and a matching method is applied. If they match, the corresponding candidates are eliminated, while the remaining ones are added to the matured detectors. This process is repeated until the termination condition is reached.

3. Incoming samples are continually matched against the detectors in D. In case the sample matches with any detector of D it is considered a *nonself* element, thus in this context an *anomaly*.

Detector Generation. Considering the Euclidean space, a detector consists of the coordinates of a center and a radius. The goal is to cover the complementary space to the self-set entirely by such detectors. Therefore, the detector generation has the decisive influence on the performance of the whole system. Primarily, two criteria are particularly crucial, the completeness of coverage and their generation must take place in finite time.

The original approach of the NSA [10] was strongly modeled on the process from nature, in which detectors were actually randomly sampled from the respective feature space and then tested against the self-set. These detectors had a uniform fixed radius, which required a sometimes redundant, large number of detectors to cover a space. This was improved with the introduction of V-Detectors [16], in which an additional attribute was added per detector to indicate the respective radius, thus significantly reducing this number (illustrated in Fig. 2). However, these approaches were still based on a generate-delete cycle over many generations and thus had an almost exponential runtime complexity.

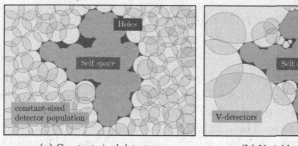
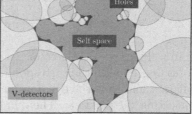

(a) Constant-sized detectors   (b) Variable-sized detectors

Fig. 2. Concept of NSA with V-Detectors (authors own illustration, based on Fig. 1 in [16])

The method used in this work is the *Antigen Space Triangulation Coverage (ASTC)*, presented by Fan et al. [7], which is a recent method to generate detectors, and the first to show significant improvement in time complexity to a logarithmic level. The ASTC algorithm is based on a method from the field of computational geometry, the *Delaunay Triangulation (DT)*, which basically divides a given set of points $p \in P$ into simplices (triangles/tetrahedra/hypertetrahedra respectively), which satisfy certain criteria, in particular the *empty circum-circle* property, which states that the circum-circle of a given simplex does not include any other $p \in P$.

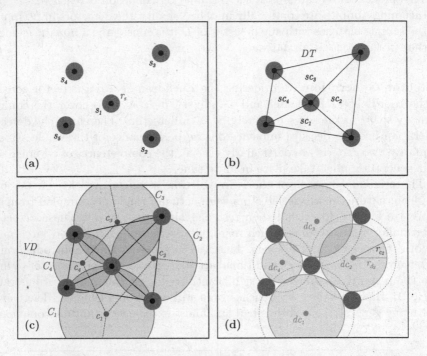

Fig. 3. ASTC detector generation process (authors own illustration, based on Fig. 3 & 4 in [7])

Figure 3 illustrates the detector generation for the points $s \in \mathbb{R}^2$. (a) depicts the self-set ($s \in S$) with the corresponding self-radius r_s. (b) shows the Delaunay Triangulation and thus the division into evenly distributed simplicial cells (sc_i) interconnecting the points s_i. Then, in (c), the circum-circle centers c_i and their circum-circles C_i are determined, for example, by using a Voronoi Diagram (VD), which is the dual graph to DT generated by the center perpendiculars. Since all points of the respective simplicial cell naturally lie on the circum-circle, the circum-circle radius can be adjusted in (d) to compensate for the overlap with the self radius. After the radius has been adjusted ($r_{d_i} = r_{c_i} - r_s$), the newly created detector ($d_i = \{d_{c_i}, r_{d_i}\}$) can be added directly to the detector-set as matured detectors, since they do not need to be further checked for self-tolerance. This omission provides further runtime advantage.

2.2 Related Work

In Yang et al. [35], the non-self space for the NSA is examined and high-density regions are identified with the help of a clustering process, whose centers are used directly as detectors. A second type of detectors are centers of further non-self instances in low-density regions. Further detectors are established via the traditional NSA. This reduces effectively redundant detectors and provides coverage of significant clusters of anomalies. Experiments have shown that this algorithm yields good detection rates with low false positive rates and even performs better in time complexity in high dimensions than the ASTC algorithm by Fan et al. [7] used in this paper. However, an application to the problem confronted in this study is not possible, since we assume a one-class classification task in which no anomalous data is available.

In Zhang et al. [36], a method to improve the time cost of traditional negative selection algorithms is proposed. As in the ASTC algorithm, they use an approach from geometric computation. The proposed algorithm adapts the idea of V-detectors. First, the distribution of the self set is analyzed, based on which a grid is generated, which successively halves the given self space, if there are still free self instances, until a minimum size of a cell is reached. With the help of this subdivision, a randomly generated detector no longer has to iterate through the entire self set, but only through the cell in which it is located and its neighboring cells. Afterwards it is censored against already generated detectors. This method successfully reduces the time cost of the detector generation considerably and prevents redundant detectors.

An approach to improve the performance of the NSA, based on hierarchical clustering of self sets, is presented in Chen et al. [2]. The real-valued negative selection algorithm based on hierarchical clustering of self set, in short HC-RNSA, uses the PCA method to reduce the data dimensions and then applies hierarchical clustering for the generation of detectors on the self set. The detector generation process is applied recursively, starting from the higher cluster level to the lower levels until the desired self radius is reached. In experiments, this method has been compared with the tradition NSA, RNSA and V-Detectors, and it has been shown that HC-RNSA performs better in higher dimensional datasets than the others, while these have in a slight edge in the lower dimensional datasets. It was also shown that this method successfully reduces the cost of distance calculations between detectors and observed candidates significantly.

Another work that uses the dimension reduction capability of an Autoencoder is proposed by Guo et al. [14]. They have developed an model of combining a dimension-reducing AE and a KNN (K-Nearest Neighbor Algorithm), hence the name AEKNN. Their results too confirm a more effective use of the, in this case binary K-Nearest Neighbor algorithm, after this preprocessing. Experiments were performed on 3 known UCI datasets[1] where the results confirm its effectiveness.

---

[1] https://archive.ics.uci.edu/ml/datasets.php (last access: 27/07/21).

3   Immune-Inspired Anomaly Detection

In the following section, the data set and its origin will be presented first, followed by excerpts of its implementation, the concepts used and the results of the anomaly detection approach.

3.1   Dataset

The dataset used in this paper was obtained from the IAEA[2] project *Enhancing Computer Security Incident Analysis at Nuclear Facilities* (CRP J02008) [27], in the context of which the *Asherah NPP Simulator (ANS)* [1] was developed.

Typically, the internals and information about their operations of Pressurized Water Reactors (PWR) are not known. In 1979, however, an accident occurred at Three Mile Island (TMI) Unit 1 [33]. This incident was widely reported and documented, enabling the derivation of certain details for implementing the ANS. Therefore, ANS is based on the same 2.772 MWt two-loop so-called Babcock & Wilcox design as in TMI Unit 1. ANS is implemented as a MATLAB/SIMULINK simulation intended to serve as a simplified reference power plant for conducting security exercises and investigations [1]. In the development process of ANS, care was taken to ensure that it is as flexible and modular as possible, especially in the sense that it has to function as a hardware-in-the-loop system with the possibility of integrating physical devices such as Programmable Logic Controllers (PLCs) in the control logic.

With the help of this simulator, four different hazards were simulated and recorded. These hazards stand for scenarios that can occur if certain components of the pressurizer fail or misbehave. The four selected scenarios comprise:

1. The *spray valves* mistakenly turn on and the *backup heater* fails to engage at the crucial time. This results in *underpressure* in the pressurizer vessel.
2. The *spray valves* fail while the *main heater* is wrongly engaged. The result is *overpressure* in the pressurizer vessel.
3. Failure of the *main heater* and *backup heater* will result in *underpressure* in the pressurizer vessel.
4. The *main heater, backup heater* and *spray valves* all turn on when they should not. The combination of these components causes opposite effects and therefore lead to *rapid fluctuations* of the pressure in the pressurizer vessel.

The described hazards do not represent cyber-attacks by themselves, but show readings that indicate possible tampering with the components, in this respect also potentially as a consequence of a cyber-attack. In this cyber-physical context, it is now a question of being able to draw conclusions about anomalies on the basis of the available physical data, the cause of which may also lie in the cyber world.

---

[2] International Atomic Energy Agency.

Both the benign dataset, which was obtained in an unmanipulated simulation, and the four listed hazards are described with 4,130 instances each and comprise seven attributes: (1) Reactor Power PR, (2) Pressurizer Pressure, (3) Pressurizer Level, (4) Reactor In Cool Temp, (5) Reactor Out Cool Temp, (6) Total Heater Output, (7) Total Spray Output.

3.2   Data Pre-processing

Prior to the actual generation of the detectors certain pre-processings are conducted on the dataset. This includes the normalization of the data, the addition of boundary points, but also the generation of new features to map the temporal dependency in the time series.

Normalization. Since the Euclidean distance is used as an affinity metric, different magnitudes, units and ranges of the individual features pose a significant problem in determining this distance, as higher magnitudes would have significantly higher weight on the affinity than others. To address this problem, a *Min-Max Scaler* is used:

$$x' = \frac{x - \min(x)}{\max(x) - \min(x)} \tag{1}$$

Delta Values. Additional features are required that map the temporal dependencies that are inevitably present in time series. These can be represented by both, the change to the immediate predecessor but also over a period of time. Both variants are applied in this paper. For the determination of the respective delta value the Mean Squared Error (MSE) is applied:

$$MSE(X, \hat{X}) = \frac{1}{n} \sum_{i=1}^{n} (x_i - \hat{x}_i)^2 \tag{2}$$

Here X stands for the considered instance, whereas $\hat{X}$ stands for its predecessor. The result is then appended to the original data as an additional feature.

Boundary Points. DT, which is the basis for the generation of detectors, is based on tessellation starting from a convex hull. If the self-set is seen as the initial set, its boundary represents this convex hull and accordingly detectors are generated almost exclusively in the interior of this set, the outer boundary however cannot be fully described by DT. Therefore, the DT generation must be supported by additional points, the so-called *Boundary Points*. These Boundary Points by themselves represent the new convex hull from which the tessellation is performed on. As shown in Fig. 4(b), the description of the self-area can be approximated by detectors from the outside of the initial set.

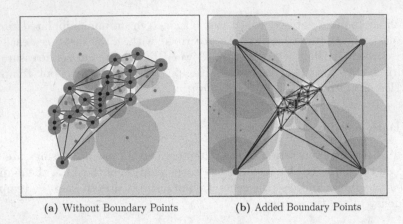

(a) Without Boundary Points   (b) Added Boundary Points

Fig. 4. Adding boundary points (authors own illustration)

3.3 Implementation

The implementation of this proof-of-concept was developed in Python 3.8.5 in a Jupyter-Lab [21] environment and uses mainly libraries and well-known repositories for Data Science, which include *sklearn* [26] for preprocessing and PCA, *keras* [3] for AE and *scipy.spatial* [34] for Delaunay/Voronoi tessellation tasks.

In the following, the two most important functions are illustrated. The *generation process* can be roughly divided into three steps (see Algorithm 1): (1) In the first step, the data set is supplemented by the boundary points described in Sect. 3.2, which enable a coherent DT. (2) In the second step, the actual DT is performed. (3) In the third and final step, the Voronoi diagram is used to determine the center of the circumcircle of the respective simplices, whereas the radius, the distance between the new detector and one of the vertices is calculated and constrained by the self-radius. Provided this radius is larger than the minimum radius, this new detector is added to the matured detector set.

Once the detectors have been generated, they are now used to *detect* anomalies (see Algorithm 2). Generally a candidate c must be matched with all detectors, since this is not very efficient it is first checked whether c lies outside the boundary points, which enclose all self instances of the training. Assuming a well-fitted model, samples lying outside these boundaries must represent anomalies. If this is not true, the distance to each detector must be calculated and checked if it is within the detector radius and if so, the sample is interpreted as an anomaly.

3.4 Analysis of the ASTC Algorithm

Evaluation Metrics. Throughout this paper, the metrics used are primarily the True Positive Rate (TPR), also called the *Detection Rate* (DR), defined as: $DR = \frac{TP}{TP+FN}$ and the *False Positive Rate* (FPR), defined as: $FPR = \frac{FP}{FP+TN}$, where TP stands for a True Positive, i.e. a true recognition of an anomaly as an anomaly, and FP for a False Positive, an interpretation of a normal instance as

---

Algorithm 1: Pseudocode of the Detector Generation

Input: Self-Set S, Self-Radius r_s, Minimal-Radius $r_{\min}$
Output: Detector Set D

1 Add Boundary Points to Self-Set:
   $B \leftarrow Calculate\_Boundary\_Points(S)$
   $S_{Train} \leftarrow S \cap B$

2 Generate Delaunay Triangulation:
   $DT \leftarrow Delaunay(S_{Train})$

3 Generate Detectors:
   foreach *simplex* $T \in DT$ **do**
   │ Calculate Circum Center:
   │ $(x, y)_d \leftarrow Voronoi(\text{vertices } v \in T)$
   │ Calculate Detector Radius:
   │ $r_d \leftarrow Euclidean\_Distance(v, (x, y)_d) - r_s$
   │ **if** $r_d > r_{min}$ **then**
   │ └ Detector Set $D \leftarrow D \cap \{(x, y)_d, r_d\}$

---

an anomaly and therefore a false alarm (the same applies to TN and FN, while N stands for Negative, i.e. benign instances).

Results of the ASTC Algorithm on the ANS Dataset. Using the validation process presented in Sect. 3.6, the ASTC algorithm was tested on the ANS dataset (see Sect. 3.1), with no distinction made between the respective hazards (i.e., all four are generally simply considered as *anomalies*). In the shown results Table 1, the *dim*-header row represents the input dimensions to the ASTC algorithm, i.e. the number of selected features of the original ANS dataset.

What stands out in the results is the dataset-complexity-dependent resulting strongly increasing number of detectors, indicated in row $|d|$. This factor is eventually also the one that makes an application of the ASTC algorithm in 7 or more dimensions infeasible, since this causes a significant memory limitation in the determination of DT. Assuming a similar growth as for the previous dimensions, a detector count between $600,000$ and the upper bound of 1 million, defined as $\lim |d| = n^{\lfloor d/2 \rfloor}$ [28], would be expected for the 7th dimension with 100 training samples. To counteract this effect, the number of training self-instances was reduced starting from the 5th dimension, see row n_{train}. But even a reduction to 100 instances did not lead to any result in the 7th dimension (the computer used for this test series has 32 GB RAM). Likewise, the number of slivers, i.e. the failed generation of simplices, increases with an increasing number of simplices, i.e. resulting detectors.

However, with the goal in mind to keep the F_1-score above 90% it was not possible to achieve a DR above 90%. It should be mentioned that the balance between DR and FPR can be controlled to some extent by the self-radius and the min-radius, where the self-radius indicates a tolerance region around the

---

Algorithm 2: Pseudocode of the detection mechanism

Input: Candidate Instance c, Detectors $d \in D$, Boundary Points $b \in B$

1 **foreach** *Dimension dim* **do**
  if $c[dim] < \min(b[dim])$ **or** $c[dim] > \max(b[dim])$ **then**
    Output: *anomaly*

3 **foreach** d **do**
  Verify if c is within range of d:
  $dist_{d,c} = Euclidean\_Distance(d, c)$
  if $dist_{d,c} < d_{radius}$ **then**
    Output: *anomaly*

Output: *benign*

---

training samples to be considered as benign and the min-radius indicates the minimum radius of the generated detectors, thus controlling how many detectors are generated in-between the self-samples. However, the FPR of this algorithm yielded very good results. Due to the shown limitation, it is consequently also not possible to use the complementary delta features and thus to map the temporal dependency that would possibly benefit the DR.

Another disadvantage stemming from the complexity of the dataset is the slow detection time, which directly correlates with the number of detectors. A sample, especially a non-anomaly sample, has to pass through all detectors one by one and has to be checked for a match. The more detectors there are the more time this process takes.

3.5 Proposed Models with Dimensionality Reduction

Since, as shown in the previous section, the ASTC algorithm is subject to certain limitations, especially concerning the complexity of the data set, two models were created that address this problem and potentially allow an application of the ASTC on the given data set. Both of these models still employ the ASTC algorithm for detector generation, but they are each supplemented by another method applied during the respective pre-processing in order to reduce the complexity of the dataset:

"ASTC + PCA". In this model, the ASTC is complemented by a dimensionality reduction by applying *Principal Component Analysis* (PCA) [29] and is performed before the Delaunay tessellation. In a strict sense however, PCA is rather a data-transformation technique than a method for dimensionality reduction, where the data is projected onto a new basis set. Thereby, the goal of PCA is to compute the most meaningful basis to filter out noise and reveal hidden structures. For this purpose it uses the eigenvectors and eigenvalues to form new axes, each consisting of linear combinations of the original features, the so-called

Table 1. Results on the ANS dataset

Model	dim:	Original ANS dataset						+ Δ	
		2	3	4	5	6	7	8 (4)	9 (4)
ASTC	$DR_⊘$	85.65	83.17	82.26	81.05	88.05			
	$FPR_⊘$	0.90	0.08	0.10	0.43	1.01			
	F_1	91.83	90.77	90.22	89.32	93.14			
	n_{train}	600	600	600	300	300	Not feasible under		
	n_{sliver}	0	0	12	109	1,281	available resources		
	$\lvert d \rvert$	93	1,586	8,112	22,281	132,272			
	t_{train}	1.32	4.03	13.88	27.18	272.80			
	t_{detect}	0.0006	0.01	0.05	0.16	0.78			

Legend	DR	100%–92%		92%–84%		84%–76%		<76%	
	FPR	0%–2%		2%–4%		4%–6%		>6%	

F_1 The harmonic mean between *recall* ($= DR$) and *precision*, which stands for the fraction of true positives among all samples classified as positive. This score allows better comparability of results without having to decide between higher DR or lower FPR.

$DR_⊘$ Since the validation uses a k-fold cross-validation, results are generated per split in each case, $DR_⊘$ indicates the mean of the DR over all splits.

$FPR_⊘$ The same applies to the evaluation of the FPR, here the individual measured values are also averaged.

$\lvert d \rvert$ Indicates the average number of generated detectors.

n_{train} Denotes the number of benign instances used for the training of the model.

n_{sliver} Denotes the number of failed detector generations.

t_{train} Denotes the average training time in seconds of the complete detector generation. This and the following time measurement was collected by enclosing the code section containing the actual function by two time points; thereafter the mean value was calculated over the difference, depending on the number of processed samples.

t_{detect} Denotes the average detection time in seconds per observed sample.

Principal Components (PCs). These new PCs are sorted by the magnitude of variance they account for, which allows the actual dimension dimensionality by utilizing only the first r PCs.

This model can lead on the one hand to a potentially better description of the data through projecting it to another basis set and reduces the data's complexity by projecting it to a lower dimension if necessary.

"ASTC + AE". In the second model, an Autoencoder (AE) [24] is employed for the task of dimensionality reduction. An AE is a special manifestation of neural networks, which basically consists of an input and an output layer, each containing the same number of nodes, and at least one hidden layer with significantly fewer nodes. The task of the AE is to learn a corresponding representation in the so-called *latent space* for given inputs and to restore the original data on the output layer with as little loss of information as possible. In the course of training, this network develops new relevant features that represent the input in a compressed way. If an AE is to be used for dimensionality reduction, the decoding layers of the model are discarded after training and only the encoding part is used to map new data to the corresponding latent features.

The AE used in this model is trained in 100 epochs each, using the so-called Scaled Exponential Linear Unit [20] or SELU for short as the level-wise activation function. The reason for choosing the SELU function stems from the fact that none of the latent features may have a 0 value, otherwise the Delaunay tessellation is not possible.

Unlike the PCA approach, which is based on linear combinations, an AE works out non-linear relationships by using the activation functions, which potentially allows this model to be superior to the other approaches in terms of performance. Unfortunately, however, this model comes with a disadvantage in advance in terms of training time, because this model requires a separate training for the so-called hyperparameters of the AE network.

These models exclusively use the defined benign-states to perform the dimensionality reduction. The hope is that potential anomalies will find a mapping in the new feature space in the same way. However, it cannot be excluded that the dimension reduction may mask certain anomalies, e.g. a coefficient in a PCA reduction may suppress a significant feature of a new anomaly. This constitutes a further research question and needs to be investigated in the future.

3.6   Evaluation

Evaluation Process. The test setup for the evaluation of the proposed models is as shown in Fig. 5. (a) First the respective delta-values are calculated and added to the dataset. In order to obtain a meaningful result, a k-fold cross-validation with 10 splices (b) is used. However, since only the benign data are used for the training of the system, only these are split. The respective slice is used to calculate the extreme values (c), which are used for normalization. With the training and test data available as feature vectors in the value range between 0 and 1, these are now processed according to the respective model (d). Afterwards, the boundary values are added (e) and the ASTC algorithm is applied to generate the detectors (f), which are finally used to classify new samples (g).

Results on the ANS Dataset. In the results of these test series in Table 2, please note that the dim-header row now has a different meaning; since these models perform a dimension reduction, they were always fed with the full number of features (7), the dimension specified in the header in this case refers to the output dimension. A direct comparison with the pure ASTC model is therefore not viable.

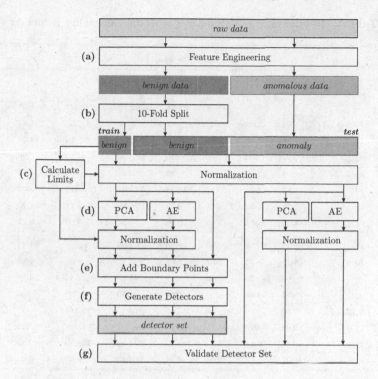

Fig. 5. Outline of the evaluation process (authors own illustration)

As with the previous test series, an F_1-score of 90% and above was targeted. However, it can be clearly seen that the DR is significantly improved compared to the pure ASTC model (maximum value was 88.05%). The FPR, on the other hand, seems to be inferior to the predecessor in these models. This seems to depend strongly on the training instances used. As the number of training instances decreases, the FPR increases, which is not surprising since the detectors gain less information about the self-set when it is described by fewer points. However, these were again adapted so that it was still possible to use higher complexities of the dataset, which was also successful in this case. Even if only with 50 training instances and a relatively high FPR, it was possible to use the 7th dimension in both models.

Influence of Number of Training Instances. What is remarkable is that the reduction of the training inputs, in order to address the memory limitation, i.e. the reduction of information about the self-area itself does not have a clearly negative effect on the recognizability and the DR, respectively. This can be explained by the fact that randomly selected samples mainly fall within the boundary of the self-area and the outer edge is thus little influenced. In addition, the method of DT leads to a generalization which can fill the holes between the samples and to an approximation of the outer edge which can also tolerate the

Table 2. Results on the ANS dataset with dimensionality reduction

Model	dim:	Original ANS dataset						+ Δ	
		2	3	4	5	6	7	8 (4)	9 (4)
ASTC	$DR_\oslash$	83.51	88.68	90.76	89.64	89.53	98.47	91.31	96.00
+	$FPR_\oslash$	1.50	3.26	3.01	3.12	3.98	8.50	1.87	1.49
PCA	F_1	90.28	92.40	93.67	93.00	92.53	95.15	94.53	97.22
	n_{train}	300	300	300	150	150	50	300	300
	n_{sliver}	0	0	11	99	1,121	10,393	9	9
	$|d|$	83	1,043	6,791	13,136	74,494	120,315	3,666	3,522
	t_{train}	0.32	1.00	4.22	9.32	96.86	342.14	3.75	3.94
	t_{detect}	0.0002	0.003	0.02	0.06	0.34	0.60	0.02	0.01
ASTC	$DR_\oslash$	77.10	85.56	92.85	94.70	94.05	92.85	91.46	95.94
+	$FPR_\oslash$	0.42	1.75	3.67	2.00	3.17	8.00	1.93	2.02
AE	F_1	86.86	91.36	94.49	96.29	95.38	92.46	94.58	96.93
	n_{train}	600	600	300	300	150	50	300	300
	n_{sliver}	0	0	2	66	1,913	23,348	7	9
	$|d|$	109	2,999	5,120	26,787	69,365	174,237	4,416	4,048
	t_{train}	17.75	16.68	14.34	42.69	123.32	528.18	12.20	12.38
	t_{detect}	0.0007	0.01	0.04	0.21	0.42	0.93	0.03	0.03
Legend	DR	100%–92%		92%–84%		84%–76%		<76%	
	FPR	0%–2%		2%–4%		4%–6%		>6%	

omission of individual points. However, as seen in the 7th column in Table 2, if the value falls below a certain level, the FPR increases rapidly.

Addition of Delta-Values (Δ). Since both models are able to reduce the dimensions, the additional delta features could be added. Where column 8 in Table 2 shows the delta to the direct predecessor and column 9 additionally shows the average delta over 10 predecessors. Again, the model was fed with the 8 and 9 features respectively, but then reduced to 4 output dimensions. Adding this temporal component resulted in improved performance in both models in terms of detection rate and reduction in FPR. In both models, the 9th column in Table 2 yielded their top results.

PCA vs. AE. The non-linear combination of features by using an AE does not show apparent advantages in terms of the achieved DR or FPR. Furthermore, another factor, namely that of the longer training time, even clearly speaks against the use of an AE. The model that uses PCA to reduce the complexity of the data on the other hand, delivers similar good results in detection whilst showing an improvement of the training time compared even to the pure ASTC algorithm and is therefore the preferred model.

A major disadvantage of any NSA in general (concerns the pure ASTC approach as well as both augmented models) is the long detection time compared to other machine learning algorithms. These usually need a much longer training time, but are mostly linear when evaluating new samples. For example, an AE that identifies anomalies based on a threshold on reconstruction errors requires a long time to calculate the corresponding weights of the node connections, whereas the detection itself corresponds to a single calculation. However, as stated before, in the case of an NSA approach, in the worst case, which is unfortunately also the case in which a *non-anomaly* (i.e. a benign instance) is tested, they have to iterate through the entire detector set by the NSA detection method and have to calculate the multidimensional Euclidean distance for each of these detectors.

Results on the Iris Dataset. Since the ANS dataset is not a publicly available dataset, additional test series were performed on the Iris[3] dataset. Since this is a dataset consisting of 3 classes traditionally used for an evaluation of classification problems, one of the classes was considered benign and the others were considered anomalies. Likewise, the dataset was also used by other papers allowing comparability with similar approaches (e.g., ASTC).

In general, the DRs are similar to those of the comparison work shown in Table 3. It is noticeable, however, that the methods used in this paper, show a higher FPR and the resulting number of detectors are much higher compared to the other works. It must be noted, that it is not apparent how it would be possible to achieve, for instance a DR of almost 100% whilst having no false positives with only 8 detectors as the ANSA model seems to do. The results

Table 3. Comparable results from other work on the Iris dataset (the results shown were taken directly from the original papers)

benign:	Setosa [0]			Versicolour [1]			Viginica [2]		
Model [*Reference*]	DR	FPR	$|d|$	DR	FPR	$|d|$	DR	FPR	$|d|$
ASTC (original) [7]	100	12	–	90	0	–	94	36	–
HNIS [12]	100	0	–	88	2	–	95	2	–
FB-NSA (m = 6) [22]	100	0	83	92	0	299	94	0	207
FFB-NSA (3–6) [22]	100	0	20	91	0	117	91	0	62
iCSA [8]	100	0.36	–	93.91	0.31	–	95	0.07	–
ANSA [18]	99.56	0	8	89.98	0	41	93.23	0	32
MPSO-DENSA [23]	98.21	7.21	12	99.98	4.16	9	98.88	3.68	11
ASTC	100	6.00	488	94.55	10.00	621	94.70	14.00	695
ASTC+PCA	100	0	403	91.92	8.00	492	90.40	8.00	508
ASTC+AE	100	8.00	551	89.60	6.00	426	93.60	6.00	495

---

[3] Available at: https://archive.ics.uci.edu/ml/datasets/Iris [9].

were directly taken from the original publications. However, during reading the publications, the authors sometimes omit information on how the models were trained and tested. This comparison allows therefore only a rough assessment and shows that our approach is of the same magnitude.

4 Conclusion

This paper proposed an immune-inspired anomaly detection approach for CPS. The artificial immune system approach references the principles from the natural immune system. In our paper, we investigated the ASTC algorithm for its applicability to CPS. Our initial analysis showed that the ASTC algorithm shows potential in terms of computability but shows bottlenecks when it comes to increasing number of selfs and the complexity of the dataset. Therefore, in our approach we introduced two models that deal with dimensionality reduction. We evaluate the models using a CPS dataset but also the public iris data set. Both models show high potential to address the complexity of the dataset for NSA approaches, whereas the model extended by PCA is the preferred one due to its better runtime and its overall better performance, yielding a DR of 96% while having a FPR of only 1.5%. This can potentially be further improved by using the detection processing in a distributed fashion and represents the basis for future work. Furthermore, an operational anomaly detection system for CPS can be developed from this basic model.

References

1. Busquim E Silva, R.A., Shirvan, K., Piqueira, J.R.C., Marques, R.P.: Development of the Asherah nuclear power plant simulator for cyber security assessment. In: International Conference on Nuclear Security (ICONS), Vienna, Austria, February 2020
2. Chen, W., Liu, X.J., Li, T., Shi, Y.Q., Zheng, X.F., Zhao, H.: A negative selection algorithm based on hierarchical clustering of self set and its application in anomaly detection. Int. J. Comput. Intell. Syst. **4**(4), 410–419 (2011)
3. Chollet, F., et al.: Keras (2015). https://keras.io
4. Cross, S.S., Harrison, R.F., Kennedy, R.L.: Introduction to neural networks. The Lancet **346**(8982), 1075–1079 (1995)
5. Dasgupta, D., Attoh-Okine, N.A.: Immunity-based systems: a survey. In: 1997 IEEE International Conference on Systems, Man, and Cybernetics. Computational Cybernetics and Simulation, vol. 1, pp. 369–374 (1997). https://doi.org/10.1109/ICSMC.1997.625778
6. Dasgupta, D., Forrest, S.: An anomaly entection algorithm inspired by the immune syste. In: Dasgupta, D. (ed.) Artificial Immune Systems and Their Applications, pp. 262–277. Springer, Heidelberg (1999). https://doi.org/10.1007/978-3-642-59901-9_14
7. Fan, Z., Wen, C., Tao, L., Xiaochun, C., Haipeng, P.: An antigen space triangulation coverage based real-value negative selection algorithm. IEEE Access **7**, 51886–51898 (2019)

8. Fang, X., Li, L.: An improved artificial immune approach to network intrusion detection. In: 2010 2nd International Conference on Advanced Computer Control, vol. 2, pp. 39–44. IEEE (2010)
9. Fisher, R.A.: The use of multiple measurements in taxonomic problems. Ann. Eugenics **7**(2), 179–188 (1936)
10. Forrest, S., Perelson, A.S., Allen, L., Cherukuri, R.: Self-nonself discrimination in a computer. In: Proceedings of 1994 IEEE Computer Society Symposium on Research in Security and Privacy, pp. 202–212. IEEE (1994)
11. Goldberg, D.E.: The genetic algorithm approach: why, how, and what next? In: Narendra, K.S. (ed.) Adaptive and Learning Systems, pp. 247–253. Springer, Boston (1986). https://doi.org/10.1007/978-1-4757-1895-9_17
12. González, F., Dasgupta, D.: A study of artificial immune systems applied to anomaly detection. Ph.D. thesis, University of Memphis Memphis (2003)
13. Greensmith, J., Whitbrook, A., Aickelin, U.: Artificial immune systems. In: Gendreau, M., Potvin, J.Y. (eds.) Handbook of Metaheuristics. ISOR, vol. 146, pp. 421–448. Springer, Boston (2010). https://doi.org/10.1007/978-1-4419-1665-5_14
14. Guo, J., Liu, G., Zuo, Y., Wu, J.: An anomaly detection framework based on autoencoder and nearest neighbor. In: 2018 15th International Conference on Service Systems and Service Management (ICSSSM), pp. 1–6. IEEE (2018)
15. Hofmeyr, S.A.: An interpretative introduction to the immune system. In: Design Principles for the Immune System and Other Distributed Autonomous Systems, vol. 3, pp. 28–36 (2000)
16. Ji, Z., Dasgupta, D.: Real-valued negative selection algorithm with variable-sized detectors. In: Deb, K. (ed.) GECCO 2004. LNCS, vol. 3102, pp. 287–298. Springer, Heidelberg (2004). https://doi.org/10.1007/978-3-540-24854-5_30
17. Ji, Z., Dasgupta, D.: Revisiting negative selection algorithms. Evol. Comput. **15**(2), 223–251 (2007)
18. Jinquan, Z., Xiaojie, L., Tao, L., Caiming, L., Lingxi, P., Feixian, S.: A self-adaptive negative selection algorithm used for anomaly detection. Prog. Nat. Sci. **19**(2), 261–266 (2009)
19. Kim, J., Bentley, P.J., Aickelin, U., Greensmith, J., Tedesco, G., Twycross, J.: Immune system approaches to intrusion detection-a review. Nat. Comput. **6**(4), 413–466 (2007). https://doi.org/10.1007/s11047-006-9026-4
20. Klambauer, G., Unterthiner, T., Mayr, A., Hochreiter, S.: Self-normalizing neural networks (2017)
21. Kluyver, T., et al.: Jupyter Notebooks? a publishing format for reproducible computational workflows. In: Loizides, F., Scmidt, B. (eds.) Positioning and Power in Academic Publishing: Players, Agents and Agendas, pp. 87–90. IOS Press (2016). https://eprints.soton.ac.uk/403913/
22. Li, D., Liu, S., Zhang, H.: Negative selection algorithm with constant detectors for anomaly detection. Appl. Soft Comput. **36**, 618–632 (2015)
23. Nemati, L., Shakeri, M.: Negative selection based data classification with flexible boundaries. J. Comput. Robot. **11**(2), 69–85 (2018)
24. Ng, A., et al.: UFLDL tutorial (2013). http://ufldl.stanford.edu/tutorial. Accessed 12 Apr 2021
25. Nuclear Energy Institute (NEI): Digital: The new word in nuclear power plant control rooms (2016). https://electricenergyonline.com/article/energy/category/generation/52/583260/digital-the-new-word-in-nuclear-power-plant-control-rooms.html. Accessed 21 Mar 2021
26. Pedregosa, F., et al.: Scikit-learn: machine learning in Python. J. Mach. Learn. Res. **12**(85), 2825–2830 (2011). http://jmlr.org/papers/v12/pedregosa11a.html

27. Rowland, M.T., Busquim e Silva, R.A.: Enhancing computer security incident analysis at nuclear facilities (2015). https://www.iaea.org/projects/crp/j02008. Accessed 23 Mar 2021
28. Seidel, R.: The upper bound theorem for polytopes: an easy proof of its asymptotic version. Comput. Geom. **5**(2), 115–116 (1995). https://doi.org/10.1016/0925-7721(95)00013-Y
29. Shlens, J.: A tutorial on principal component analysis. Computing Research Repository (CoRR) abs/1404.1100 (2014). http://arxiv.org/abs/1404.1100
30. Slowik, J.: Evolution of ICS attacks and the prospects for future disruptive events, February 2019. https://www.dragos.com/resource/evolution-of-ics-attacks-and-the-prospects-for-future-disruptive-events/. Accessed 22 Mar 2021
31. Stibor, T.: On the appropriateness of negative selection for anomaly detection and network intrusion detection. Ph.D. thesis, Technische Universität Darmstadt (2006)
32. Stibor, T., Bayarou, K.M., Eckert, C.: An investigation of R-chunk detector generation on higher alphabets. In: Deb, K. (ed.) GECCO 2004. LNCS, vol. 3102, pp. 299–307. Springer, Heidelberg (2004). https://doi.org/10.1007/978-3-540-24854-5_31
33. U.S. Nuclear Regulatory Commission: 1979 annual report (1979). https://tmi2kml.inl.gov/Documents/4e-NRC-Annual/1979%20NRC%20Annual%20Report%20(NUREG-0690).pdf. Accessed 23 Mar 2021
34. Virtanen, P., et al.: SciPy 1.0: fundamental algorithms for scientific computing in Python. Nat. Methods **17**, 261–272 (2020). https://doi.org/10.1038/s41592-019-0686-2
35. Yang, C., Jia, L., Chen, B.Q., Wen, H.Y.: Negative selection algorithm based on antigen density clustering. IEEE Access **8**, 44967–44975 (2020)
36. Zhang, R., Li, T., Xiao, X.: A real-valued negative selection algorithm based on grid for anomaly detection. In: Abstract and Applied Analysis, vol. 2013. Hindawi (2013)

RQ Labs: A Cybersecurity Workforce Talent Program Design

Clinton Daniel(✉), Matthew Mullarkey, and Manish Agrawal

School of Information Systems and Management, University of South Florida,
Tampa, FL 33594, USA
{cedanie2,mmullarkey,magrawal}@usf.edu

Abstract. This research contributes to the knowledge of how Information Systems (IS) researchers can iteratively intervene with practitioners to co-create instructional programs for fast-paced, rapidly changing IS fields such as cybersecurity. We demonstrate how complex fields such as cybersecurity have the need for a talented workforce which continues to rapidly outpace supply from Universities. IS researchers partnering with practitioners can use this research as an exemplar of a method to design, build and evaluate these innovative co-curricular IS programs.

Keywords: Cybersecurity workforce · Program design · Elaborated Action Design Research

1 Introduction

Cybersecurity workforce talent shortage is a global problem that is being studied by academia, practice, and government [8]. The growth and complexity of emerging technologies and cyber threats motivates the demands of a capable cybersecurity workforce. On October 2nd of 2018 the CEO of the cybersecurity firm Reliaquest (RQ)[1], Brian Murphy, committed $1 million to the University of South Florida (USF) for the purpose of preparing students for careers in cybersecurity. Murphy's motivation was clear in his statement, *"In the face of what the industry refers to as a talent shortage, we believe that cybersecurity is actually suffering from a skills shortage"* [17].

Along with the financial contribution from RQ, additional commitments were made by both USF faculty and RQ technical staff to co-create a training program called "RQ Labs" that would continuously operate over a 5-year period. This co-created program would offer USF researchers with a unique opportunity to answer the following research question:

How can a cybersecurity workforce talent training program be co-created as an industry-university partnership which will effectively generate an instructional product that rapidly adds value to a cybersecurity practitioner firm and to a University student?

---

[1] Reliaquest: https://www.reliaquest.com/, website accessed on 8/19/2021.

© Springer Nature Switzerland AG 2022
R. Krishnan et al. (Eds.): SKM 2021, CCIS 1549, pp. 171–185, 2022.
https://doi.org/10.1007/978-3-030-97532-6_10

Value-added contributions of the program to the cybersecurity firm and under-graduate or graduate University student would include measurable outcomes such as:

- Increased number of part-time or full-time hires in a security operations center
- Curricular changes in internal cybersecurity firm training practices
- Employable cybersecurity skills to graduating University undergraduate and graduate students

These measurable outcomes would not only define the measurable success of the cybersecurity training program, but further motivate the evolution of its program design and implementation.

2   Motivation

Government agencies, private firms, and academic institutions have been motivated to study the challenges associated with the problem domain of cybersecurity workforce shortage [1]. There is a significant amount of evidence that has been collected which indicates that a cybersecurity workforce talent shortage problem exists across multiple domains and technologies. It has been argued within government, academic, and practical journals that cybersecurity education initiatives are a critical solution to this problem domain. Specifically, extensive research projects have been motivated to understand what type of cybersecurity instructional program can be designed and implemented to effectively address the cybersecurity workforce skills shortage. Additionally, researchers agree that the effectiveness of the program design and implementation must be measurable and capable of dynamically adjusting to the current demands of the practical applications observed in cybersecurity [2].

Initiatives, such as the National Initiative for Cybersecurity Education (NICE) and the National Centers of Academic Excellence (CAE), have been established to form partnerships between government, academia, and private firms for the support of standards and best practices within cybersecurity training, education, and workforce development [5]. These initiatives have had a significant impact on educational program development by establishing a set of criteria based on the concept of a knowledge unit (KU). These KUs consist of knowledge groupings which identify skills in specific cybersecurity topics. Although academic programs can use these standards-based approaches to design a training program, Conklin et al. cites that "*industry wants workers to arrive ready to work day one, on their equipment, configured as they have configured it, and able to immediately add to the team strength*". Therefore, structured guidance from initiatives such as NICE and CAE provide an excellent foundation for high level program design theory, knowledge, and skills required for the cyber-security workforce. However, the depth of the knowledge and skills delivered by an educational program will require a closer engagement of knowledge exchange and guidance from a practicing cybersecurity firm.

Some researchers have reported that depth of cybersecurity knowledge and practical skill with an educational program can be achieved through a "*stackable curriculum*"

[13]. A stackable curriculum allows students to *"earn shorter-term credentials with clear labor market value and then build on them to access more advanced jobs and higher wages"*. This can be achieved through offering students' programs which promote industry recognized certifications in cybersecurity. Additionally, Katz reports that education programs can promote depth in practical knowledge by having students participate in hands-on cybersecurity competitions. These competitions allow the student to independently apply what they have learned in the classroom to a challenging practical scenario. Our research on the results of our academic approach to incorporate both stackable curriculum and promote participation in cybersecurity competitions identified a persistent, significant gap in the students' knowledge and skills required for success in hiring in a typical cybersecurity firm. Consequently, we chose to engage with a leading cybersecurity firm to build and evaluate an extra-curricular cybersecurity instructional program that could address our research question.

Our research describes a cybersecurity training program design which has been co-created with a team of practicing experts from a cybersecurity firm, RQ, and academic researchers from USF. RQ is motivated to collaborate with USF academic researchers to co-create and co-deliver a cybersecurity training program that integrates the body of theoretical and standards-based knowledge with the proprietary knowledge and operating environment of a partner firm to address the cybersecurity workforce shortage class of problem. We conduct our research using the paradigm of Design Science Research (DSR) [10–12] and focus on the design, build and evaluation of an innovative artifact in the form of a cybersecurity training program targeted at employing students in a Security Operations Center (SOC). We approach the primary research effort through a series of iterative interventions as detailed in the elaborated Action Design Research (eADR) methodology [18].

3 Literature Review

The principle goal of our literature review is to identify specific cybersecurity program curriculum and designs which have been implemented to address the problem domain of cybersecurity workforce skills shortage. We conducted a comprehensive search for academic and practical research articles across multiple disciplines and databases which describe how cybersecurity education programs are designed and what motivates their curriculum. Upon review of 36 articles that met our search criteria, we selected 15 published between 2013 and 2019 which align closely with the problem domain.

In general, many cybersecurity training programs consider standards and best practices promoted by the National Initiative for Cybersecurity Education (NICE), led by the National Institute of Standards and Technology (NIST), when determining a curriculum which could address the current and future cybersecurity challenges [1]. The NICE publishes the National Cybersecurity Workforce Framework (NCWF) as a guide for cybersecurity training program development. The framework organizes specialty areas of cybersecurity into groups that identify specific knowledge, skills, and abilities (KSAs) needed to fulfill workforce roles.

In addition to the NICE initiative, the literature supports the use of the National Security Agency (NSA) Centers of Academic Excellence (CAE) program to promote higher education and research in cyber defense and operations [5]. The application of the CAE can often be observed within academic programs which align accredited Information Systems (IS) core curriculum objectives with requirement demands from those firms hiring the graduating students. Hence, there is a trend among IS education programs in higher level institutions to manipulate their curriculum content so that it aligns with the demands of operational activities conducted within cybersecurity firms.

Another approach argued within the literature for cybersecurity program design considers *"organizations in which hiring personnel and technical leads are communicating well and understand the complex nature of the cybersecurity field will be in the best position to identify talent with the correct qualifications"* [16]. This collaborative combination of cybersecurity practitioners along with formal education programs is considered critical to the success and sustainability of cybersecurity program design and implementation. The complete summary of our literature review is documented in Table 1.

Table 1. Summary of literature identifying cybersecurity education program designs and curriculum implementation approaches

Author (s)	Education program design	Program curriculum	Year
Murphy et al. [19]	Core cybersecurity concept; Minimum of five optional knowledge units	Supply Chain security knowledge	2013
Manson et al. [15]	NIST National Cybersecurity Workforce Framework	Cybersecurity team competitions through real-world simulations	2014
Conklin et al. [5]	Align an accredited core Information Systems program objectives with hiring firm's requirements; Use NSA curriculum based model	NSA Knowledge Units (KU)	2014
McDuffie et al. [16]	Collaborative communication between hiring personal and cybersecurity technical leads with formal education programs	Standards and best practices promoted by the National Initiative for Cybersecurity Education (NICE)	2014
Endicott-Popovsky et al. [7]	Kuzmina-Bespalko-Popovsky (KBP) Pedagogical model	Economic and political environments; Constantly evolving set of threats, vulnerabilities, and operational systems	2014
Caulkins et al. [4]	Pilot education program designed to address unique challenges of human dimension in cybersecurity	Multidisciplinary approach; Operations; Behavioral; Emerging issues; Research methods and practicum	2016

(continued)

Table 1. (*continued*)

Author (s)	Education program design	Program curriculum	Year
Spidalieri et al. [21]	NSA and DHS National Center of Academic Excellent (CAE), Cyber Defense Research (CAE-R), and Intelligence Community Center of Academic Excellence (IAE)	Extend cyber-related coursework for both technical and non-technical career paths; Extracurricular activities with hands-on experience; cybersecurity-related internships	2016
Beuran et al. [2]	A framework automatically defines the training content and instantiates a cyber range that corresponds to the given activity	Dynamic based on framework; Considers: Training Specification, Content Definition, and Cyber Range Specification	2016
Baker [1]	Computer Emergency Response Team (CERT) appoach to cybersecurity workforce development	Knowledge building; Skill building; Experience building; Evaluation	2016
Tang et al. [23]	Automated hands-on training using a test environment that mimics vulnerabilities and cyber attacks	Vulnerability database; Exploit database; Instantiation database; automated cyber attacks	2017
Knapp et al. [14]	Certification marketplace used to maintain industry relevancy and guide specialized curriculum	Standard knowledge courses specified by various cybersecurity educational frameworks; Specialized courses are driven by industry certifications	2017
Dill [6]	Establish a Civil Cyber Force (CCF), modeled after the Civil Air Patrol, that would include youth members who are mentored by adults; Youth attend year-round programs that test leadership, technology, and fitness	NSA outreach to STEM programs employed throughout the public school system and their National Centers of Academic Excellent in Cybersecurity serve as the foundation for curriculum development	2018

(continued)

Table 1. (*continued*)

Author (s)	Education program design	Program curriculum	Year
Cabaj et al. [3]	Masters programs that were evaluated in this study demonstrate updates with curriculum content and available courses are aligned with available faculty and expertise	Core cybersecurity knowledge is universal and suitable for any geography; Some special topics	2018
Katz [13]	Stackable curriculum which allows students to earn shorter-term credentials with clear labor market value and then build on them to access more advanced jobs and higher wages; Courses are mapped to NSA-CAE Knowledge Units	Integrates the pillars of people, process, and technology; Labs, Case Studies, exercises, and role-playing scenarios involving non-technical aspects of the discipline;	2018
Gonzalez-Manzano et al. [9]	Recommends topic choice, level choices, teachers commitment, gender adaptation, regional adaptation, interaction design, age impact, suitability of content design, activities review, students video commitment	All 35 programs analyzed included a mixture of curriculum based on the NICE (National Initiative for Cybersecurity Education) framework	2019
Cyber2yr2020 Task Group [22]	Task force developed used Cybersecurity Curricular Guidelines (CSEC2017), NSA-CAE knowledge units, and NICE Cybersecurity Workforce Framework	Associate Degree Programs; Security concepts in Data, Software, Components, Connections, Systems, Humans, Organizational, and Societal	2020
Ward [24]	Uses Action Design Research (ADR) to add Organizational Context with an Institutional Advisory Board	Learning approaches include role-based, challenge-based, scenario-based, and inquiry-based	2021

Overall, the articles reviewed did not present evidence of an instance where a practicing cybersecurity firm was actively involved in co-creating a cybersecurity education program with an academic institution. However, recently researchers have recognized that industry can advise the design of a cybersecurity workforce development program. Additionally, the literature did not reveal a single research study which documented a program design where the practicing firm is motivated to hire the students into a Security Operations Center upon successful completion of the training. Therefore, this gap within the current literature offers our research team with an opportunity to contribute new knowledge within the cybersecurity workforce talent shortage problem domain.

4 Program Design Methodology

The "RQ Labs" training program offered a co-creation engagement between USF research faculty and RQ staff. Throughout the development of the program, USF research faculty were embedded with RQ cybersecurity engineers and education specialists. This collaborative relationship between researcher and practitioner offered an opportunity for an Action Design Research (ADR) [20] project. ADR is a research method traditionally used to build an IT artifact through a guided, emergent in situ intervention build and evaluation process. In this research, we adapt the ADR methodology from the traditional use of creating an IT artifact to the creation of a cybersecurity training program. Specifically, we use an elaborated version of Action Design Research (eADR) [18] methodology to iteratively design and implement an innovative cybersecurity training program. The eADR methodology offers both researcher and practitioner an ADR process continuum using iterative diagnosing, design, implementation, and system evolution stages. Each iterative eADR cycle within a stage offers an opportunity for a researcher to formulate the problem (P), create an artifact (A), evaluate the artifact (E), reflect on the results of the evaluation (R), and learn from the reflection (L). An iterative eADR cycle can be used by a researcher to inform the diagnosis, design, implementation, or evolution stages of an ADR process.

Due to prior research of the problem domain during a faculty externship that confirmed the significant skills gap between graduated students and those of successful hires and consequential executive decisions by RQ to support an extra-curricular University activity, it was decided by the research team that an initial diagnosis stage was not required to begin the eADR process. RQ had firmly positioned the project to begin immediately designing the structure of the cybersecurity training program as a co-creation activity with University researchers. Therefore, the flexibility of the eADR process model allowed the researchers to begin their research by entering at the design stage of the ADR process. In the Fall of 2018, an eADR cycle was initialized to design a version 1 program structure which would be used for the first cohort of University students. Version 1 of the program structure was planned for implementation in late Fall of 2018. The program structure continued a 6-week cycle of implementation throughout the Fall of 2018. Upon completion of the first cycle, data was collected and evaluated to understand the pros and cons of the implemented structure. This 6-week cycle continued to iterate in future University semesters from 2018 to 2021. In each iteration, RQ practitioners intervened on the program structure and an evolution of the program was created in the form of Version n (see Fig. 1).

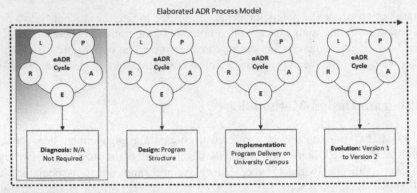

Fig. 1. Illustrates the interventions at each stage of the eADR method used to design the co-created cybersecurity training program. Adapted from [18]. Note: in the eADR cycle: P = Problem Formulation/Planning, A = Artifact Creation, E = Evaluation, R = Reflection, and L = Learning

5 Cybersecurity Workforce Talent Program Design

The eADR methodology used collaboratively between practitioner and researcher was instrumental in the development of a cybersecurity workforce talent training program called RQ Labs. RQ Labs can be described as a comprehensive cybersecurity training program implemented as an extra-curricular college student engagement which provides a solution to a class of problem within the cybersecurity workforce talent shortage domain. The RQ Labs program design is summarized in Table 2.

Table 2. RQ labs program design summary

Week	Activity	Description	Timing
1	Pre-Boot Camp	Introduce program purpose and general understanding of cybersecurity domain. Designed to filter out students who are not interested in cybersecurity training program	3 h
2	System Admin Boot Camp	Cybersecurity and networking Fundamentals	4 h
3	Attack Surface	Enterprise networking, security tools, data security, and kill chain	4 h
4	Anatomy of an Attack	Application Security	4 h
5	Detect, Response, & Mitigate	Incident Response Fundamentals	4 h
6	Capstone Assessment	Capstone Analysis using cyber investigation analysis methodologies	4 h

The summarized program design in Table 2 describes a training program that includes a total of 23 h of classroom instruction over a 6-week period of time. Each classroom instructional session includes individual hands-on activities, group activities, industry case studies, and mentoring sessions. In week 1 of the program design, approximately 100+ students from any major across the University are recruited through various communication channels to participate in a pre-boot camp. The pre-boot camp is designed to introduce any student to the cybersecurity domain. Pre-boot camp content includes cybersecurity terminology, the CIA (Confidentiality, Integrity, and Availability) triad, careers in cybersecurity, expectations of the program, and testimonies from RQ Security Operation Center analysts. Students are given an opportunity to participate in a question and answer session with the practicing analysts so that they have a complete understanding of what the cybersecurity workforce does on a daily basis.

Since the capacity of the RQ Labs Program in weeks 2 through 6 is limited to approximately 50 students per program iteration, students are offered an opportunity to compete for a slot or decline to move forward. If students would like to pursue the opportunity for the program, they are asked to complete an online general cybersecurity knowledge assessment and sign up for a behavioral interview. Students will compete for one of the available slots in weeks 2 through 6 through an initial behavioral interview conducted by a RQ human resource specialist team. In any given cycle, a human resource specialist team could conduct up to 80 or more interviews between weeks 1 and 2 of the program. The initial interviews are designed to select the best candidates from the students who elect to move forward in the program. The interviews are designed to get a general sense of the student's potential fitness in the cybersecurity workforce. At this stage, fitness is measured subjectively based on the student's responses to behavioral questions. Technical questions are not used within interviews at this stage.

Once the human resource team selects the student candidates for weeks 2 through 6, students are invited to an optional Systems Administration boot camp in week 2. This boot camp is designed for those students who do not have an extensive technical background in systems. Those that elect to participate in the week 2 Systems Administration boot camp are given hands-on classroom instruction using a Linux virtual machine by a University professor. The content covered in the Systems Administration boot camp includes Linux operating system and networking commands and concepts. Additionally, students are exposed to how the content is directly linked to the context of fundamental cybersecurity concepts such as application, data, and network security.

Weeks 3 through 6 of the RQ Labs program are designed to immerse the student in hands-on cybersecurity training that is focused on activities typically experienced by a practicing security operations center analyst. The training in weeks 3 through 6 is completely conducted by practicing RQ cybersecurity analysts and engineers with varying levels of experience.

In week 3, students are broken up into 5 groups of 10 students each. Each group is assigned 2 RQ cybersecurity practitioners which serve as direct mentors to all students in the group. Each mentor sets up a Slack channel using the Slack app on their mobile devices so that students can communicate questions in between weekly training sessions. The mentor's responsibility to is explain and reinforce all concepts covered in the content of the program each week to any student within their assigned group. Each week, during weeks 3 through 6, students are assigned homework activities on a Learning Management System (LMS) that are evaluated by their mentors for reinforced feedback. Furthermore, the mentors are incentivized with a reward from RQ if their group out performs all other groups in the program during the semester cycle. Performance of the mentor is directly measured by how many students within their group are converted to a full-time or part-time position upon completion of the program.

The content covered in week 3 of the program includes an understanding of the Attack Surface. To understand the Attack Surface, a student must gain competency in enterprise architecture to includes its networking and tools used to manage or evaluate its functionality. Students are instructed on how data flows through an enterprise and can be used as a means for motivating an attack. Finally, students are introduced to cases with scenarios that demonstrate the structure of an attack through a cyber kill chain. The cases are then reproduced in a custom virtual lab environment hosted in Amazon Web Services (AWS).

In week 4, students are introduced to the anatomy of an attack by examining security vulnerabilities experienced in various applications. Essential training in this week will include an introduction to exploits, web server security, and offensive security concepts. Students will then link the types of attacks to the parts of the attack surface which were covered in week 3. Additionally, various types of attacks, the attack lifecycle, and an understanding of threat actors is covered. These concepts are then reproduced as online hands-on labs within the AWS environment.

Week 5 content is designed to introduce the student how to detect, respond, and mitigate cybersecurity events which have been generated by a security information and event management (SIEM) system. Students are introduced to a cybersecurity investigation analysis methodology that helps to guide them through the analysis process. Initial iterations of the program used third-party SIEM and End Point Detection (EDR) tools hosted on AWS as learning mechanisms. However, recent iterations of the program now require students to learn on the RQ proprietary platform. Due to the design of the proprietary RQ platform, this evolution of the program was added to improve the likely success of the student's ability to implement the desired cybersecurity investigation analysis methodology.

Finally, week 6 of the program includes a comprehensive capstone assessment of the student. Program mentors assign cybersecurity event scenarios to students with simulated data based on prior RQ customer experiences. Students are expected to evaluate the cybersecurity event scenario using all of the tools and technologies exposed to them throughout the program. Upon completion of the analysis of the event, students submit a comprehensive report of their findings to their mentors for evaluation. Mentors then score the students level of success completing the comprehensive capstone assessment.

6   Evaluation of Program Design

Upon completion of each 6-week program iteration, data is collected to measure the value added to RQ and the University students. Value-based data is recorded for program evaluation at 8 different stages during and following the completion of a program iteration. Table 3 summarizes the data points captured at different stages of the program evaluation process.

Table 3. RQ labs evaluation 8-stage process

Stage	Evaluation description	Value measure description	Data	Metric
1	Completion of Week 1	General Cybersecurity Knowledge Assessment	Online cybersecurity baseline assessment quiz	Score
2	Completion of Week 1	Behavioral Interview	Verbal interview	Fit/Not Fit
3	Completion of Week 6	Final Capstone Assessment	Rubric based on capstone tasks	Score
4	Completion of Week 6	Technical Interview		Acceptable technical knowledge or Not
5	Personality Assessment Online	Personality type	Vendor assessment results	Personality type
6	Cultural/Behavioral Fit	Behavioral/Cultural Interview	Verbal interview	Cultural/Behavioral Fit/Not fit
7	Final Interview	Mixed Interview: Technical/Behavioral/Cultural	Verbal Interview	Full-time or Part-time Job Offer
8	Full-time or Part-time job offer	Verbal or written response	Verbal or written response	Students accepts offer or declines

Table 4 summarizes the data collected after completion of five program iterations. During each program iteration, a total count of students was collected as each University semester program iteration advanced to the next stage.

526 USF undergraduate and graduate students from various colleges were sampled to begin Stage 1 of the RQ Labs program. Prior to the design of this program, RQ had reported trivial success with USF undergraduate and graduate students passing the initial technical interview - essentially no students hired in prior four years. Upon completion of Week 1 in all program iterations, Stage 1 of the RQ Labs was completed and the total sample size had been reduced to 369 students. 157 of 369 students did not attempt to pursue a required effort to complete Stage 1 evaluation for advancement into Week 2 of the program. Upon completion of the Stage 2 evaluation process with all program iterations combined, RQ had selected 238 students to participate in Stage 3 of the RQ Labs program. During Stage 3, a minimal number of students quit the program for various reasons such as receiving other job offers, personal, or difficulty with the academic load.

Table 4. Number of students from # RQ labs program iterations

Stage	Fall 2018	Spring 2019	Fall 2019	Spring 2020	Spring 2021	Total
1	82	66	91	107	180	526
2	52	56	70	80	111	369
3	34	43	50	53	58	238
4	29	27	47	37	39	179
5 & 6	18	13	11	37	29	108
7	16	11	11	37	29	104
8	10	4	10	12	9	45

Upon completion of Stage 3, Stages 4 though 8 of the program evaluation process involve a progressive set of interviews by RQ staff. During Stage 4 evaluation, a total of 59 students were eliminated due to poor technical interview responses reducing the total number of students between all program iterations to 179. All students passing Stage 4 of the evaluation process were required to complete Stage 5 for a personality type classification. This was completed to better place them in teams if they pass the entire evaluation process. Upon completion of Stage 6 evaluation, 4 students were judged as being culturally unfit for RQ reducing the total number of students to 104. Finally, of the 104 students evaluated in Stage 7, 59 were eliminated due to lack of cultural/behavioral fit or lack of in-depth technical knowledge. The Stage 7 final interview was designed to revisit and elaborate further on questions asked in Stages 4 and 6. This left the final pool of students in Stage 8 with 45 part-time or full-time cybersecurity job offers by RQ.

Once the program evaluation process was completed, RQ practitioners collaborated with University researchers to make improvements in the program structure for the next iteration. This engagement resulted in continuous improvements of the program design. These program improvements were further used to modify the internal training processes of RQ employees.

7   Discussion and Conclusion

Upon evaluation of the data collected from two iterations of the RQ Labs program, we can observe that there is value added to the University student and cybersecurity firm. RQ benefited directly from adding 45 new cybersecurity employee hires, as a result of the program, to work in their security operations center. The remaining students who did not get hired by the cybersecurity firm directly benefited from the program by adding an employable skill to their resume. For instance, several students who did not get hired by RQ at the end of the program iteration were hired for a cyber security job in another firm. Additionally, RQ directly benefited from the program design by improving their own internal training practices and curriculum.

The following summarizes the improvements reported by RQ staff, undergraduate students, and University faculty based upon what was learned throughout the various evaluation stages.

RQ reports the following upon evaluation of the program design:

- Improved hiring efficiency
- Improved onboarding efficiency
- Community partnering demonstration for near-peer companies
- Impact on future University curriculum as the faculty re-integrate the lab curriculum

Students report the following upon evaluation of the program success:

- Practice knowledge gained
- Work-like product and work experience
- Opportunities for Certification
- Guaranteed job interview with a company hiring upon successful completion
- Opportunity to present to other near-peer companies hiring similar roles

Faculty report the following upon evaluation of the program success:

- Relationship engagement with a cybersecurity firm
- Growth in content with practitioner examples
- Innovative program structure and design
- Student preparation for roles
- Student satisfaction with program, department, college
- Student recruiting into the University of South Florida
- Research access to people, data, and innovative services and products

Finally, we suggest that the RQ Labs program provides a solution to a class of problem within the cyber security workforce talent shortage domain. Additionally, we suggest that the eADR methodology allows the flexibility to begin an innovative artifact creation research activity at any point of entry in the ADR process.

Although the artifact has addressed a well diagnosed and understood class of problems, more research is required to understand if this design can be implemented at other academic institutions with a similar opportunity for collaboration. The evolution of the RQ Labs program can and should continue through the Evolution stage of the eADR.

8   Contributions and Future Research Direction

In fast paced industries, such as this cybersecurity environment, it should not be surprising that standard University curriculum will not keep up and provide students with currency in the discipline and its requisite skill sets. In these cases, a collaborative co-creation with practitioners serves to ensure the content is relevant. To co-create in this environment, our research identifies an iterative guided emergent program design artifact, in or out of the traditional University curriculum, where an approach like the eADR can work well. The evaluation of the program design artifact thus developed must show benefit not only for the student and the faculty, but also for the partnering practitioner organization.

This research clearly addresses the research questions presented at the outset. The approach taken in this research also contributes to the knowledge of how IS researchers can iteratively intervene with practitioners to co-create instructional programs for fast-paced, rapidly changing IS fields – including cybersecurity, artificial intelligence, distributed ledger, virtual reality, social, mobile, and cloud. In each of these fields the need for skilled workers continues to rapidly outpace supply from Universities. IS researchers partnering with practitioners can use this research as an exemplar of a method to design, build and evaluate these innovative co-curricular IS artifacts.

We find that the iterative interventions within cycles also add to our knowledge of the distinct roles that can be played by faculty and practitioners in the co-create activities for these innovative IS artifacts. A methodology that embraces the co-creation design of Information Systems (IS) program curriculum between practitioners and academia is necessary to respond to rapidly changing problem domains such as cybersecurity workforce shortage. More research is needed to better understand how the eADR methodology can be used to motivate the future of IS curriculum design.

References

1. Baker, M.: Striving for Effective Cyber Workforce Development, pp. 1–26. Carnegie Mellon University, Software Engineering Institute (2016)
2. Beuran, R., Ken-ichi, C., Yasuo, T., Yoichi, S.: Towards effective cybersecurity education and training. Japan Advanced Institute of Science and Technology, School of Information Science. Japan Advanced Institute of Science and Technology (2016)
3. Cabaj, K., Domingos, D., Kotulski, Z., Respicio, A.: Cybersecurity education: evolution of the discipline and analysis of masters programs. Comput. Secur. **75**, 24–35 (2018)
4. Caulkins, B.D., Bockelman, P., Badillo-UXXuiola, K., Leis, R.: Cyber workforce development using a behavioral cybersecurity paradigm. In: 2016 International Conference on Cyber Conflict (CyCon U.S), pp. 21–23. IEEE, Washington, DC (2016),
5. Conklin, W.A., Cline, R.E., Roosa, T.: Re-engineering cybersecurity education in the US: an analysis of the critical factors. In: 47th Hawaii International Conference on System Science, pp. 2006–2014. IEEE Computer Society (2014)
6. Dill, K.J.: Cybersecurity for the nation: workforce development. Cyber Def. Rev. **3**(2), 55–64 (2018)
7. Endicott-Popovsky, B.E., Popovsky, V.M.: Application of pedagogical fundamentals for the holistic development of cybersecurity professionals. Cybersecur. Educ. **5**(1), 56–68 (2014)
8. Furnell, S.: The cybersecurity workforce and skills. Computers and Security, TC 11 Briefing Papers, vol. 100, pp. 1–7 (2021)
9. Gonzalez-Manzano, L., de Fuentes, J.M.: Design recommendations for online cybersecurity courses. Comput. Secur. **80**, 238–256 (2019)
10. Hevner, A.R.: Design science research. In: Tucker, A., Topi, H. (eds.) Computing Handbook, pp. 22-1–22-23, 3rd edn. Chapman and Hall/CRC, New York (2014)
11. Hevner, A.R., March, S.T., Park, J., Ram, S.: Design science in information systems. MIS Q. **28**, 75–105 (2004)
12. Hevner, A., Chatterjee, S.: Design research in information systems. In: Sharda, R., Vob, S. (eds.) Springer, New York (2010). https://doi.org/10.1007/978-1-4419-5653-8
13. Katz, F.H.: Breadth and depth: best practices teaching cybersecurity in a small public university sharing models. Cyber Def. Rev. **3**(2), 65–72 (2018)

14. Knapp, K.J., Maurer, C., Plachkinova, M.: Maintaining a cybersecurity curriculum: professional certifications as valuable guidance. J. Inf. Syst. Educ. **28**(2), 101–114 (2017)
15. Manson, D., Pike, R.: The case for depth in cybersecurity education. Cyber. Educ. **5**(1), 46–52 (2014)
16. McDuffie, E.L., Piotrowski, V.P.: The future of cybersecurity education. Comput. Educ. **47**(8), 67–69 (2014)
17. Morelli, K.: USF/Reliaquest partnership aims to fill the talent gap in the emerging cybersecurity field. USF Muma College of Business Newsroom Articles (2018). https://www.usf.edu/business/news/articles/181002-reliaquest-partnership.aspx
18. Mullarkey, M., Hevner, A.: An elaborated action design research process model. Eur. J. Inf. Syst. **28**(1), 6–20 (2019)
19. Murphy, D.R., Murphy, R.H.: teaching cybersecurity: protecting the business environment. In: Information Security Curriculum Development Conference 2013, pp. 88–93. ACM, Kennesaw, GA (2013)
20. Sein, M.K., Henfridsson, O., Purao, S., Rossi, M., Lindgren, R.: Action design research. MIS Q. **35**(1), 37–56 (2011)
21. Spidalieri, F., McArdle, J.: Transforming the next generation of military leaders into cyber-strategic leaders: the role of cybersecurity education in US service academies. Cyber Def. Rev. **1**(1), 141–164 (2016)
22. Tang, C., et al.: (Cyber2yr2020 Task Group). Cybersecurity Curricular Guidance for Associate-Degree Programs, Cyber2yr2020. ACM, Committee for Computing Education in Community Colleges (CCECC) (2020). https://doi.org/10.1145/3381686
23. Tang, D., Pham, C., Chinen, K.-I., Beuran, R.: Interactive cybersecurity defense training inspired by web-based learning theory. In: IEEE 9th International Conference on Engineering Education (ICEED), pp. 90–95. IEEE, Kanazawa, Japan (2017)
24. Ward, P.: Constructing a methodology for developing a cybersecurity program. In: Proceedings of the 54th Hawaii International Conference on System Sciences 2021 (2021). https://doi.org/10.24251/HICSS.2021.006

Do Fake News Between Different Languages Talk Alike? A Case Study of COVID-19 Related Fake News

Lina Zhou[1]([✉]), Jie Tao[2], Evan Lai[3], and Dongsong Zhang[1]

[1] University of North Carolina at Charlotte, Charlotte, NC 28233, USA
{lzhou8,dzhang15}@uncc.edu
[2] Fairfield University, Fairfield, CT 06824, USA
jtao@fairfield.edu
[3] St. Mark's School of Texas, Dallas, TX 75230, USA
221aie@smtexas.org

Abstract. Social media fuels fake news' spread across the world. English news has dominated existing fake news research, and how fake news in different languages compares remains severely under studied. To address this scarcity of literature, this research examines the content and linguistic behaviors of fake news in relation to COVID-19. The comparisons reveal both differences and similarities between English and Spanish fake news. The findings have implications for global collaboration in combating fake news.

Keywords: Fake news · Language · Topics modeling · Content-based behavior linguistic behavior

1 Introduction

Social media is transforming the process of spreading news, increasing its dissemination speed and outreach [1], it also contributes to the proliferation of fake news. Fake news has widespread impact on individuals, organizations, and the society. It has the potential to influence political outcomes, lure consumers into deceptive marketing schemes, defame business firms or celebrities, and so on [2]. Unfortunately, social media platforms provide limited mechanisms to assess the credibility of news propagated through them. Moreover, fake news spreads across the globe in different languages, multiplying its impact.

Existing fake news research has predominantly focused on English (e.g., [3, 4]). Given that culture, language, and other factors such as political views and religion may influence the way that news is generated, perceived, and disseminated, understanding the similarities and differences between fake news across different contexts such as languages is crucial. How the characteristics of fake news may differ between different languages, however, remains largely under studied. Thus, to address the above-mentioned literature gap, this study examines the language effect on fake news characteristics by answering the following research questions: 1) How does the content behavior differ

© Springer Nature Switzerland AG 2022
R. Krishnan et al. (Eds.): SKM 2021, CCIS 1549, pp. 186–199, 2022.
https://doi.org/10.1007/978-3-030-97532-6_11

between the fake news in different languages? A related question is how to extract content behavior from online news effectively. 2) Does the linguistic behavior of fake news differ between different languages? If so, how?

The uncertainty around the emergence of COVID-19 has led to numerous fake news, which can serve as an ideal case for studying fake news. The pandemic is a global problem, heightening the need to understand fake news in different languages. Thus, we answer the research questions about fake news by using COVID-19 as the context and by choosing English and Spanish as different languages for comparisons. By analyzing COVID-19 related fake news in both English and Spanish, this study makes multifold research contributions. For the first time, we identify both differences and similarities in content-based behavior between English and Spanish fake news. Additionally, we discover differences in linguistic behaviors between fake news of the two languages. Finally, we develop a transformer-based topic modeling method by extending a state-of-the-art technique for natural language processing, and design a multi-method approach to evaluating the performance of topic models.

The rest of the paper is organized as follows. We first review related work in Sect. 2 and then introduce our method design in Sect. 3. Subsequently, we report results in Sect. 4 and finally conclude the research with Sect. 5.

2 Related Work

We review two streams of related literature: fake news in multiple languages and deception behavior in different languages.

2.1 Fake News in Multiple Languages

Social media platforms, like Facebook or Twitter, augment the speed at which content spreads across a broad audience [5]. For instance, countries have endorsed the cross-regional statement on "infodemic" in the context of COVID-19, and its spread is regarded "as dangerous to human health and security as the pandemic itself." When compared with English fake news research, studies on fake news in other languages are sparse. For example, FIRE 2020 hosted the first shared task focusing on fake news detection in the Urdu language [6]. Al-Ash et al. [7] deployed ensemble learning methods for Indonesian fake news detection. Recognizing the importance of studying fake news in many non-English languages and the challenges of doing so, many have concentrated their efforts in collecting fake news datasets in different languages (e.g., [1, 8, 9]).

A few recent studies have explored detecting fake news across multiple languages. For instance, by developing a generic detection approach, Faustini and Covoes [10] investigated fake news detection in three different languages: English, Portuguese, and Bulgarian. They used the following types of features as inputs to machine learning algorithms: frequency counts of features of textual units (e.g., proportion of uppercase characters, number of sentences, words per sentence), Word2Vec representations, and bag-of-words with tf-idf. Their results demonstrate that text length and Word2Vec consistently ranked among the most important features across different languages. The study, however, does not provide insights into the characteristics of fake news content between different languages. Similarly, Abonizio et al. [1] evaluated language-independent textual features for fake news detection using news corpora written in American English, Brazilian Portuguese, and Spanish through traditional machine learning techniques such as Support Vector Machines, Random Forest, and Extreme Gradient Boosting. Their work was focused on identifying generic text features but not cross-language differences. In addition, they mainly used complexity and stylometric text features. Dementieva and Panchenko [11] proposed an approach that used multilingual evidence to detect fake news. Nevertheless, instead of using raw fake news in different languages, they relied on an online translator to match English news titles to non-English counterparts.

2.2 Deception Behavior in Different Languages

Given that fake news intends to mislead, authoring fake news can be considered as a type of deception. Deception theories (e.g., [12]) suggest that deceivers are engaged in information, behavior, and image management. Building on the extensive research on deception behavior in face-to-face communication [13], there has been a surge of interest in online deception behavior over the past two decades. Given the source of text, deception behavior can be grouped into content and linguistics-based behaviors, depending on whether the behavior identification requires domain knowledge [14]. For instance, an earlier study illustrates that online asynchronous deceptive communication used less self-references, more group references, less complex language, and in general involve more affective language [15].

Compared with the studies on deception behavior in English, the studies on deception behavior in other languages are much fewer. One study of Chinese online deception behavior found that deceivers exhibited a tendency to communicate less and use less complex and diversified texts in their messages [16]. Another study examined cross-cultural deception detection by comparing the performance of classifiers trained on datasets collected from one culture and tested them on datasets collected from a different culture (i.e., United States, India, and Mexico) [17]. Another study of deception behavior of Spanish speakers suggested that linguistic and psychological processes would be most relevant for discerning between true and deceptive statements [18]. It is worth noting that the datasets used in the above two studies were collected from lab environments instead of the real world; and importantly, none of the studies has focused on fake news.

This research aims to address the above-mentioned limitations by comparing the content and linguistic behaviors between the fake news of different languages.

3   Methods

3.1   Dataset

In this study, we used a multilingual fact check news dataset on COVID-19 [19], which used Snopes and Poynter as news sources and collected data from 92 fact-checking websites. The international fact-checking network at the Poynter Institute leads the #CoronaVirusFacts Alliance that joins the efforts of more than 100 fact-checkers around the world on facts regarding the coronavirus [20]. Snopes is a fact-checking website, which helps sort out myths and rumors on the internet [21]. According to a 2020 report [22], English and Spanish are the first and third most common languages used on the Internet, respectively. Thus, we selected fake news in English and Spanish for the case study. After filtering the dataset based on class rating (e.g., false, mostly false), the final dataset contains 2,747 fake news in English and 1,210 in Spanish.

3.2 Data Preprocessing and Behavior Extraction

The news data first went through some common text preprocessing steps, including tokenization, lower-case transformation, and the removal of punctuation, symbols and non-letter characters.

To answer the research questions, we extracted both content and linguistic behaviors from fake news. Specifically, we operationalized content behavior with topics and linguistic behaviors with language complexity, personal pronoun, and affect features in this study. The extraction of linguistic features leveraged LIWC (Linguistic Inquiry and Word Count) 2015 [23]. The tool has the capability of handling English and many other languages such as Spanish. Although each language may have its own unique features, different languages share a large set of common core, enabling us to perform cross-language comparisons. We introduce topic extraction separately next.

3.3 Transformer-Based Topic Modeling (TM^2)

Topic extraction was accomplished through building topic models. Traditional topic modeling techniques (e.g., Latent Dirichlet Allocation (LDA), Non-negative Matrix Factorization (NMF)) are limited mainly in two aspects. Firstly, these traditional techniques rely on patterns from the language space built with the specific text data used in the analysis, which may lead to poor generalizability and coverage. Secondly, these techniques capture context as simple co-occurrence (e.g., bag-of-words), which is difficult to capture the sentence-level context.

To address the aforementioned limitations, we proposed a topic modeling method by extending a state-of-the-art transformer-based model (TM^2)—BERT (Bidirectional Encoder Representations from Transformers), which was pre-trained on a large amount of generic text data, and used the self-attention mechanism to capture the contextual information embedded in the text data. Figure 1 depicts the architecture of TM^2. The method consists of three main components: text representation, topic modeling, and post-hoc handling.

- **Text Representation.** We employed BERT to learn the representation of textual content of fake news. Specifically, we selected Sentence-BERT (SBERT) as the embedding model [24] to ingrain the input text at the sentence level (rather than at the word level as does Word2Vec). In view of the multilingual nature of the input text, we adopted the teacher-forcing strategy in TM^2, following the suggestions of [24], to ensure the alignment between different languages. In the model, text data in different languages (i.e., English and Spanish) was fed into both the teacher and the student models. The teacher model was used to embed the English version of the text, whereas the student model was used to embed both the English and Spanish texts. Using the mean squared error as the loss function, we calculated the loss between the embedding of the English texts from both the teacher and student models and between the embedding of the English texts from the teacher model and the Spanish texts from the student model. To this end, we selected the SBERT-paraphrase as the teacher model and the XLM-R [25] as the student model because of their performances on both the English and Spanish texts [24]. Then the embedding from the XLM-R model was used as the representation of the input texts. The downstream tasks (i.e., topic modeling and post-hoc handling) mainly focused on measuring text semantic similarity.

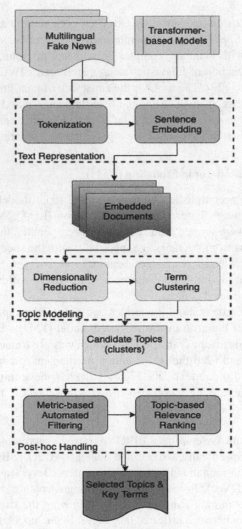

Fig. 1. Transformer-based Topic Modeling (TM²)

- **Topic Modeling**. Given the high dimensionality of document embedding (e.g., 768), it is desirable to perform *dimensionality reduction*. To this end, we selected Unified Manifold Approximation and Projection for Dimension Reduction [26] because it preserves the global structure of original features and does not require extensive running time and computational restrictions. The *clustering* process groups text representations (i.e., vectors in a language space) into different clusters (i.e., candidate topics). Since the topics in a language space can be at levels of different density, we selected a density-based clustering method, specifically HDBSCAN [27], for identifying candidate topics because it is able to identify the most important clusters with interpretable representations.

- **Post-hoc Handling**. This component aims to select a final set of topics and their associated key terms by filtering candidate topics. This component contains two types of post-hoc handling strategies: *metric-based automated filtering* and *topic-based relevance ranking*. Given that clusters represent candidate topics, we measured how one cluster differs from the rest of the clusters for topic optimization. We developed *metric-based automated filtering* by employing a variant of the traditional tf*idf metric that treats all texts belonging to the same cluster as a single document. The equation for the modified metric, namely topic-based tf*idf (T-tf*idf), is shown in Eq. (1):

$$T - tf * idf = \frac{t_i}{w_i} \times \log \frac{m}{\sum_j^n t_j} \tag{1}$$

where t_i is the frequency of term t for each topic i, w_i is the total number of terms in i, m is the average number of terms per topic, and $\sum_j^n t_j$ is the frequency of t across all n topics. The T-tf*idf metric, compared to tf*idf, can better measure the importance of each term, to the cluster collectively. By using the T-tf*idf metric, we were able to obtain the loadings of each term on its respective associated topics, similar to the word-topic matrices in LDA. However, there are key differences between our term loadings and the word-topic matrices in LDA: 1) the T-tf*idf measures the importance of a term to a certain topic rather than the entire dataset, and 2) the calculation of the metric uses the SBERT embedding, which captures more contextual information in text compared to the word2vec counterpart. The *topic-based relevance ranking* aims to ensure that the topics differ from one another. To maintain the coherence of all the terms belonging to the same topic, we introduced the topic optimization step by employing Maximal Marginal Relevance (MMR) [28], as shown in Eq. (2):

$$MMR = Arg \max_{D_i \in T}[\lambda(sim_1(w_i, T) - (1 - \lambda) \max_{D_j \notin T}(sim_2(w_i, w_j)] \tag{2}$$

where w_i and w_j denote a term in document D_i and D_j, respectively. D_i contains topic T, whereas D_j does not. sim_1 measures the maximal pairwise similarity between w_i and all terms in T, while sim_2 measures the similarity between w_i and w_j. $\lambda \in [0, 1]$ is a constant. MMR, as introduced in the field of information retrieval, ranks query results by their relevance. In this study, we extended MMR to topic modeling by finding the most relevant terms within each topic, while reducing the redundancy between different terms. For each topic, the top-N terms ranked in a descending order of MMR scores, were selected, where N was determined heuristically [29]. Finally, we obtained a set of unique stabilized topics and their associated terms, which were coherent for each topic, as the final outputs.

3.4 Evaluation Setting and Measures

We focused the evaluation on the performance of topic models. We selected traditional topic modeling methods—LDA [30] and NMF [31] as the baselines for comparison.

- For the LDA models, we tuned the parameters of document-topic density and topic-word density in the range of (0.5–1), and averaged five different LDA models for each setting for the number of topics to determine its optimal value.
- For the NMF models, we applied Bayesian optimization using the grid search method to search for the optimal hyper-parameters automatically.

For the baseline models, we constructed bi- and tri-grams from the textual content of fake news; then used term-frequency-inversed-document-frequency (tf*idf) as text representations. We applied to the elbow method to determine the optimal number of topics for the baseline models.

The interpretation and evaluation of topic modeling results depend on the requirements of real-world applications [32]. Given that the main goal of topic modeling is to extract latent topics from fake news, we designed a multi-method approach to evaluating the extracted topics for triangulation. The method consists of three components: coherence score, level of agreement, and quality rating.

- **Coherence Score.** It is the most commonly used metric for assessing the quality of topic modeling results [33]. Specifically, the coherence of a topic measures the degree of distributional similarity between top terms in the topic. A topic with a higher coherence score tends have a higher semantic interpretability.
- **Level of Agreement.** The level of agreement was calculated on labelled topics. We first labelled each of the extracted topics manually. A group of coders who were familiar with the respective languages and had experience with assessing the credibility of fake news performed the manual labelling. Specifically, two coders manually analyzed and labelled each of the topics extracted from the English fake news based on their associated key terms independently, and another two coders followed the same procedure to label the topics extracted from the Spanish fake news. Subsequently, for each language, we consolidated the two sets of labels and merged identical topics through meetings with the coders. For instance, Donald Trump and President, response to intervention and RTI, President Rodrigo Duterte and Philippine President, cleaning and sanitizing and sanitization, fact checker and fake detector were merged into the same topics. The topic consolidation was also informed by the similarity between the topics generated by the different topic models. To this end, we applied the cosine similarity metric by embedding the texts in the same language space (i.e., customized word2vec model trained on English and Spanish texts, separately). Finally, we computed the percentage of agreement between the coders based on the consolidated topics. A higher level of agreement indicates a better model performance.

- **Quality Rating.** The coders first met to resolve inconsistent labels and reached a consensus on the fake mews topics. Then, for each topic, they were asked to rate the relevance of each of its top-N terms to the topic on a 3-point Likert scale with 0 being not at all relevant, 1 moderately relevant, and 2 extremely relevant. Finally, we averaged the relevance ratings of all the selected terms for each topic to derive the quality rating of the topic, and further averaged the quality ratings of all the topics generated by a topic model as its overall quality rating.

For quality rating of the content-based behavior, we applied independent-sample t-tests to examine whether there was any difference between the performances of TM^2 and each of the baseline topic modeling methods separately, and whether there was any difference between the two baseline methods. We also applied the t-tests to compare the linguistic behavior of the fake news between the two selected languages.

4   Results and Discussion

We first present the extracted topics and their evaluation results. Then, we report the statistical analysis results for the comparison between English and Spanish fake news.

4.1   Results for Content-Based Behavior: Topic Modeling

Using the elbow method, the number of topics for both LDA and NMF models of the English fake news was set to 9; and the number of topics was set to 9 and 5 for LDA and NMF models of Spanish fake news, respectively. The plots of the coherence scores for varying numbers of topics based on the outputs of LDA models are shown in Fig. 2. Ten topics were selected for the both English and Spanish TM^2 topic models.

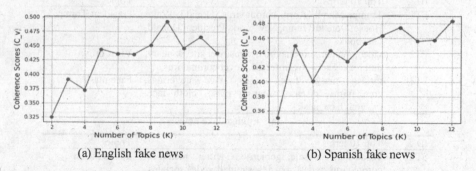

(a) English fake news   (b) Spanish fake news

Fig. 2. Elbow method for selecting the number of topics

The evaluation results of the topic models are reported in Table 1. We select the top-10 topic terms from the outputs of all topic models, which is a common practice in evaluating topic modeling results [33]. The results show that, among the three models, the percentage of agreement for the TM^2 models are consistently the highest across both English (100%) and Spanish fake news (73%). The other two models produced similar performances with NMF models performing slightly better than the LDA counterparts for English. In addition, the coherence scores were also the highest for the TM^2 model.

The results of independent sample t-tests on quality rating show that, for English fake news, both the TM^2 model and the NMF model achieved a higher quality rating than the LDA model (p < .001). However, the difference between the TM^2 and NMF models was not significantly different (p > .05). Similarly, for the Spanish fake news, the TM^2 model generated higher-quality topics than the LDA model (p < .05) and NMF model (p < .001); however, the LDA model generated topics of marginally higher-quality topics than the NMF model (p < .1 in the two tailed results).

Table 1. Evaluation results of the extracted topics

Language	Metrics	TM^2	NMF	LDA
English	Coherence score	0.581	0.572	0.501
	Percentage of agreement	100%	66.7%	60%
	Quality rating (mean [std.])	1.51 [0.23]	1.33 [0.3]	1 [0.14]
Spanish	Coherence score	0.601	0.594	0.532
	Percentage of agreement	73%	60%	60%
	Quality rating (mean [std.])	1.48 [0.211]	0.96 [0.207]	1.22 [0.249]

Table 2. Sample fake news topics and their top-10 terms

ID	Top 10 terms	Topic
ET1	Trump, March, April, coronavirus, Donald, White House, Donald Trump, New York, President Donald, Facebook	President Trump
ET2	video, Wuhan, coronavirus, virus, website, January, outbreak, Facebook, infected, novel coronavirus	Virus origin
ET3	masks, mask, face masks, face coverings, coronavirus, disease, wearing mask, cloth face, oxygen, face mask	Face mask

(a) English fake news

ID	Top 10 terms	Topic
ST1	Whatsapp, mensaje, gobierno, Twitter, mensajes, coronavirus, redes, sociales, sanidad, redes sociales	Social media
ST2	alquiler, impuesto, pequenas_medianas, PYME, macron, dificultar, tendran, gas, aguar, pelear	SME
ST3	dioxido, mascarilla, carbonar, gas, hipoxia, mascar, azufrar, oxigenar, cubrebocas, CO	Face mask

(b) Spanish fake news

We observed the following differences between between the topics extracted from the English and Spanish fake news.

- English fake news touched on the topics of virus origin and flu virus; whereas Spanish fake news focused on community efforts and/or general efforts in combating coronavirus.
- English fake news covered a broad set of intervention mechanisms, whereas Spanish fake news mainly focused on vaccine.
- Spanish fake news tended to focus on topics at the regional level, whereas English fake news did not.
- Only English fake news covered the topics of violence, unrest, government, and data privacy, whereas only the Spanish news covered those of SME, hospital, and breathing issues in relation to the coronavirus.

On the other hand, our comparison between the topics of English and Spanish fake news detected some similarities: coronavirus, social media, and vaccine. Table 2 lists three sample topics extracted from the English and Spanish fake news, respectively, along with their top 10-terms.

4.2   Results for Linguistic Behavior

Table 3 reports the results of independent sample t-tests on linguistic features. The results reveal that there are significant differences in language complexity and personal pronouns, psychological features between the two languages ($p < .001$). Compared with English fake news, the language complexity of Spanish fake news is higher in terms of word count, words per sentence, long words (6 letters or more), and cognitive processing. We also observed interesting pronoun usage patterns. Although Spanish fake news overall uses more pronouns ($p < .001$), English fake news uses more first-person pronouns (e.g., *I* and *we*) ($p < .001$). Spanish fake news uses more second-person ($p < .05$) and third-person pronouns (e.g., *she/he* and *they*) ($p < .001$) than the English fake news.

Table 3. Comparisons of linguistic features between English and Spanish fake news

	Features	English	Spanish	T statistic (E-S)	p-value
Language complexity	Word count	684 [382.6]	835.8 [684.6]	−7.229	***
	Words per sentence	43.4 [17.2]	65.4 [59.1]	−12.725	***
	Long word	25.2 [3.87]	29.9 [3.09]	−40.856	***
	Cognitive processing	8.95 [2.4]	17.93 [2.59]	−102.678	***

(continued)

Table 3. (*continued*)

	Features	English	Spanish	T statistic (E-S)	p-value
Personal pronoun	Personal pronoun	2.26 [1.59]	6.65 [1.26]	−92.644	***
	I	0.16 [.294]	.063 [.196]	11.829	***
	We	.757 [.746]	.579 [.661]	7.144	***
	You	.509 [.738]	.565 [.665]	−2.275	*
	She/He	.456 [.619]	6.05 [1.221]	−151.02	***
	They	.382 [.412]	1.75 [.765]	−58.649	***
Affect	Affect	2.75 [1.06]	3.04 [1.545]	−5.932	***
	Positive emotion	1.56 [.826]	1.51 [.718]	1.865	
	Negative emotion	1.11 [.712]	1.57 [1.188]	−12.619	***
	Anxiety	.182 [.241]	.168 [.237]	1.59	
	Anger	.333 [.395]	.979 [1.159]	−18.891	***
	Sadness	.124 [.221]	.152 [.243]	−3.4	**

Spanish fake news overall used more affective words than the English counterpart (p < .001). After taking into account the polarity of emotions, the difference was observed for negative emotions (p < .001) only but not for the positive emotions (p > .05). Further, Spanish fake news exemplified a higher level of negative emotion in two specific categories: anger (p < .001) and sadness (p < .01).

5 Conclusion

This study compared the content and linguistic characteristics between English and Spanish fake news in the context of COVID-19. Despite some topics in relation to COVID-19 shared by the two languages, fake news in each language had its unique coverage in terms of breadth of intervention measures, geographical regions, and other topics (e.g., virus origin, violence, and hospital). In addition, English and Spanish fake news differed significantly in linguistic complexity, personal pronoun usage, and affective expressions. Moreover, there were nuanced differences in terms of negative emotions between English and Spanish fake news. Furthermore, our proposed topic modeling method not only outperformed traditional topic modeling techniques (e.g., LDA, NMF) but also wass more streamlined than the latter.

The findings of this study have implications for both human and automated detection of fake news across different languages. On one hand, it is possible to leverage the common characteristics of fake news across different languages to build a language-independent component of an automated fake news detection model. On the other hand, it is important to factor in language-dependent features in constructing fake news detection models for individual languages. The findings on both similarities and differences in topic and linguistic characteristics of fake news between different languages underlie the importance of collaboration between international communities in combating fake news.

This study has some limitations that could present future research opportunities. Both English and Spanish receive widespread use in many different countries around the world. Thus, for each language, it requires fine-grained analysis (e.g., at the country level) to provide better explanations for the observed content behaviors. On a related note, there are nuanced differences in the linguistic features between different dialects of the same language (e.g., American vs. British English). We examined three types of linguistic behaviors of fake news in this study. One natural next step is to examine and compare other types of linguistic deception behaviors (e.g., expressivity, diversity, and uncertainty [15]) between fake news in different languages. It would be interesting to improve the performances of fake news detection models for English and Spanish by incorporating the fake news behaviors validated in this study.

Acknowledgements. This research was partially supported by the National Science Foundation [Award #s: CNS 1917537 and SES 1912898] and the School of Data Science at UNC Charlotte. Any opinions, findings, and conclusions, or recommendations expressed in this paper are those of the authors and do not necessarily reflect the views of the above funding agency.

References

1. Abonizio, H.Q., de Morais, J.I., Tavares, G.M., Barbon Junior, S.: Language-independent fake news detection: English, Portuguese, and Spanish mutual features. Future Internet **12**(5), 87 (2020). https://doi.org/10.3390/fi12050087
2. Akhter, M.P., Zheng, J., Afzal, F., Lin, H., Riaz, S., Mehmood, A.: Supervised ensemble learning methods towards automatically filtering Urdu fake news within social media. PeerJ Comput. Sci. **7**, e425 (2021)
3. Pérez-Rosas, V., Kleinberg, B., Lefevre, A., Mihalcea, R.: Automatic detection of fake news. In: Proceedings of the 27th International Conference on Computational Linguistics. Association for Computational Linguistics, Santa Fe, New Mexico, USA (2018)
4. Shu, K., Wang, S., Liu, H.: Beyond news contents: the role of social context for fake news detection. In: Proceedings of the Twelfth ACM International Conference on Web Search and Data Mining, pp. 312–320. Association for Computing Machinery, Melbourne VIC, Australia (2019)
5. Blanco-Herrero, D., Calderón, C.A.: Spread and reception of fake news promoting hate speech against migrants and refugees in social media: research plan for the doctoral programme education in the knowledge society. In: Proceedings of the Seventh International Conference on Technological Ecosystems for Enhancing Multiculturality, pp. 949–955. Association for Computing Machinery, León, Spain (2019)
6. Amjad, M., Sidorov, G., Zhila, A., Gelbukh, A., Rosso, P.: UrduFake@FIRE2020: shared track on fake news identification in urdu. In: Forum for Information Retrieval Evaluation, pp. 37–40. Association for Computing Machinery: Hyderabad, India (2020)
7. Al-Ash, H.S., Putri, M.F., Mursanto, P., Bustamam, A.: Ensemble learning approach on indonesian fake news classification. In: 2019 3rd International Conference on Informatics and Computational Sciences (ICICoS) (2019)

8. Kishore Shahi, G., Nandini, D.: FakeCovid – A Multilingual Cross-domain Fact Check News Dataset for COVID-19. arXiv:2006.11343 (2020)
9. Posadas-Durán, J., Gómez-Adorno, H., Sidorov, G., Escobar, J.J.M.: Detection of fake news in a new corpus for the Spanish language. J. Intell. Fuzzy Syst. **36**, 4869–4876 (2019)
10. Faustini, P.H.A., Covões, T.F.: Fake news detection in multiple platforms and languages. Exp. Syst. Appl. **158**, 113503 (2020)
11. Dementieva, D., Panchenko, A.: Fake news detection using multilingual evidence. In: 2020 IEEE 7th International Conference on Data Science and Advanced Analytics (DSAA), pp. 755–756 (2020). https://doi.org/10.1109/DSAA49011.2020.00111
12. Buller, D.B., Burgoon, J.K.: Interpersonal deception theory. Commun. Theory **6**(3), 203–242 (1996)
13. DePaulo, B.M., Lindsay, J.J., Malone, B.E., Muhlenbruck, L., Charlton, K., Cooper, H.: Cues to deception. Psychol. Bull. **129**(1), 74–112 (2003)
14. Zhou, L.: An empirical investigation of deception behavior in instant messaging. IEEE Trans. Prof. Commun. **48**(2), 147–160 (2005)
15. Zhou, L., Burgoon, J.K., Nunamaker, J.F., Twitchell, D.: Automated linguistics based cues for detecting deception in text-based asynchronous computer-mediated communication: an empirical investigation. Group Decis. Negot. **13**(1), 81–106 (2004)
16. Zhou, L., Sung, Y.: Cues to deception in online chinese groups. In: Hawaii International Conference on System Sciences (HICSS-41). Big Island, HI, USA (2008)
17. Pérez-Rosas, V., Mihalcea, R.: Cross-cultural Deception Detection. n: Proceedings of the 52nd Annual Meeting of the Association for Computational Linguistics, pp. 440–445. Association for Computational Linguistics, Baltimore, Maryland (2014). https://doi.org/10.3115/v1/P14-2072
18. Almela, Á., Valencia-García, R., Cantos, P.: Seeing through Deception: A Computational Approach to Deceit Detection in Written Communication. In: Proceedings of the Workshop on Computational Approaches to Deception Detection, pp. 15–22. Association for Computational Linguistics, Avignon, France (2012)
19. Shahi, G., Nandini, D.: FakeCovid – A multilingual cross-domain fact check news dataset for COVID-19. In: Workshop on Cyber Social Threats (CySoc 2020) at 14th International Conference on Web and Social Media 2020 (2020)
20. Fighting the Infodemic: The #CoronaVirusFacts Alliance. Cited on 10 Aug 2021. https://www.poynter.org/coronavirusfactsalliance/
21. Snopes.com: Debunking Myths in Cyberspace. 27 August (2005). https://www.npr.org/templates/story/story.php?storyId=4819108
22. Statista. Internet: most common languages online (2020). https://www.statista.com/statistics/262946/share-of-the-most-common-languages-on-the-internet
23. Pennebaker, J.W., Chung, C.K., Ireland, M., Gonzales, A., Booth, R.J.: The development and psychometric properties of LIWC2007. LIWC.net, Austin, TX (2007)
24. Reimers, N., Gurevych, I. Making Monolingual Sentence Embeddings Multilingual using Knowledge Distillation. In: Proceedings of the 2020 Conference on Empirical Methods in Natural Language Processing, pp. 4512–4525. Association for Computational Linguistics (2020)
25. Conneau, A., et al.: Unsupervised Cross-lingual Representation Learning at Scale. In: Proceedings of the 58th Annual Meeting of the Association for Computational Linguistics, pp. 8440–8451. Association for Computational Linguistics (2020)
26. McInnes, L., Healy, J.: UMAP: Uniform Manifold Approximation and Projection for Dimension Reduction. arXiv:802.03426 (2018)
27. Campello, R.J.G.B., Moulavi, D., Sander, J.: Density-based clustering based on hierarchical density estimates. In: Pei, J., Tseng,, V.S., Cao,, L., Motoda, H., Xu,, G. (eds.) Advances in

Knowledge Discovery and Data Mining. PAKDD 2013. LNCS, vol. 7819. Springer, Berlin (2013). https://doi.org/10.1007/978-3-642-37456-2_14

28. Carbonell, J., Goldstein, J.: The use of MMR, diversity-based reranking for reordering documents and producing summaries. In: Proceedings of the 21st Annual International ACM SIGIR Conference on Research and Development in Information Retrieval, pp. 335–336. Association for Computing Machinery, Melbourne, Australia (1998)

29. Aletras, N., Stevenson, M.: Evaluating Topic Coherence Using Distributional Semantics. In: Proceedings of the 10th International Conference on Computational Semantics (IWCS), Potsdam, Germany, Association for Computational Linguistics, pp. 13–22 (2013)

30. Blei, D.M., Ng, A.Y., Jordan, M.I.: Latent dirichlet allocation. J. Mach. Learn. Res. **3**, 993–1022 (2003)

31. Emre Celebi, M. (ed.): Partitional Clustering Algorithms. Springer International Publishing, Cham (2015). https://doi.org/10.1007/978-3-319-09259-1

32. Chang, J., Boyd-Graber, J., Gerrish, S., Wang, C., Blei, D.M.: Reading tea leaves: how humans interpret topic models. In: Proceedings of the 22nd International Conference on Neural Information Processing Systems, pp. 288–296. Curran Associates Inc., Vancouver, British Columbia, Canada (2009)

33. O'Callaghan, D., Greene, D., Carthy, J., Cunningham, P.: An analysis of the coherence of descriptors in topic modeling. Expert Syst. Appl. **42**(13), 5645–5657 (2015)

Author Index

Printed in the United States
by Baker & Taylor Publisher Services